The Keys
to your
Dreams

An A to Z guide
to over 11,000 dreams

R. M. Soccolich

A&B

A&B Publishers Group
1000 Atlantic Avenue
Brooklyn, New Y9ork
11238

COVER DESIGN: *A & B PUBLISHERS GROUP*
COVER ILLUSTRATION: *INDUSTRIAL FONTS & GRAPHIX*

Library of Congress Cataloging-in-Publication Data

Soccolich, R. M., 1963
  Night symbols: 11,001 dreams interpreted / R. M. Soccolich
          p.   cm.
  Includes bibliographical references and index.
  ISBN 1-886433-19-4
  1. Dream Interpretation—Dictionaries. 2. Dreams—Dictionaries.
3. Symbolism (Psychology)—Dictionaries. I. Title.
BF1091.S62   1999   99-40762
154. 6'3 09—dc2   CIP

Published
by

A&B PUBLISHERS GROUP
1000 Atlantic Avenue
Brooklyn, New York,
11238
(718) 783-7808

00 01 02 03 6   5 4 3 2 1

Manufactured and Printed in Canada

To

R. K., T. K., D. A., L. A., D. S & L. P.
Thank you for your profound inspiration
and undying love.

Why I Wrote this Book

This book was written to clarify the language of our dreaming mind. This vernacular, presented in lucid images while we sleep, communicates our internal variables of personality. In the course of this work, we will explore how these tenets of self, including and especially our personal fears, frustrations, desires and hopes, are revealed in the format of our dream landscapes. That is to say, the visual reality field of our dream impression. Moreover, we will separate the metaphoric dream down to its individual, symbolic elements. Doing so, the reader may explore each separate component of the dream as it pertains to his or her personal circumstances in daily life. The reader is then asked to cross-correlate each dream reference and find the overall connective theme as it relates to their larger, waking experience.

There is an assumption made that our unconscious mind brings together these disparate dream references in a similar fashion to words which are combined to form sentences and finally, language. We hope to uncover exactly how the language communicated from the deepest part of our human memory illuminates a building understanding about who we are and why we behave in our own unique fashion. In this sense, we are instructed about our mind, body and soul by the greatest teacher of all.

Ourselves...
R.M.S

Introduction

Long before Sigmund Freud wrote that dreams were mental windows opening wide before the landscapes of our psyche enigmatically called 'the u nconscious', tribal shaman, orishas, medicine-men and temple priests the world over guided their people by symbols found in the divine visions of their sleeping mind.

Far from being a fruitless practice, these magic men translated the instructions of the gods who spoke through the incarnate forms of their specific creations. For instance, in the Celtic tradition, the 'Oak Tree God', acted as the vortex or spiritual power point of the ceremonial circular dances around its formidable and age-old trunk. When this mighty Oak appeared in the dreams of the northern shaman, it was clear that the 'Supreme One' had miraculously spoken to them and expected in turn the full and undivided attention of ITS one and only community of mortal children.

Correspondingly, in the Old Testament, Moses (in a dream-vision) is summoned and overcome by a burning bush, in other words, a flaming mountain 'Tree of Divinity.' Further into the biblical tradition, every western child is keenly aware of Adam and Eve's 'Tree of Knowledge' which brought forth man's apple of reason and subsequent suffering, guilt and shame.

Carl Gustav Jung , originally a student of Freud's, branched off from the elder mentor's teaching and founded a new school of psychological thought based upon the foundation of complete dream analysis and individual interpretation. This later led him to theorize his unique viewpoint of a universal 'collective unconscious'.

To Carl Jung, the Oak Tree of the Celtic shaman, Moses' burning bush and the wisdom of the 'Tree of Life' followed by the ancient kabbalists, became ALL collective 'archetypes' which meant 'eternal' symbols etched in the mind of all human beings.

In the mind of man the 'Tree' has persisted as a symbol of human transfiguration and spiritual uprightness while remaining deeply rooted in the earth or 'flesh experience.' The intriguing follow-up to Jung's thinking is that symbols are not merely man-made creations, but transcendent messages recorded within the very matrix of our DNA and RNA composites, a built-in language of being as old as our formulative gene-pools.

In accordance with this line of thought, we travel back in time away from Jung's thinking (and with his full permission to do so) to primitive cultures who naturally and fluidly traveled the vital landscapes of their sleeping mind's eye from the pre-cultures of Great Asia in the Far East to furthermost points south to the wind-swept interiors of Silent and Sacred Africa and Aboriginal Austra-lia. We venture to return west to the Earth Natives of the Americas and, completing the compass circle, we land upon the frozen northern mounts where prehistoric Celtic freemen walked steadily in the ice-age trances of divine illumination, the vision of heaven and earth gods heavy on their furrowed brows.

In Asia sat Siddharta, the Silent One, who dreamt under the Bodhisattva Tree the dream of the Buddha who was dreaming the far reaches of the universe itself, an illusionary test-ground for mortal men. Men like Chang Tsu who dreamt of a butterfly and then understood that it was he, the butterfly, who dreamt of a man dreaming about himself, the unknown and the unknowable.

Accordingly, the unknowable men who built the Great Pyramid altars to the firmament of heaven in Ancient Egypt along with their not-altogether- distant neighbors, the Assyrians, took to writ-ing the tale of their dreams in elaborate 'Dream Texts' that mapped out the meaning of their divine-inspired existence. Further south, existence was pure and idyllic in the so-called 'Dream-Time' of the Australian Aborigines, a Garden of Eden where the "Extraterrestrial Ancestors" had descended upon a barren planet and willingly trans-formed themselves into all the lush species of plants and animals encircling the primordial horizon lines.

Following suit to the majesty of the dream vision, Ancient Greeks erected Incubation Temples where the sick and suffering in-gested herbal sleep-inducing extracts which invoked and conjured inevitable dreams which the temple priests awaited to interpret. It was understood that the dream would reveal the medicine and therapy necessary for the individual twisted in the unyielding arms of the wicked illness.

Just north, and years earlier, in Jerusalem, Jacob dreamt of a lad-der to heaven where angels and saints ascended and descended lightly and without effort as the ancient Hebrews became further aware that Yahweh was communicating to them by way of dreams, the voice of the 'One True God' persistent in their mind both day and night. Across the globe, the highest and most holy God of the ancient and illuminated Aztec chieftains was himself the 'Maker of Dreams' and led men with the guidance of his dream creations, dream innovations which helped outline a thousand-year culture of rare and efficacious human society.

This brings us back to the Celts, who carved niches in their mighty Oaks where young warriors could sleep and dream the dream of the Oak God who existed in a timeless place within the tree spirit of a young warrior's soul transfixed in the eternal limbs and far-reaching branches of mankind, the animal of dreams...

As the reader reads the pages of this book he or she should keep in mind the pure vision of his or her primordial ancestors, remembering that the language of dreams is not mere pictures provided by a sleeping brain, but the intense personal images that complete the psyche of self. As we travel through the interpretations of universal dream symbols found in this book and make the connections which link the meaning to our personal lives of experience, we should be comforted in the realization that dreams have guided our human kind for as long as we can remember and that same memory brings us closer to ourselves, and our deepest elusive purpose in life, the dream within the dream, within the dream...

Dream Interpretation

As human beings, we possess a brain and physiological system
which slowly developed an increased potential over the
course of countless millennia and successive generations.
From the earliest forms of man's predecessors, a steady evolutionary learning and adaptation transformed the extraordinary ability of
neural consciousness into the worldly perception we enjoy today.

However, the story doesn't end there. Researchers have found
the human brain's long evolutionary process of development has
traveled an unfolding and progressive course. The implications of
such a miraculous progression involve the singular retention of
each successive stage of neural completion. Hence, within our
brain's activity, or consciousness, resides an innate comprehension
of all stages of human development and a subsequent memory of
an entire, living history.

Herein, we begin the examination of the very crucial reality of
dreams. The mysterious component of consciousness which retains
the aforementioned collection of memory, Jung referred to the as
the Unconsciousness. In the course of his life, Jung pointed out
how this unconscious is not at all limited to the temporal or spatial
conceptualization of waking consciousness.

He further expounded how this vast information storehouse
does not communicate via a normal language, which is grounded
inexorably in a linear and scientific understanding of reality. Instead, the complex and ancient unconscious translates feelings and
psychological states through an elaborate and boundless series of
dynamic visual memories. Consequently, the dream, which is the
projection screen of this limitless unconscious, presents images appropriate to their symbolic meaning. For example, in the language
of the dream, fire is not just flame, but also burning passion, anger
or heated confrontation. Hence, a man's head may be on fire all
night and not sustain any real injury or even pain. Simply put,
physical reality takes a back seat to symbolic reality. Accordingly, in
dreams, people can fly, cry and die with equal ease, and monsters,
serpents and mermaids can play a real part in a serious individual's

night-by-night existence.

In this sense, we examine in the context of this dictionary the symbolic language of the unconscious revealed to us in dreams and nightmares. Moreover, we follow the guidance of an age-old mental framework which elucidates its wisdom to us each and every night; with sharp precision, fierce passion and the profound insight of humanity's grandiloquent and immense history.

R. M. Soccolich

How To Use This Dream Book

The five steps to dream interpretation

1) Upon waking, write down every aspect of the dream including colors, backgrounds, characters and objects.

2) List these separate components in the order of their significance within the dream.

3) Refer to this guide book for specific and possible meanings for each of these entries. It is recommended that the dreamer add his or her own personal feelings about each item, since all of us in one form or another, has experienced a unique history of intimate memories and associations regarding life's perception.

4) The combined symbolic references will begin to unravel and reveal a psychological portrait of the dreamer's overall concerns, desires and, perhaps, innermost aspirations.

5) This complete procedure should be conducted over an extended series of nights to illustrate central intellectual and emotional conceptualizations and, perhaps, the aim and heading in one's waking life of experience.

Contents

ABANDON: A feeling of desperate isolation. This isolation stems from the childhood 'feeling' of parental separation felt from infancy when the guardian parent left the room or immediate field of vision. In adult life, Abandonment translates into the fear of an unknown which must be faced entirely alone, for instance, embarking on a business proposition on one's own that is risky or otherwise perilous. This isolation or abandonment can also express sexual or emotional transitions in life, which tends to make one unsure of his or her footing in a new or changing relationship. The fear of abandonment is an unconscious metaphor that the dreamer may need to make an entirely 'individual' decision in their life.

ABBEY: Hopes and schemes will fall under religious scrutiny of a 'higher' order. An individual is faithful in the merit of a decision made, however he or she may harbor feelings of guilt or spiritual repercussion for the act chosen upon. If the dreamer is female the Abbey may represent spiritual or emotional cleansing. The abbey therefore, is a double-edged sword which may represent purity, or conversely, repressed guilt, dependent upon the psychological make-up of the dreamer.

ABBESS: A feeling of spiritual leadership and comradeship is applied to this dream form. Responsibility and social vision usually accompanies this figure. A woman, upon placing herself unconsciously as a spiritual leader, may be experiencing the wisdom of her matriarchal character as it pertains the context of her community. This incorporates various formulations of selfless love including the acceptance of worldly suffering, analogous to child-birth and unconditional devoted behavior toward the innocent and vulnerable. If she is simply an outsider addressing the abbess, the dream vision may imply devout or religious trust in some 'outside' female figure in her own life; including, but not necessarily, her own mother. (*see* Angel)

ABBOT: To dream that you are an Abbot, may signify a suspicion that others are misjudging you, or conversely, that others are jealous of your position of social power. In essence, you have a platform and a pulpit in community and others in your immediate social sphere, may not enjoy this real influence over their respective peers. However, the dream vision of oneself in the clergy may also indicate hiding something immoral about oneself. These repressed thoughts are masked behind the hard stone walls and thick robes of organized religion and its accepted standards of morality. To further understand the significance of the abbot, the dreamer must note the exact appearance and manner of this religious figure and determine the nature of that figure's motivations concerning an ethical platform. Moreover, the dreamer needs to clarify the message given by the abbot himself in this dream formulation. The unconscious finds various and dynamic ways to translate its advice into our consciousness. For many, an abbot reflects real wisdom and spiritual meditations upon the worldly plain. Gestalt therapy may be advised if this dream is recurring.

ABDOMEN: All dreams relating to the stomach or stomach regions can be observed metaphorically as a physical center of anxiety, or unnatural pain. If the dreamer is a woman, a natural fear or anxiety about childbirth, which itself may not signify birth, but sexual consequences, should be examined thoroughly. Another series of dream interpretations reveal that dreams of abnormal abdomen conditions infer an 'unattainable' hunger or longing. However, therapists agree that since the unconscious is revealing something about the exact nature of the goal of the dreamer, that particular goal may indeed be VERY attainable. We also find references to 'gut' feelings, which defy our logical determination, yet seem to ring true on another level of our awareness. The dreaming consciousness may be well aware of these instinctual urges and their viable involvement in our ence.

ABHOR: A person dreaming that they are Abhorred demonstrates a feeling of self-disgust or chastisement. It is a conscious reflex and reaction to feelings of guilt or interpersonal wrong doing. It may also signify a deeply repressed social fear. A young child thrives on the POSITIVE attention and acknowledgment of his or her parents. When this attention is not forthcoming or the child receives NEGATIVE attention, the child associates that it has done something absolutely wrong and is now being punished. Therefore, simply put, to be 'abhorred' represents a refraction, or social castigation, which may need to be examined. In order to function as a well adapted individual in culture, we need to adopt a feeling of belonging from our social peers. In this sense, we may need to confront our feelings of alienation, simply to erase any forms of self-guilt, or a general lack of personal self-worth. In order to build loving relationships, we must first determine ourselves fully deserving of this love.

ABJECT: To dream that one is Abject refers to a feeling of loss or loss of resources. This human symbolism or archetype refers to weakness or a general inability to defend oneself against the 'natural' hardships in life. The implications of this archetype involve a complex series of repressive emotions that signal the 'giving up' of certain responsibilities. Conversely, if the dreamer is abject, yet elated, this may signal a 'cleansing' of soul and release of 'earthly shackles.'

ABODE: To dream that you can't find your Abode, may signify a loss of personal belief and may signify a huge transition in your life. The abode is symbolically understood as a place of comfort, familiarity and sanctity in one's state of mind, therefore to erase one's abode implies a nervous 'plunge' into the future, which is of course, unknown. Working away from the absolute loss of one's abode, we may categorize fundamental changes in the 'look', 'familiarity' and overall functionalism found within the confines of the abode. As an archetype the abode varies in meanings from the unified family to a satiated sexual or loving experience of emotion.

ABORIGINAL: Many researchers note that the Aboriginal figure represents the unconscious itself, a primal look into the human heart, brain and soul. In more practical terms, the aboriginal represents a dual quality within ourselves. The first quality is the untamed, natural self that exists hand in hand with 'the wild' world or landscape. He or she has no restrictions and no parameters other than pure and fluid existence. This figure is an extremely clear vision of the dreamer choked by the responsibilities or the fear of accountability posed by the 'civilized' world. The second quality of the aboriginal dream figure is an innocent return to divine faith with child-like, yet immensely powerful conviction. Conversely, to fear the aboriginal demonstrates the unconscious warning against the overabundance of this same behavior by the dreamer, who may be harming him or herself with this unrestrained exuberance.

ABORTION: The complexity of the Abortion dream relates to the exact nature of what is being 'aborted' in the psyche of the individual dreamer. A project or original idea of one's own making which is abruptly 'cut-off' or even challenged by some overpowering force is unconsciously felt as the pain of 'loss of life.' In reality, the life lost is fundamentally the stunted 'life-force' of the dreamer. The abortion signifies a very personal loss which cannot be wholly understood, felt or even appreciated by others. Naturally, because of the intense individuality of the abortion image, every other aspect of this dream should be honestly approached and systematically interpreted in order to better understand the nature and source of the dreamers anxiety.

ABOVE: When something is hanging over your head and about to fall, the obvious implication is that something, or some force, is out of reach, yet can cause immense and irreparable psychological harm. The dreamer may need to remember that the laws of physics do not apply in dreams and therefore the unconscious may be stating that what is above is simply above, and can easily be reached, overcome and absorbed. Our feelings of helplessness in dreams is equally combated by the knowledge that our dreams are 'given' to us by our minds to better understand and eventually master our own human obstacles. Therefore, we should not only look at the 'motivation' of the dream, but also the 'implication' and 'conclusion' of the respective dream.

ABROAD: To be Abroad is a concept which refers to, or symbolizes, a unique and separate country or land. It may symbolize one's past or 'homeland' which a person longs for (or more commonly) needs to escape to, in order to regain psychological freedom or sanctity (see ABODE). It may also represent travel or the traveling toward some foreseeable goal which is strange yet pleasurable. Conversely, the concept of abroad may signify that contact with old friends is desired and that preparations to make this happen need to be made.

ABSENCE: To dream about the absolute Absence of a particular individual in your dreams may signify that this same individual has been upset or set apart from yourself by some 'wrongful' behavior done to him or her by you, perhaps unintentionally. Unconsciously, you need to 'find' this individual again and perhaps seek atonement for your abnormal behavior.

ABSORB: When one is Absorbed in the context of the dream it is once again necessary to know what being or force is doing the absorbing. The symbolism of absorption is personal defeat or personal surrender to some anxiety-provoking power or nemesis. Another aspect of the dream is the implied 'disappearance' of self which indicates that some important aspect of yourself is changing. Furthermore, the disappearance of self usually denotes a change in the perception of 'others' in society who may be perceiving you differently or perhaps can no longer 'see' you at all, due to your new emotions or psychological changes.

ABUNDANCE: To dream that you are possessed with an Abundance of goods represents one of two possible meanings dependent on the psychological feeling placed upon the goods themselves, within the context of the dream. For instance, if an individual is comfortable and entirely at ease in the midst of his or her abundance, the notable significance of the opulence is satisfaction or personal achievement, the pride of the fruits of labor, in other words, a hard-earned prize. If however, the dreamer is stressful and anxiety-ridden in the midst of their abundance, it usually signifies that the dreamer has not 'earned' the abundance and therefore feels it can be taken away just as easily as it came. Alongside this latter definition, we also find guilt in the dreamer because of his or her fragile self perception, which is falsely inflated to grandiose proportions in order to compensate for a repressed and extraordinarily low level of self-esteem.

ABUSE: To dream that you are Abusing an innocent person represents an uncanny way for the unconscious to illustrate that you are harming or psychologically mutilating different aspects of yourself and consequently, injuring others by the sheer imbalance of your personality. On the other hand, if you are the abused, or victim in the dream, the symbolism is unjust punishment and a cry for help. Moreover, elements of helplessness versus defensive behavior should be interpreted for waking similarities concerning victimization. Accordingly, it is crucial to understand the 'conclusion' of the dream vision, as well as the initial 'motivation.' In the case of a recurring abuse dream, professional therapy is strongly suggested to aid in the understanding of its source and to develop a means to its end its interference with our psychological development.

ABYSS: The Abyss may represent a complete loss of control in one's waking life. The notion of 'falling' into a place of no fixed reference can be devastating to the conscious mind which needs something, some REASON to grasp, to align itself with a perception of reality. The reason why the abyss appears so often in dreams is because dreams are unconscious and boundless, a natural terrain for the expression of the infinite. Accordingly, positive associations of the abyss reflect individual freedom, a tearing away of limiting parameters and a fearless step into the exhilarating unknown.

ACADEMY: To attend an Academy in your dreams has diverse meanings dependent on your age and associations with education and possibly discipline on the whole. An older individual may be experiencing feelings of regret about the opportunities that passed them by through sheer indifference or possibly difficult economic times. A young person on the other hand may feel locked-up in an institution and unable to 'free' him or herself out of the complicated maze. It is interesting to note, in both cases, the academy appears as an 'obstacle' which needs to be overcome by the mental processes of the dreamer.

ACCEPTED: For a lover to dream he or she has been Accepted by a desirable counterpart, may signify something lacking in the way of personal self-worth. This overcompensation may be projected toward an individual's loved ones or potential lovers. This dream-inspired acceptance can be looked at as ego-guarding 'wish fulfillment.' This of course, is not a hard rule and 'acceptance' can and does in fact, signify in certain cases, a comfortable feeling of well-being within one's social group, respective peers and of course, within the context of a relationship itself.

ACCIDENT: In general, Accidents are understood as aggressive events which occur suddenly and are completely uncontrollable. It is the uncontrollable aspect of the accident dream which symbolizes an abnormal anxiety or fear of 'things getting out of hand' in a very short time. Accident dreams, by and large, express an internal struggle based on new and sudden events occurring in the otherwise organized and consistent life of the dreamer. Conversely, if the dreamer is NOT personally involved in the accident itself, but merely (or casually) observing it, the implication may be one of hidden and very turbulent feelings of aggression. Individuals who are unable to express their hostility in everyday life often require violent dreams as a necessary outlet for their overload of physical tension. There is some controversy over the nature of prophetic, or visionary, accident dreams. To better understand these arguments, we ask to reader to study the sections on Clairvoyance, The Collective Unconscious and Lucid Dreaming. (*see* Crash)

ACCORDION: The playing of music or a musical instrument suggests the invocation of intense emotions. Strangely enough, there is a subtle connection between the shape and sound of the instrument itself and the emotion it most often reflects in test cases. For instance, the acoustic guitar, with its feminine shape and lush sweeping tones suggests sensuality and eroticism, while the bugle with its short, stout, piercing shrill seems to suggest an almost adolescent fear or alarm involving human contact. Accordingly, the Accordion is a rather large instrument involving the continuous physical movement of squeezing and pulling, roughly synonymous with ones own breathing. Taken together, the symbolism of the accordion is one of intense 'physical' emotion demonstrating a kind of bodily weariness involved in sustaining a certain powerful emotion. Since the accordion 'breathes' it is only natural to assume that the dreamer 'becomes' the instrument of music, dance and merriment. Moreover, if the dreamer dances while he or she plays the accordion may be an illustration of an emotion which the dreamer is 'juggling in uncertainty' to the point of exhaustive delirium.

ACCOUNTANT: To 'count-up' ones belongings is roughly akin to weighing or accessing oneself. In dreams, we express concepts like 'value' and 'worth' or conversely, 'greed' and 'misfortune' with human-like figures who visually represent our desired thought constructs. One such figure, known as the accountant, may be perceived as a negative force who projects our deepest fears of worthlessness or social shame, or conversely, a virtuous presence who reminds us to 'surrender our greed' etc. If the dream of the accountant is recurring, it may be necessary to confront the figure and determine his (your?) complete intentions.

ACE OF SPADES: In a deck of cards the Ace of Spades is the card given the highest value, dominating even the vainglorious king of diamonds. Spontaneous, mischievous and heartless, the powerful ace comes crashing down on all 'games' with an all-seeking and all-possessing authority. Consequently, the ace card is a very peculiar dream symbol representing extreme competitiveness complicated by an equal fear of loss and ultimate submission. Many analysts have argued that this kind of submission is actually sought after by the dreamer. (*see* Sigmund Freud)

ACHAEMENEDS: The Zoroastrians in the period of Acheameneds followed the theory of Sifat-i-Sirozah who posed that dreams could only be interpreted in accordance to the day of the year in which that dream occurred. Each day of the year coincided with a prophet and/or religious event, which significantly colored and shaped the overall meaning of the dream and moreover, how it effected the immediate waking life of the dreamer within that active society.

ACHILLES HEEL: In Greek mythology Achilles represented a turning point in dream symbolism when he broke the Homeric tradition of receiving dreams solely from Gods. Instead, Achilles dreams of Patroclus who demands a decent burial for his deceased body. This sensitive mortality of Achilles is echoed in his infamous wound which could never heal. When we dream of a wounded Achilles heal which prevents us from escaping an enemy, we are implying that our own humanity may be allowing others to take advantage of us in the rich and complex battlefield of our psyche.

ACID: In dreams, Acid represents simmering feelings of revenge or long-standing rage or hatred. An alternate viewing of an acidic substance refers to introversion and insecurity. These dream symbols require immediate analysis. It is our unconscious' way of demonstrating the harm done by the prolonged stress of hatred and conversely, fear. Naturally, there are recorded cases where we find a combination of hatred AND a paralyzing fear of retaliation. These dreams illustrate a complicated emotional immobility, which may require some form of general counseling.

ACORN: The Acorn is the archetype of potential as it is a seed which grows into the formidable adulthood of a mighty tree. Potential is also a representation of a brand new beginning in one's life. Human nature detests change because new environments are fearful, alienating and disorientating. The Acorn dream is the psyche's way of providing hope in order to build up the courage necessary to create changes which may be needed in life.

ACROBAT: There is a duality in the Acrobat dream figure based on the skill of the acrobat. If the acrobat is bungling and falters in

her performance risking harm to either herself, her fellow per-
formers or the audience itself, a deep distrust in ones own abilities is being expressed rather colorfully. The indication of this illustrious symbol is an apparent lack of discipline in ones own
life. This unfocused behavior may be causing a psychological or
emotional imbalance which the dreamer is struggling (perhaps
in public) to change. Conversely we find the alternate side of the
dualistic Acrobat which is poised, talented and innately coordinated. She represents a balance in ones life in dealing with psychological and emotional obstacle with apparent ease.

ACTIVE IMAGINATION: A technique developed by Carl Jung
where a dreamer is encouraged to spontaneously play with and
otherwise fantasize upon a remembered dream. This technique
often involves 're-creating' characters within the dream and es-
tablishing a 'conversation' with them. The power in this technique lies in the agreement of the dreamer that all thoughts
should come naturally into the mind and not be 'forced' or 'concentrated' upon. This way, the elaborate and explanatory images
perceived are considered to emerge from the unconscious.

ACTOR: Primarily, an Actor in ones dream refers to feelings of personal deception, in other words, not expressing ones true self.
Implied in this symbol is a deep concern about the repercussions
of ones own recent 'actions.' In this sense the audience represents our peers, the people who we care about. An interpretation of the actor or actresses dialogue in the performance and
the audience reaction to it is crucial in the understanding of the
dream symbolism. An alternate archetype of the actor is a com-
pensatory need for public acclaim in ones waking life.

ADAM AND EVE: This biblical figure may represent moral guilt
and a metaphoric fall from grace. However, the complexity of
the dualistic nature of male and female is also explored in this
dynamic archetype. Crucial in the understanding of this dream
is the temporal element involved in its re-enactment. Are we
observing, the paradise before the fall, or the sudden awareness
of the harsh reality of life, after the ingestion of the fruit of
knowledge? In any case, our innocence is thrown into question
and we may need to determine the spiritual implications of our
own waking behavior. (see Apple)(see Tarot Major Arcana)(see
Paradise)

ADDICT: The dream of an addiction demonstrates anxiety about something unshakable in ones life. There are many powerful intrusive forces in a persons life, therefore, the addiction symbol is not necessarily drug or alcohol related. Rather, the dreamers unconscious is clearly warning against escapism in the face of seemingly unstoppable obstacles or extremely seductive influences. To dream of an addict is to dream of a person in trouble who may need to defiantly face and finally overcome his or her personal demons. In this sense it is a very powerful and uplifting dream symbol, which instills hope into a personal darkness.

ADVENTURE: When there is an Adventure in a dream landscape it is an example of compensation in a persons waking life which may be uneventful or even dull. The adventure dream is a call for danger, peril and uncertainty. Conversely, if a person is already living a dangerous life; and DANGER as we all know is a very relative term, then his or her adventure dream may be a warning to slow down the pace, which may have become too perilous and may cause irreparable harm. The subtle environment and its physical and psychological impact upon the dreamer, need to be analyzed with great detail to aid the dreamer in the understanding of its personal and perhaps prophetic message.

AESCULAPIUS: In ancient Greek mythology Aesculapius was a mortal doctor who was trained in the art of healing by the centaur Chiron. His healing ability became so great that soon Aesculapius was bringing the dead back to life. This of course angered Hades, who in turn petitioned Zeus, who 'dealt' with the problem by striking Aesculapius dead with a bolt of lightning. Subsequently, INCUBATION temples were erected in Greece in the name of Aesculapius where sick and dying Greek citizens were encouraged to sleep and dream (sometimes for weeks and months) in order that temple priests could later analyze and interpret the dreams and find within their context a suitable medical treatment for the disease empowered by the help of Aesculapius. Sometimes, one of his two daughters Panacea and Hygeia, were summoned as well by the dream priests.

AFRICA: In our unconscious we think of Africa as the birthplace of mankind. In this context we are expressing feelings of our inner 'free' and 'natural' being unconstrained by the stressful and dehumanizing modern world and being set free into a vast primordial earth. Added to this, there is also an illustration of submission and love for this immense and life-giving landscape which symbolizes the mother of our race. Mother earth is an archetypal symbol which spans virtually every culture known to man and therefore cradles our people's entire psyche.

AGE: A major concern in the dreams of aged men and women entail a loss of resources. For example, numerous studies have shown that elderly women often dream of running out of food to serve to their relations. In this we find a complex feeling of loss regarding the nurturing abilities built into the fabric of women-kind who are blessed with the right to bring life into this world. Therefore, a main archetype of old age in dreams is loss of vitalness and usefulness. The unconscious is demonstrating for us an image of regret, which can and should be altered. Another symbol of age is sense which guides us with the eyes of experience. Taken together in our dreamscape, the wisdom to patiently learn the lessons of life in order to avoid regret may be imperative in our waking life.

ALBATROSS: The Albatross flies high above the horizon line with the widest wingspan of all birds and therefore represents freedom hampered by an almost extreme vulnerability. In ancient times, it was believed that a dying or dead albatross signified harsh and immediate bad luck for the dreamer. This makes sense when one determines that the dreamer is feeling exposed and vulnerable in his extremely visible, slow glide through the heavens. We find in this figure, the exact opposite of the notion of 'a cloud with a silver lining.' As such, we witness a peaceful tranquillity, which may be threatened, or susceptible, to a negative outside force.

ALBINO: In dreams, the Albino represents the 'spirit being' who allows transcendence through the purity of his or her appearance and demeanor. He/She symbolizes the walk past death into eternal life. This archetype is perhaps as old as mankind itself and should be taken very seriously. If the albino figure is feared, there may be an implication of irrational worry concerning a loved ones health and/or the acceptance of a loved ones passing. The albino symbol may need to be embraced and followed via Active Imagination in the dream landscape. (see White)(see Aboriginal)

ALCHEMIST: Dreams themselves are representations of Alchemy, in that they are separate elements which combine to bring together greater meaning and comprehension of a coherent psychological whole. However, dreams of alchemy usually refer to (both psychologically and archetypically) a significant change in ones life toward something considered far better, either materially (turning stone to gold) or spiritually, which is more often the case, since alchemy is significantly tied to magic and the ancient art of hierophantry.

ALLEY: A normal Alleyway has only two means of entrance and/or exiting, therefore, to dream of an alley refers to a difficult emotional situation where a person is forced to make an important decision where there are very few options to choose from. Moreover, since an alley is symbolic of a dangerous isolated space, difficult choices are viewed as potentially harmful to the dreamer, or his or her immediate associates. The dreamer is advised to take a stand and choose a way out of the alley and begin the therapeutic process of dealing with the consequences.

ALLIGATOR: The image of the Alligator involves an emotional threat which lurks just below the surface of our perception. Nevertheless, the unconscious illustrates our subtle awareness of the potential jeopardy. As such, we may need to interpret surrounding signs in the overall dream landscape, in order to determine the exact specifics of this personal and conceivably difficult emotional predicament in our waking day to day experience. (see Reptile)(see Water)(see Jaws)

ALPHA WAVES: Brain wave patterns are measured on a sophisticated piece of equipment known as an electroencephalograph or EEG. These EEGs measure electrical energy released by the brain in terms of amplitude and frequency. These recorded brain waves assist researchers in understanding patterns of sleep (NREM Stages 1-4) and (REM stage 1) and wakefulness (A1-A2). Alpha waves appear when a person is awake yet falls into a very relaxed and meditative state (A2). Furthermore, Alpha waves are characterized by a frequency of 8-12 cycles per as compared to Delta waves (occurring in deep sleep) which demonstrate high amplitude but very slow frequency, in the range of 1-2 cycles per second.

AMAZON: The image of a large and powerful female warrior is complex and certainly dependent on the gender of the dreamer. If the dreamer happens to be an elderly woman, the vision of the Amazon symbolizes inner strength still felt and perhaps requiring a sympathetic audience of peers. If on the other hand, the dreamer is a very young girl, the vision symbolizes an archetype of wish-fulfillment in terms of body growth and health and/or power. In the case of a man dreaming about an amazon warrior, there is an indication of insecurity and unsure feeling towards a particular woman or women in general. In these latter cases the symbol is usually a recurring one, finding itself in many different dream landscapes. There is an added dimension of free-spirited or aggressive sexual symbolism present in this archetype, expressing itself fully and equally for both genders.

AMPUTATE: Dreams of Amputation, which are quite common, refer to a very serious and perhaps permanent loss. In general, the 'body' is symbolic of the 'true' person or 'inner' self. On the body, ones legs refer to movement and travel, hands represent possessions or motivations and sex organs illustrate sex-drives or unspoken desires. The removal by amputation of these body parts represents the loss of their symbolic psychological status.

ANALYST: To dream about an Analyst is to observe oneself in a symbolic third person. It is an attempt to record a self-expression upon ones own submerged and otherwise repressed feelings. Accordingly, all other aspects of the dream landscape containing the analyst, as well as a detailed account of every opinion brought forth by the analyst figure, is necessary to interpret the dreamers' graphic unconscious message.

ANCIENT ARCHITECTURE: The archetype of Ancient structures involves the very real arena of human transcendence, replete with the struggle of beauty, mortality and physical sacrifice. The building of the Great Pyramid, the arrangement of Stonehenge and the eloquent horizon line of the Parthenon in Athens all reflect the need for earth-bound man to align his soul with an eternal beyond. In dreams, these ancient edifices become symbolic of the dreamers longing for an eternal spiritual existence. In short, this architecture represent a rallying cry against the absolute silence associated with worldly parting. (*see* Tarot Major Arcana: Judgment (20) and The World (21))

ANGEL: The Angel is a symbol for moral decision making, as opposed to the 'little devil' or Demon which represents an immoral choice. If the angel symbol is angry or annoyed, feelings of personal guilt are apparent in the dreamer. The winged angel is also symbolic of ones 'Holy' or 'Guardian' Spirit. In most test cases, the angel is entirely illuminated in light and remains faceless, however, if the angel is recognized as someone known, either living or dead, a need to determine the dreamers relation to, or feelings about that person, may be entirely necessary to determine the dreams meaning.

ANIMA/ANIMUS: Carl Jung developed an ideology postulating men and women continually observing dream figures of their opposite sex, in order to elaborate on their converse feminine and masculine natures. In other words, men possess recurring 'dream-women' or Anima, to act out their own internal stereotypical and perhaps repressed feminine natures. A few superficial examples would include: moodiness, sensitivity and emotionalism. While women externalize their same repressed masculine natures of stubbornness, aggression and fierce competitiveness, with replete 'male figures' or Animus.

ANT: The image of the Ant denotes hard work and a practical focus toward a difficult goal. However, if the poor, little ant confronts insurmountable obstacles, for example, a mighty river or deep canyon in its path, we may be witnessing a symbolic fear of ones tangible ability to provide for oneself, or moreover, ones family. The extent of this phobia may be vividly implied within the harsh landscape of the dream vision. We may need to note any conditions in the environment, which assist the ant (ex: wind, raft etc.). These variables each have their own vital significance, crucial to the dreamer's personal acknowledgment and overall awareness.

ANTARCTICA: The archetype of a world of ice is deeply rooted in our unconscious and genetic memory. The idea of extreme cold and all its obstacles against survival is relevant in our understanding of a battered and paralyzed emotional state. Any and all elements in the antarctica dream are extremely crucial in the interpretation of the unconscious' answer or psychological course of action regarding this fearful, isolated emotional state of being. (see White)

APE: The symbol of erratic, mischievous behavior which is intelligent yet 'over the top' illustrates the Ape archetype. The meaning of this dream implies 'compensation' on the part of the dreamer who may feel too stiff or rigid in his or her day to day actions. In many REM tests male dreamers report being chased by the ape or somehow sexually competing with the ape or 'hairy man.' Therefore, the ape refers to a wild 'inner' nature, especially sexual, which has been repressed and now seeks expression in the dreamers outward life.

APPLE: In Greek mythology the image of the apple is symbolic of sexual awareness or sexual pleasure. In the Judea-Christian world, the apple continues to be the representation of human sin based on the bible's story of Adam and Eve. Both of these interpretations are valid. Other focused elements in the dream landscape containing the 'apple' will readily reveal the significance of the 'forbidden fruit.' Incidentally, this fruit is taken from the tree of 'wisdom', which the apple also represents, in the expression of 'Opening ones eyes, and seeing the whole world around oneself.'

ARCHETYPE: Archetypes, in the sense that Carl Jung incorporated them into his theory of the human unconscious refers to instinctual genetic memories held by man. Archetypes are 'visual symbols' which portray deeply embedded human concerns such as 'life after death', 'sexual awakening at puberty', 'a conceptual madonna or mother image', 'relations to environment', 'elaborate fears of animals' and countless other subtleties of the human experience. Archetypes have existed as long as recorded and unrecorded human history and are well documented from cave drawings to computer animation. Archetypes represent the modern understanding of the soul's travel into the infinite source of its primal consciousness.

ARROW: While Arrows are in fact weapons, as dream symbols they take on far more 'romantic' notions of love (aka Cupid) and skill (aka Robin Hood). There is an alternate view of the arrow as phallus which 'finds' the target of sexual union based not only upon its shape, but also its launcher, 'the bow', which creates (sexual) tension and then releases it.

ARTEMIDORUS (A.D.150): A Roman, Artemidorus wrote the first 'comprehensive' and 'modern' book on the interpretations of dreams. In his enormous five volume work entitled the Oneirocritica, Artemidorus demonstrated how dreams were dependent upon the uniqueness of the dreamer. He explained how the concerns of the dreamer, such as his status, health and family figured greatly into the working fabric of the dream figures and dream landscape.

ARTIST: The dream figure of the artist usually refers to untapped creative potential (in any of the arts) which has remained un-tested or unfulfilled. The painting created by the artist should be analyzed thoroughly because it may hold some indication as to why the dreamer has repressed his creativity and what the dreamer may need to fulfill, before tapping into his or her artis-tic pool.

ASHES: Although there is an allusion to death in its symbolism, the predominant meaning of Ashes seems to be change, thoughts scattered into new worlds and transfiguration without regret. Ashes symbolize a spiritual 'letting go' of the fire of suf-fering, found in an all too real human mortality. In the words 'Ashes to ashes, dust to dust' an implication is made wherein the earth accepts worldly flesh back into its sacred folds. There-fore, Ashes represent a hopeful return to ones environment and one's 'true' self.

ASTROLOGY: Primarily, dreams focusing on Astrologers refer to a concern about the future, a sort of sought after, dream horo-scope. Should the astrologer in the dream give advice or a pre-diction, the message given should be thoroughly analyzed as the zodiac involves within its parameters the four seasons, the four elements (fire, air, water, earth), and the birth sign of the dreamer, each with very significant references to the dreamer. In the case of the astrologer dream, every astrological facet of the dream needs to be considered for a proper interpretation. This includes, the date on which the dream occurred, which may it-self be the single motivating psychological factor, involved in this specific dream symbol.

ASYLUM: The idea of a 'crazy house' is symbolic for disorder and 'apparent' chaos in ones emotional life. Actual mental illness is rarely a factor, instead the image of mental anguish illustrates an emotional or psychological anomaly which the dream com-municates, can be returned back to normal. The asylum in this regard, is a mirror to a hospital where sick patients arrive, re-cover and then return home. There is also an indication of emotional sacrifice found in the surreal and nightmarish asy-lum dreamscape.

ATHLETIC: Dreaming about Athletics primarily involves a symbolic contest and competition in general. This competition is rarely pitted against another person, instead the event is representative of overcoming our own obstacles. In a very real sense, success in sports revolves around individuals who are able to surmount inner dissension. When this is achieved and only when this is achieved, can the athlete function at his or her maximum level and as a focused team player. The unconscious utilizes these doctrines of athletics and illustrates their metaphoric analogy to the outward percussions of inner conflicts found in every day life. As such, we need to interpret the colors worn in the game, intention and ethics of opponents and our own strengths and weaknesses in the tournament on the whole. (*see* Acrobat)

ATTACK: The Attack dream is very common and reflective of the stressful society in which we live. This is because the attack dream demonstrates an assault upon our 'waking' selves, that is, our character, personality and outward social behavior etc. In most cases our feelings of guilt cause this self-chastisement, which is why in a large majority of dreams, attackers' faces and intentions cannot be identified. In other cases, attackers may be people known to us, in which case, a need to understand feelings held about those individuals is critical in interpretation. If the attacker is an animal, it should be noted what species it belongs to and its appropriate symbolism. This way one may understand, its psychological intrusion upon the dreamer's awareness.

ATTORNEY: The ideas of 'law', 'guilt' and 'punishment' rely heavily on this dream figure. There is also a notion of frustration involved in having ones affairs handled by a stranger in this dream. The symbolism is an intellectual impotence to defend ones own actions and moral integrity.

AURA: In the dream sense of the word, Aura depicts a viewpoint about an individual or object which is multi-layered and multi-dimensional. For example, a man in a dream who is simultaneously happily married, father of five children, avant-garde artist, visionary, hockey player, world class bicyclist AND an all-around nice guy, must possess an aura. This is because of the superimposition of all these separate 'attributes' which the dreamer has placed upon him and which convert into emotional 'sensations' about this subject. This does not mean that the subject is a 'holy' man in the mind's eye (although this sometimes is the case), but rather a 'complicated' and 'out of reach' force which must be dealt with carefully and emphatically.

AUTHORITY FIGURE: Our childhood life is by and large dominated by Authority Figures who instruct our behavior by either sheer force or good sound reason. We are taught how to behave socially first by our parents and then our teachers, next our religious leaders and finally our financial leaders, otherwise known as 'the boss.' In dreams, authority figures are representations of what we may have learned from the original authoritative influence in our life. It is our unconscious' way of targeting a lapse in our responsibility and\or direction. Conversely, the dream may be demonstrating our own tyranny, in taking on the role of Authority Figure in our waking daily lives and wrongfully harming people around us. Whether they be employees, friends or family members. The message communicated by the authority figure in the dream, will aid in the understanding of the dream symbolism, when combined with the analysis of ones feelings toward the commanding figure focused upon in the overall dreamscape.

AWAKE: To dream oneself sleeping and then in the dream suddenly awakening is an allusion to the mind's awareness of its own dream state. In other words, the conscious and unconscious overlap and bridge respective functions and concerns. The conscious mind is immediate and rational, 'organizing' as it does our day to day activities in a linear schedule based on time. On the other hand, the unconsciousness is not grounded in time and soars over and around the entirety of our human perception. Together, the rational and irrational symbols of our dream connect to reveal a deep, yet immediate guide to our current predicaments and otherwise confusing situations.

AXIS: The Axis is the center of the sphere which allows balance, rotation and overall equilibrium. Therefore, to be interacting fluidly with the axis found in the dreamscape may signify a psychological and emotional balance in ones personal and vulnerable infant found in our dream suckling or crying, perhaps hungry is a clear description of our fragile inner selves which require professional life.

BABY: The immediate gratification in the form of care or attention. This unconscious dramatization was referred to as 'The ID' by Sigmund Freud. When situations in our waking life become overbearing and overly complicated we have a tendency or desire to revert back to our childlike self (in the form of a baby) whose needs are cared for by another. The shift from responsibility to dependence, occurs quite often in the psyche as a defense mechanism against decision-making, which may have an affect upon the overall well being of loved ones.

BACKGROUND: It is essential in the understanding of dreams to be fully aware of every element found within the dream itself. The background of a dream is in no way incidental. The environments chosen as 'landscapes' for dreams reflect subtle psychological states of mind and are not necessarily consistent with 'waking' life. In dreams, skies may be green, turtles may be purple and trees may be rainbow-colored and able to walk, talk and laugh hysterically. Therefore, it is necessary to isolate and then analyze each element of a dream on its own terms. When the separate psychological facets are understood, then and only then, can they be pieced together to form a symbolic 'storyline' which reveals something about the dreamer which may be hidden or repressed from the waking conscious itself.

BACON: The symbolism of Bacon is wealth and excess as remarked in the quote, 'The head of the family brings home the bacon.' The image of thick, fatty meats frying on the stove and filling the house with certain sumptuous aromas is not lost on the unconscious. This concentrated symbol reminds us that material life is plentiful but should not overshadow our spiritual lives. In many cases men and women dream of burnt bacon, or meat which falls to the floor and is immediately swallowed up by hungry dogs. The implication here is a loss of wealth due to unnecessary greed (over-cooking) and/or distrust of our peers and associates (hungry dogs).

BAG/BAGGAGE: The symbolism of a Bag lies in what one carries. A person may carry the responsibility of faith, trust or even love. Therefore, if the bag is too heavy or tears apart, a reflection is given of a burden too difficult to 'carry out.' A person may need to examine his or her waking life to determine which of their obligations is tearing away at the fabric of their psyche.

BALD: The image of Baldness is entirely different from the image of losing ones hair. Hair is a symbol of sexuality, virility and strength. Therefore losing ones hair, or having ones hair cut off against ones will, is a representation of anxiety felt about ones sexuality or overall good health. On the other hand, 'normal' or intentional baldness signifies purity and personal sacrifice, a kind of surrendering of ones cloak of deception.

BALANCE: The dream of maintaining ones balance is central to erect-standing human beings who must sustain balance in order to stand, walk and perform daily functions. Our equilibrium has therefore become a symbol for proper, upright behavior. Since we fear 'falling down' in our tasks and responsibilities we go to great lengths to create fluid equilibrium in every aspect of our lives. We court love, money, friendship, skill and security, hoping to acquire an equal and healthy 'share' of each gift of life. However, if one of our 'gifts' is absent we experience stress about the possibility of 'falling down' into the darkness of human failure. In most cases the dream character maintaining balance indicates which psychological limitation of oneself is threatening the whole. (*see* Tarot Major Arcana: Justice (11))

BALLERINA: Lyrical beauty, innocence and subtle coordination are all features present in the archetype of the Ballerina. In the dream landscape, a ballerina is the representation of a smooth, flowing musical life with no obstacles and no restrictions. The ballerina is thought to be so light and agile that she can leap up into the night sky and land again weightlessly into the waiting arms of her many admirers. Therefore, in a dream, the ballerina represents fluid order in ones own life which depending on the other elements of the dream landscape may be threatened by a new and unforeseen force. In some cases, the Ballerina is simply representational of unreachable and divine beauty which weighs heavily on a dreamer's waking life.

BALLOON: The balloon is a double-archetype of childhood innocence and total freedom. Therefore, there can be negative associations with the balloon symbolizing children who are so 'free'
that they are left alone and placed into jeopardy. Supporting this
approach is the fragile nature of the balloon which can 'burst' or
become 'lost' at any time. However, notwithstanding its apparent and perhaps misleading vulnerability, the balloon primarily
illustrates merriment, mirth and brightly colored emotional jubilation.

BAMBOO: The Bamboo plant is known for its strength and resil-
iency. In the dream, it signifies a strong bond or agreement with
ones associates. The bamboo plant is also symbolic of native,
and therefore, trustworthy behavior. In a dream, goods wrapped
in Bamboo may be representational of sound and fair business
transactions. In this figure, we find a further allusion to upright
and spiritual behavior on the whole. (*see* Tree)

BAPTISM: The archetypal symbol here is the fourth element (fire,
air, earth...) Water, is the clear and unpolluted purifier, the
cleansing away of sins and the attainment of spiritual rebirth.
Psychologically, we need to purify or renew ourselves after, or
prior to, periods of intense emotional difficulty. The dreamer
may be experiencing guilt for wrong behavior which has left
them feeling 'unclean' in the moral sense. The image of Baptism is one of intense character transfiguration replete with a
new lease on life, a second chance to provide atonement. This
archetype also contains elements of regression, as it may be a return to childhood innocence and absolute purity.

BAR: The dream image of the Bar is a common one, in that it contains within its well-structured landscape, an array of deeply
seated human rituals. A primary example of this is the 'right of
passage' critical in the development of young men moving into
'adulthood.' A young man is encouraged to 'drink' himself into
a state of 'mental disorder', an entirely preconceived yet 'irrational' step into the beyond, akin to young native warriors who
are cast into the 'wild' to prepare their souls and bodies for the
responsibilities of age and/or tribal leadership. This formal ritual sometimes leads to alcoholism (in young men in bars, not
warriors) which is certainly an anxiety reflected in the dream ex-
ile of the pub and ale house. As it concerns sexuality, the bar is a
'stage' or 'forum' for both men and women to reveal and perform their social poise and sensual posture to an audience of

their peers. Taking all this into account, the bar archetype provides an ideal landscape to demonstrate a characterization of ones 'inner' self and personal desires, dependent upon ones actions or 'performance' within its well-defined parameters. To succeed, fail or remain anonymous in a particular bar ritual represents a psychological message about that liturgy's significance in ones waking life.

BARREN: The clear symbolism of the Barren field is a lack of fertility or the lost harvest. However, this dream landscape indicates not only infertility and its masculine counterpart impotency. Sometimes the barren symbolism rather dramatically reflects desperate isolationism, loss of relationship or hanging on to changing (perhaps outdated) methods. The dream may also represent a simple overview of the personal anxiety of enduring a plain and otherwise flat lifestyle that seeks the lifeblood waters of emotional challenge combined with 'seeds' of new and wondrous experience. In other words, a call to go out and brave existence.

BASEMENT: The Basement archetype often refers to our unconscious which 'stores' within its unknown depths the long file of our living memories, some of which may be unpleasant and entirely repressed. In our dreams we may experience unspeakable horrors hidden (or hiding) in the basement which are waiting to return to our surface lives seeking dreadful revenge. In dreams we sometimes experience a turning point in a repressed emotion which suddenly may need to re-emerge into the conscious psyche. The basement represents fear tinged with acknowledgment and most importantly, confrontation. In the therapeutic sense, the dreamer is expressing a need to free his Shadow figure in the basement, this to undo its presumed fearful and vengeful harm.

BASIN: The symbol of the Basin depends heavily on the fullness and contents of the vessel itself. For example, a wash basin filled with dirty water which cannot be drained out, is a clear indication of an emotional predicament which is stagnating and refuses to go away such as illness, tragedy, or a bad relationship. Perhaps even, a pregnancy, or the related burden of child-rearing. On the other hand, when the basin is empty and drains everything poured into it, the dreamer may be experiencing an extreme fear of loss, or losing a sane, yet fragile perception, or 'hold', on life. The empty tub is in this sense symbolic of emotional isolation and a sinking feeling of loneliness. (see Leak)

BAT: The bat as winged creature, refers to ones erratic state of mind and the distinct danger associated with that kind of unsteady 'focus' in ones everyday consciousness.' The Bat as baseball stick symbolizes hitting for glory, and otherwise, attempting to 'score' or 'win' some critical game. The 'game' itself is symbolic of life, therefore naturally, the hit or miss of the bat, singular in the game process, is significantly expressing a crucial event in ones life which has already transpired or will take place in the near future. In this sense, the bat is the archetype of promise, potency and potential; moreover, as phallus the bat can 'score', be broken (castration or impotence) or strike out (lack of self-confidence).

BATHROOM: The symbolic reference of the Bathroom landscape, entirely familiar in the modern world, concerns the absolution of the 'sins' of every day life. We remove our uncleanliness and 'recreate' ourselves through cleaning, grooming and the application of makeup. In dreams, we are expressing transition and renewal in the bathroom landscape, since it is a place to superficially free ourselves from the reality of mortality which weighs us down and brings us closer to our 'uncivilized' selves. We may be expressing a need to forgive someone who has treated us in an uncivilized manner or, conversely, we may be communicating a desire to return to 'society' with a new face. In this sense, we may also fear death and the normal changes that come with age.

BEACH: The Beach represents a borderline between two states of mind, one solid and well thought out, and the other unsteady, emotional and perhaps wrought with danger, or adventure. The interpretation is dependent on whether we are in the ocean, or on the sand, and in which direction we respectively face. If we face the ocean, we may be preparing ourselves for the unknown and vast changes in our life which may effect us, or our families, in an unalterable way. It must be noted if the ocean is calm, pleasant and inviting, or stormy, dark and forbidding. If there is a hurricane brewing we certainly need to heed the intense fear of change being expressed in the dream. On the other hand, if we are returning to land, we may be expressing a return to the familiar. Perhaps an unusual event has recently occurred in our lives and we are finally adapting to it and accepting its parameters.

BEAM: If the Beam is sturdy in the dream and supports our home which is a reflection of our body, it is a clear indication of a solid psychological framework. We are expressing a general satisfaction with our choices in life. If the beam is new, we are reflecting a recent decision which seems to give us security and a general sense of well-being. On the other hand, if the beam is cracked and shaky, we may be expressing anxiety about the health and welfare of our families or persons close to us. If the beam is crumbling and the house is falling down around us, we may be expressing a fear of sickness or a recent and tremendous personal loss, for example, losing ones job, or preparing for a divorce.

BEARD: The Beard is symbolic of virility, strength and vigor. However, the beard can also represent a mask or something to hide behind. Therefore, it is crucial to understand why the person in the dream wears the beard. If the man is a stranger and the dreamer is attracted to him, it may represent a desire to return to a natural, unhampered way of life reminiscent of the 'mountain man.' On the other hand, if the dreamer himself suddenly has a beard, he may be expressing guilt and a need to get away from himself for a short time. Conversely, the dreamer may feel out of place in a situation, therefore places himself 'undercover' in order to rationalize for the perceived intrusion incurred on his associates. If a woman dreams of wearing a beard, she may be expressing hostility about being treated 'like a woman' rather than being treated as an equal. In so doing, she becomes both sexes and can conquer all who would attempt to belittle her. In dreams, the bearded lady is more than a side show freak, but a real and formidable archetype worshipped in ancient times.

BED: The Bed is symbolic of ones most intimate self. It represents the discovery of ones sexuality in puberty, the sublime union of marriage, the recovery center in times of sickness and the place of sleep, and you guessed it, dreams. Therefore, when we refer to a bed in our dreams, we are revealing a piece of our deepest selves. We may be offering this part of ourselves to another. Needless to say, this may be a very difficult proposition in our life and we may need to examine the condition of the bed, the color of the sheets and our feelings about the bed. If the bed seems uninviting and dangerous, we could be experiencing deep emotional fear and difficulties which may require professional counseling.

BEGGAR: The Beggar is symbolic of life out of balance, a failure of society and the surrender of an individual against the harsh pressure of that society. He or she is the embodiment of poverty and the reality of mortality and its needs. To dream of oneself as a beggar indicates a drifting away from others. A dreamer may be experiencing difficulty within his or her social environment. The unconscious therefore, is calling out for help, not in the form of spare change, but rather, acceptance and honest guidance; it is a dream search for the generosity of soul.

BELL: A Bell usually signifies a call to order, command or warning. In a dream, a ringing bell illustrates a signal by the unconscious to be 'prepared' for whatever will happen next, either in the dream or in real life itself. If there is a significant occurrence in the dream after the ringing of the bell, analyze its meaning thoroughly, because it may hold the key to a pending situation in waking life. If the bell rings relentlessly in the dream and never stops, we can be certain a warning has been issued to the dreamer who may be experiencing extreme anxiety about a situation and needs to face its reality.

BETWEEN: There are moments in dreams where we find ourselves crushed Between two opposing forces. This dream situation is clearly indicative of outside forces pushing us in different directions. Each outside force desires us to join their side and not the others. In life, we realize the reality of opposing viewpoints and the pressure placed upon us to make a decision and 'choose a side.' The unconscious is illustrating our frustration in this predicament and reflecting the absurdity of non-movement which occurs from resistant, and close-minded, points of view.

BIKINI: The Bikini dream is indicative of superficial desire and an almost pre-pubescent eroticism as opposed to nakedness which may indicate more than a primal sexuality. The bikini symbolizes a return to youth and innocence, desire and connection made without consequence. It is an image of sexual and voyeuristic freedom coupled with a playful, yet nonthreatening eroticism. The bikini dream may be expressing a desire to 'lighten up' current psychological or emotional states of mind in order to re-establish a relationship with another or even with oneself.

BIRDS: Primarily, birds represent the spiritual longing of mind because of their ability to fly and their melodious song which may move our human spirit. However, there are also images of nesting in the bird archetype which may have references to our own family and homelife. It is important to observe the condition of the nest and the young within the nest. Is the nest safe? Are the chicks crying or chirping happily? Is the nest being built? All these answers are symbolic to the state of well-being in the home for the dreamer. Certain birds carry their own unique archetypical meanings. (*see* Crow, Eagle, Chicken, Owl)

BINOCULARS: In dreams, Binoculars generally refer to searching, perhaps searching for hope in the symbolic form of land. However, binoculars may conversely signify, seeing what should not be seen. In this case, binoculars represent guilt about knowledge which should not be known, perhaps gained by spying or some form of eavesdropping.

BISEXUAL: If a person is not Bisexual and dreams him or herself as bisexual, there may be an indication of sexual repression or wish fulfillment. The dreamer may be compensating for his or her lack of sexuality with a 'heightened' sense of all-encompassing eroticism. (*see* Anima/Animus)(*see* Hermaphrodite)

BITE: In a dream, to Bite someone is a complicated expression of aggression which implies 'devouring' another person's attributes or 'lifeforce'(*see* Cannibalism). However, biting some object or ones own lip may simply imply attempting to control ones own aggression. If the dreamer is bit by a wild animal, he or she may be experiencing fear or anxiety about their own natural or sexual feelings which may be repressed in waking existence. In another sense, the soul of man is often symbolized as the mouth, or in the mouth, providing the circular breath of life. In this sense, the biting motion of teeth may imply a blocking of spiritual faith. Moreover, since we ourselves perform the action of biting, we may be questioning our very own moral strength and fiber. (*see* Tarot Major Arcana: Judgment (20))

BITTER: In life, many situations leave the idiomatic 'bad taste' in ones mouth. A dream utilizes Bitterness to exaggerate this harsh anxiety. It is absolutely necessary to analyze the characters and landscape surrounding the moment or 'phase' of bitterness experienced in the dream to better understand the source from which comes the 'element', or reality, too difficult to swallow. If, as in a nightmare, the bitterness is prolonged or persistent in its agonizing, the dreamer may be experiencing guilt about betrayal or the allowance of continual abusive behavior inflicted by a loved one. (*see* Bite)

BLACK: The color Black in the dream sense is almost always indicative of the mysterious and unknown. If a figure wears a long black robe, black cape or black hood in a dream landscape we fear his power and his knowledge which is entirely unknown to us. Often, as is the case with Carl Jung's interpretation of the Shadow figure, the man in black is a reflection of our hidden or repressed desires. In this manner, all objects which are encased in shadow or black are representations of our unconscious, the dark pool of reason. As the color black is the result of all colors occurring simultaneously, so to is our unconscious the accumulation of all collective human experience. (*see* Collective Unconscious)

BLANKET: The Blanket is primarily a symbol of protection and warmth. If in a dream we wrap a cold or wet loved one in a blanket we are expressing a need or desire to care for that person. In the visual sense the blanket is the antithesis of the bikini, the former representing 'love' and the latter 'lust.'

BLAZE: The concept of the Blaze refers to passionate anger and a sudden emotional release. Moreover, the symbolism of fire is synonymous with both creation as well as, destruction. As such, we need to determine the nature of the blaze. For example, is it in the fireplace representing hearth and family, or conversely, is it burning through the woods and therefore, symbolically demonstrating the devastation of our natural and creative instincts. In any case, like passion itself, the dream indicates that the symbolic reference to blaze in our waking life, may need to be harnessed and focused toward our real desires and aspirations. As such, the rising flame should never be allowed to rage out of our complete control. In this, dreams warn us not to cross the line of blind, and potentially murderous obsession. (*see* Ablaze)(*see* Fire)(*see* Hearth)(*see* Wood)(*see* Kindling)

BLEED: In dreams, a loss of Blood implies a loss of vitality and faith in oneself. In ancient times, blood was symbolic of life itself. Therefore, to spill an enemies blood in battle was the equivalent of draining the life out of not only the soldier, but also his people. There have been accounts of tribes worldwide, throughout the years, who believed in drinking the blood of their enemies in order to absorb their respective and respected powers. As a symbol of sacrifice, blood is the physical embodiment of our spirit. This would explain why people wound themselves to show allegiance to their social organizations and sometimes far more brutally, to demonstrate their love for a potential consort. In order to interpret the blood dream properly, we must analyze both the person who bleeds and the person who has caused them to bleed. Lastly, we must determine where the person bleeds and decode the symbolism of that body part. Taken together, these three components may aid in understanding the message of the unconscious.

BLIND: To dream of Blindness implies closing ones eyes to a given truth which cannot be seen (coped with) for whatever reason. It is the symbolic equivalent of wishing for the DISAPPEARANCE of ones enemies. There is a strong rationale for this behavior in that our enemies represent a failure or limitation in ourselves. There is a psychological implication made therein, that our enemies seek to destroy us because they 'feel' we are somehow inappropriate or inferior as human beings. In dreaming of blindness, we close our eyes to what is horrendous and not at all viewable, in many cases, the hideous object of repulsion may be ourselves, and the manifestations of our own actions.

BLUE: The color Blue contains two distinct emotions revealed in subtle differences in shade. Light blue represents the sky and the morning sea, bright, limitless and eternal. All light blue objects in a dream fit well within the spectrum of birth and the infinite. On the other hand, the application of dark blue or navy blue represents deep and slow depression, a cessation of forward movement and innocent hope. A dark blue sky illuminates the beginning of night and physical uncertainty. In dreams therefore, deep blue depression can be encoded on clothing, skin tone and the entire landscape.

BOAT: The symbolism of a Boat is dependent on the movement and type of craft positioned in the dream landscape. Should the boat be sailing along effortlessly on a smooth turquoise sea, the dreamer is feeling vital, energetic, free and potent (with full blown sails which echo health and the expectant flowering of pregnancy). If instead, our dream reflects a row boat which is moored and sways unsteadily in a stormy setting, our unconscious may be illustrating fear, and uncertainty in our emotional affairs. There are social aspects to the boat archetype which 'carries' upon its deck handfuls of different individuals. In many respects, this small social arrangement upon the boat is reminiscent of family. Therefore, a boat sinking may represent a fear of losing ones children, due for instance, to a difficult and insurmountable emotional circumstance. (Ex: Divorce)

BONE: The Bone is not necessarily the symbol of death. The skeletal frame of the human body represents its infrastructure and basic form. Therefore, bones can represent life and body intact.

Since the immune system is based upon chemicals secreted from glands found within bone marrow, the unconscious may be reflecting sound and stalwart physiological and psychological health. However, in dreams, cracked bones may symbolize the reverse symptoms of poor health and shaky psychological ground. A need to analyze which bone on the body is broken and what that particular part of the body may represent to us.

BOOK: In dreams, Books represent old wisdom, memory and a collection of personal experiences. In many ways, ALL books represent the single book, or story, of our life. However, if a particular book is singled out in a dream, the dreamer needs to understand his or her feelings about that particular work. Perhaps the book angered the reader by illustrating a character development similar to a repressed trait or 'characteristic' of him or herself. On the other hand, the book might represent a significant calling, such as religious leadership, or an invitation into the field of education as teacher, or perhaps, student.

BOTTLE: A Bottle is symbolic of sensual celebration. It is the representation of the 'pouring' of life in all its spirited animation. As such, a bottle is broken on a ship to 'christen' its first journey of 'wondrous' travels. Along these same sacred lines, the bottle is thought to be symbolic of the vagina and moreso, the womb itself. Because of its shape and the free pouring of its emotional and intoxicating liquids, the bottle has in many ways become symbolic of femininity and eternal womanhood.

BOX: Since a Box is a solid structure with eight (which is the symbol of strength) corners, which 'house' ourselves and our belongings, it is no wonder it has become the symbol of our mind and psychological edifice. Out of this 'Pandora's Box' comes all human invention and unique creation. In dreams, a box may be a gift from our unconscious to our conscious, in other words, a representational transition point from internal idea, to external worldly realization. (Ex: Engagement ring which is revealed and displayed from a tiny box with emerges suddenly and unexpectedly)

BRAINWAVES:(*see* Alpha & Delta Waves)

BREAD: In dreams, Bread may be symbolic of any knowledge or physical reality which is crucial or basic to our very existence. Bread is a basic nourishment and the complement to meats, cheeses and most other food sources. Therefore, in the representational sense, bread is the symbol for the 'host body' itself.

(Compare blood as the symbol for 'spirit') In this way we understand that bread, or 'the body', is both the foundation and the completion of the stuff (animation) of life. Accordingly, when we dream of bread, we are dreaming of our physiological reality and how it may be currently effected by situations in direct contact with us.

BREATH: How we Breathe in a dream is symbolic of how we may be experiencing our psychological reality. If we find ourselves breathing rapidly, we may be expressing anxiety, tension or outright fear concerning a new situation in our waking lives. On the other hand, if we stop breathing as though submerged under water, we may be experiencing womb-like memories replete with biological or psychological dependence upon another. (Ex: Mother Figure) In this context, we may be communicating a temporary inadequacy to care for ourselves via a distinct inability to fulfill our own needs and therefore, surrendering or 'sinking' into our 'prebirth' helplessness. Another unconscious illustration, the holding of ones breath, indicates a stubborn state of mind and an almost childish reflection of our single-minded willfulness to demonstrate this resolve. The nightmarish sensation of a shortness of breath and an outright difficulty in normal breathing, may be a more direct unconscious message to examine ones physical health or the health of ones family.

BRICK: The image of a Brick, may represent psychological or emotional obstacles which pile up and create internal barriers or walls. Alternatively, bricks may represent hard labor and the mental pain of conviction. As such, we need to determine the goal and relative accomplishments associated with the bricks themselves. The final, or proposed, construction of the bricks is perhaps more symbolically conclusive, than the individual bricks. (see Wall)(see House)(see Rocks)

BRIDGE: In dreams, Bridges represent transitions in ones emotional life. Changes which may effect our delicate emotional balance are approached slowly and with great caution. We may even be asked to pay a symbolic 'toll' to enable our emotional passage. When we end a relationship, we talk about 'burning the bridge behind us' which implies enacting a clean cutaway from the person with which we were involved. The purpose of this is to remove all 'problematic' emotional ties which prevent both individuals to complete their emotional transitions intact. This may enable them to begin their own specific means of healing.

BROKEN: In a dream, any shattered ideal state, whether it be physical, psychological or emotional is represented to the psyche as a Broken symbol. In order to analyze the dream message we first need to understand the importance of the object which is broken in our dream vision. For example, if a wine glass is broken, we may be expressing superior emotional vigor; on the other hand, if a child's doll is broken, we may be depicting a deep deficiency in our most basic emotional needs which must be fulfilled.

BROTHER: In a dream, a person's Brother may represent a mirror image of the person dreaming, regardless of the dreamers gender. Because of the normal psychology in sibling rivalry, our brother may represent qualities which we may or may not possess. We may be experiencing an unconscious desire to express these traits in a more forceful manner. On the other hand, we may be experiencing guilt for recently behaving in a childish manner reminiscent of our early years of rivalry, where competing for the favor of our parents, sometimes overshadowed the human consequences of our actions. This may include the harmful and pointed physical or psychological attacks on our own brother or sister.

BUDDHA: The Buddha represents a worldly calm which he creates for himself in a dream state. Should he awake, all of reality, which is his own manifest illusion, would vanish. Therefore, when we dream of the buddha, we are dreaming of the frailty and insubstantiality of our own existence. The implication of this dream may involve the mechanics of the dream process itself. We may be observing the landscape of our living experience in order to shape and become a better figure within that reality. In essence, we are asking the dream (the unconscious) to show our place within the dream (reality). If our waking life is filled with pressure, confusion, depression and anger, the buddha may be the unconscious way of demonstrating how to turn our 'nightmare' back into a calm, purposeful and transcendent dream life.

BUG: With the exception of the ant (*see* Ant), Bugs generally refer to psychological irritations or fears. If we are annoyed by a single bug in our dream, we simply need to face our symbolic tormentor and calmly brush it away. If on the other hand, our dream pests consist of a handful of black widows, scorpions or a swarm of locust, we need to analyze what psychological fears in our life is causing this degree of anxiety. The indication of the insect/bug symbolism refers to a large number of small grievances which may have accumulated and now surrounded us, or conceivably our family.

BULL: In dreams, Bulls represent blind aggression and rage. However, unlike a tiger, which is also an aggressive powerful animal, the bull has no poise and lacks grace. Therefore in the dream, we may be referring to recent impulsive actions which may have left others with the impression of us as a 'bull in a china shop.' Conversely, because of its blind rage, the unconscious may use the bull archetype to illustrate a deeply repressed sexuality which is in need to 'charge out' and face its opponent. The extensive mythological use of a minotaur inside the labyrinth is further and undoubtedly suggestive of our repressed sexual and aggressive natures. However, the reverse definition may also hold true. In this manner, the minotaur of the labyrinth blocks the final entrance into spiritual enlightenment with its sexual and stubborn physical nature. Appropriately, we need to determine the relative physicality of the bull and how it applies to our own peculiar situation. (*see* Horn)

BUTTER: In dreams, if our bread is thick and covered with butter, we are experiencing a rich, healthy life. However, if we choke on that butter or find it spread too thick upon the bread, our unconscious may be expressing excess in our life which must be curtailed in order for us to maintain our physical, psychological and emotional balance. Conversely, if our bread lacks butter and tastes bland, we may be expressing a need to add quality (Ex: art, leisure, travel, new environment) and fullness (Ex: friends, family) into the context of our day to day lives.

BUTTERFLY: In dreams, a Butterfly is significant of fragile and beautiful, yet elusive hope. In many traditions, it is the single metaphor of the human soul. Analogous to the world dream of the Buddha, the butterfly is so delicate it nearly defies existence. It is a gift, rather than a right. To dream of capturing a butterfly is symbolic of a child who wishes to 'capture' beauty. In adulthood, we learn to cherish and respect beauty, to hold it in our hands and watch it fly free without remorse for the joy which it has given us. We have learned to return the gift of love back into the maternal arms of nature who dreams silently on the long and translucent wing of the sole butterfly as she travels faithfully on her timeless and sacred journey into night, and eternal memory.

CABIN: In a dream, a Cabin may be symbolic of protection from 'elements' in our life which may be closing in on us. There are factors in our day to day waking life which we cannot escape in the confines of our own home (Ex: bills, marriage, poverty). Consequently, we seek to escape these realities by changing our location, which is our symbolic psychological landscape. Keeping this in mind, we return to a natural setting and a simpler way of life. Dream reality does not concern itself with the waking realities of cabin cost, available vacation time or the availability of an ax to chop fire wood. The dream instead, reveals a message to the dreamer to keep things simple and approach life's difficulties one at a time, and with a straightforward manner, not entirely unlike a mountain man or pioneer.

CACTUS: A Cactus is known for its ability to survive in harsh elements with its long, hard thorns and water saving physiology. However, human beings are not cactus, and this dream may imply the utilization or lowering of ones own defense mechanisms. If the cactus defies the dreamer's need to hold it, or drink its water, the unconscious might be telling us to release someone or something which we ourselves may be pushing into a corner by our own selfish actions. Conversely, if we picture ourselves as the cactus, we may be expressing a difficulty in allowing people into our lives causing us loneliness and desperate isolation. (*see* Desert)

CADET: The image of a young soldier carries with it a complex range of emotions. This factor is primarily centered around the opposite concept of youth and innocence versus the murderous, adult reality of war. Within the nucleus of these polar opposites we find transitional roads of psychological and spiritual learning and transcendence in both directions. As such, we see a young adult step into the responsibility of full adulthood, just as we see the potential older and hardened soldier, jeopardizing his or her life for youth and freedom. Moreover, the rites of passage involved in adulthood are drastically illustrated in this dormant war-like figure. In another sense, we witness a call to duty, or a hunger for valor and/or honor, all in the name of our peers and social influences. Accordingly, the cadet dream illustrates harsh, yet productive and quite plausible possibilities found in the context of our waking experience. (*see* Bar)(*see* Warrior)

CAGE: When we are held back from expression, movement and especially, freedom, we inevitably illustrate the dream symbol of the Cage. In waking life, there are numerous laws, rules, codes, regulations and limitations which in theory provide structure and organization in society. When a dreamer feels trapped by these binding knots in the fabric of society and civilization, he or she visualizes him or herself as dislocated from choice and therefore, removed from the independence of individuality. On the other hand, if the dreamer feels that they 'belong' behind bars, it may be a clear representation of feelings of guilt over ones wild, uncontrolled and perhaps violent behavior.

CAKE: In a dream, a Cake may symbolize social or family unity. It is a food source intended for many to celebrate the honoring of a few. If the cake is sliced and the dreamer receives a wedge of cake which is in some way spoiled or inferior to slices received by other members of the celebration, it may imply jealousy on the part of the dreamer toward ones family or peer group. Conversely, if ones slice is bigger than everyone else's, guilt about ones greed or excess should be examined. If, as originally stated, the cake in the dream is intact and whole, the dreamer may be expectant of an important emotional celebration, including marriage, a better job, or perhaps, the birth of a child.

CALENDAR: In dreams, a Calendar may represent the passage of time, which may carry with it a concern about ones age. A calendar may also illustrate ones apprehension, anxiety or fear concerning an approaching date. If there is a date displayed in the dream, a need to analyze its significance may be necessary. If the date means nothing to the dreamer, he or she may be alerted that they themselves need to make something happen on that date, which may be the unconscious' way of remembering an unexpected window of opportunity, revealed long ago.

CAMEL: The Camel is symbolic of healthy, stalwart life. Because of this, and the shape of its hump, it may also indicate pregnancy or birth. Moreover, since the camel is an obedient, trustworthy animal which can carry a human being through the harshest of elements, its dream appearance indicates deep trust or spiritual transcendence in that dreamers life. We need to analyze our behavior with and acceptance of the camel in order to better understand the dream's message. For example, if the camel is dying, we may be witnessing a change in our own trustworthiness or altruistic behavior.

CANDLE: In a dream, lighting or carrying a single Candle may represent a ray of hope where there is nothing but darkness. In this, a candle is akin to a prayer for knowledge and guidance. In many cultures a candle is lit for a loved one who has passed away. The candlelight is symbolic of the loved ones soul which burns bright and flickers its warmth and light through the worldly haze. If, in our dream, a candle is blown out, we may be surrendering an important part of ourselves prematurely. If many candles are lit in a dream, we may be surrounding ourselves with a certain faith in ourselves, our loved ones, our society, or a spiritual calling.

CANNIBAL: Cannibalism implies the giving of oneself completely when a dreamer views him or herself as the human sacrifice which will be 'carved' and 'devoured' by the tribe. Because of the offering of ones flesh, their is a deep repressed sexuality which may be at the root of this dream landscape. The dreamer may be demonstrating a desire to surrender his or her own life-force for the prolonged existence of another in the most extreme form of altruism (which is a form of selfless love) imaginable. In the Christian religion, Jesus is said to have offered and given his body and blood for the redemption of the sins of man. However, if the dreamer IS the cannibal who eats or desires to eat human flesh, he or she may be seeking to absorb the vitality or perhaps, the sexuality of another.

CANYON: A Canyon is a huge natural phenomenon which dwarfs the size of a single individual. Therefore, its vastness can be approached with wonder, joy and enlightenment of being a part of it all, or, with fear, apprehension and a loss of self-importance and significance. Notwithstanding a fear of heights, the dreamer has the option of feeling in tune with 'everything' or feeling him or herself as the embodiment of 'nothingness' and hopelessness, come face to face with an almost infinite reality. How we view ourselves in the dream and how we feel about the canyon may reveal something crucial about our respective personality. Are we moved by reality, or mortified by it?

CAR: The automobile has become a major component of the American psyche. Advertisers, almost universally, have anthropomorphized the sexuality, status and dire familial necessity of the mechanical beast. It has become almost unthinkable to approach adulthood in today's society without a driver's license and accompanying shiny new, (or slightly used) vehicle of choice. This fact remains consistent even in our major cities, where driving is unnecessary and at times, environmentally crippling. Conversely, the rebuilding of America, and the world proper, to accommodate for these automobiles, via highways, byways, roads, streets, cul-de-sacs, parking zones, traffic helicopters and scooters, gas and fuel stations riddled across the landscape, not to mention motor, maintenance, exotic and classic car appreciation clubs nationwide, have unceremoniously changed the country's panorama in a very real and permanent fashion. In this psychological terrain, the automobile takes center stage and is reflected appropriately in our dream consciousness. Accordingly, the movement, freedom, sexuality and status offered by our car is examined and thrown into symbolic light by our ever-useful unconscious. In this complex symmetry of society and understanding, our vehicle becomes the single embodiment of ourself, in both its glory and limitation. Hence, we ordinarily use ordinary metaphors like, 'She's a hot, 68 Caddy with pink tails, soft cushions and plenty of bite and throttle for the long, hard open road.' or 'He's a 38 Desoto, from his short block, crop top, to his pudgy old fenders, without any hint of style, flash or imagination, whatsoever.' All this would lead us to believe that a car's appearance in a dream landscape may reveal a deeply held truth about the totality of our waking experience.

CARAVAN: The dream symbolism of a caravan may well be an expression of social union in order to withstand the harsher elements of life. The archetype of a 'journey' refers to physical and spiritual transcendence. The caravan unifies and guides the human journey, becoming a world unto itself and therefore absorbing the journey of transcendence back into its own folds. In a dream, the caravan may be the implication to organize or join others, perhaps a family, to achieve the greater good of the whole.

CASTLE: A Castle represents the myth and archetype of power, both good and bad. To be a part of the castle reflects nobility, comfort, and protection, as well as 'romantic' desire and adventurous passion. A castle is also reminiscent of the mystery of its many rooms, which may represent the complexity of the human mind or human heart. In a dream, we must analyze our 'place' in the castle and our behavior in this capacity. We may be experiencing guilt about our royal, yet pompous behavior, or we may be expressing a wish-fulfillment to be 'saved' from the high tower of our morals by some young, willful knight or some large, lustful dragon!(see Knight)(see Dragon)(see King)(see Queen)

CASTRATION: Castration may imply ones anxiety about impotence or a perceived loss of masculinity. If a person is intimidated or brought into submission by a man or woman's strong aggressive nature, that person may dream of being severely mutilated. Conversely, if the dreamer dreams of mutilating another person, he or she may be illustrating a need to strike out against unfeeling, aggressive and otherwise masculine behavior. To cut off ones own phallus in a dream implies a severe repression of ones sexuality or the inability to interact with individuals of the opposite sex.

CAT: The cat is the symbol of mystery, independence and sex. Because of these qualities, the cat has often been compared to mysterious, independent and sexual women. The author would argue that the cat is closer aligned to the unconscious which is mysterious, dark, silent and contains all the wildness of our natural selves, including our lustful sexuality and violent aggression. Accordingly, we need to follow the cat who stalks in our dreams in order to 'see' where it leads. If the cat kills, what has it killed and where has it placed its kill? If it fights other cats, what color are they, and, of who or what do they remind us? And the three most important questions, is the cat male or female, what are our feelings about the cat, and what is the cat illustrating about ourselves in its curious behavior?

CAVE: In many ways a Cave is symbolic of the womb because of its shape and protection. In dreams we may need to run back into our cave (infantile dependence) to escape the large fierce reality of every day life. On the other hand, if we fear the cave and its darkness, we may be expressing a lack of self-confidence about our ability to cope with the unknown. We need to analyze our behavior in and around the respective cave, to better determine the message related to us by our unconscious. (see Womb)(see Hole)

CELEBRATION: A Celebration in our dream primarily reflects an elation found in our psychological experience. Naturally, the ritual of celebration involves sacred rites of passage, including birthdays, weddings and sometimes even funerals. As such, the elation may involve a personal or social transfiguration into another plain of perceptive reality. Moreover, the emotional aspect of the dream imagery is centered around the support of our loved ones and encouraging admirers. In this, we find an unconscious allusion to mechanism of our well being, and that is, the understanding circle of human beings that comprise the day to day interpersonal relationships which fuel our real life's full and fertile experience. (*see* Cake)

CENOTAPH: A number of dream reports indicate individuals witnessing their own name on the marble plaque of a Cenotaph. The implication of this recurring dream image demonstrates the dreamer no longer recognizing him or herself; that gradually in the course of their life, all hopes and aspirations were forced into the background by the real pressures of every day life. The unconscious now illustrates the grim search for a displaced body and soul. Moreover, the cenotaph reflects ones real accomplishments in life, or lack thereof. In this sense, the unconscious may be instructing the dreamer to create something personal in the world, something which demonstrates the spirit of humanity and which just may live on, in the minds of future generations and kin. This concerns leaving behind a memory, other than ones own fancy tombstone.

CENTAUR: In dreams, the mythological Centaur represents music, powerful magic and lustful abandon. As is the case in most archetypical examples of Zoomorphism (half-man/half-animal), man is responding to his primal and 'animalistic' nature, which he deems to project onto a third party or fully realized synthesis of his human and animal characteristics. Unlike the minotaur (which is half bull), the centaur (being half horse), portrays graceful, nearly musical powers of persuasion. To dream of the centaur may reveal a resistance to ones personal and powerful feelings of love or passionate desires. If we ride the centaur, our unconscious may be implying that we are being 'carried away' by our sexual needs.

CENTER: The image of the Center of an object, as seen in a dream, may refer to that object's essential meaning and core purpose. As such, our unconscious may be implying that we get to the 'heart of the matter' in a particular situation. As such, the object may allude, in the sense of an archetype, to the exact nature of the circumstance involved. Moreover, the center of any physical article in space usually provides balance and support for its overall structure and relative function. Accordingly, we may witness a symbolic reference to the human soul. In this, we find a religious or spiritual allusion equated to the physical parameter of the dream impression of center. (*see* Axis)

CEREMONY: As opposed to a celebration, which involves elation and merriment, the Ceremony is a very serious event of human transfiguration and is usually met with somber dedication and commitment. The unconscious therefore may be alluding to thoughtfulness and deliberate meditation involving some event in waking life. The concept of spiritual preparation is inherent in this dream image. Accordingly, we may need to take a long look at ourselves and determine if we are ready for the fidelity and devotion required to successfully move into a higher spiritual plain. The ceremony therefore, is the proving ground of our merit and the vortex of our self sacrifice made real. (*see* Ritual)(*see* Path)(*see* Tribe)(*see* Sacrifice)

CHALICE: In dreams, any holy vessel, and most especially, the Chalice, refers to ones emotional spirituality. The unconscious may be rhetorically asking us if we have been offering enough from the 'cup' of our spirit and good will to the people who surround us in our life. In the infamous legends of King Arthur, all the knights of the round table were sent out to find the Holy Grail (chalice) in order to restore England to her former glory. The symbolic implication was that England's spiritual cup had been emptied and only the 'highest' of all spiritual vessels upon being found and refilled could restore the spirit of England herself. In dreams, when we drink from a chalice, we may be illustrating a preparation to take on a major emotional and spiritual responsibility, for instance, the adoption of a child. On the other hand, to spill blood from a golden chalice may imply an emotional sacrifice which has terribly wounded us and left us feeling dry, empty and desolate. However, as the Arthurian eventually learned, ones spiritual cup will always be refilled and poured faithfully, and indeed infinitely, in the name and cause of helping those less fortunate than ourselves.

CHARGE: To seize a moment with ardent passion and wild instincts is a figurative illustration of our primal self. In this, we witness the release of our repressed pre-ancestral nature. As such, we act on our inner most drive of attacking our opponent before he or she may attack us. In the primal sense, the opponent may have been our quarry and once killed provided our valid sustenance for survival. Alternatively, when the charge is organized, as in an army, we find the social aspects of our primal self. In this, we witness the level of evolutionary intelligence, via language, and its relative effectiveness in the survivalist battle field. (*see* Bull)

CHASED: The Chase dream implies running from ones own fear. Therapists recommend turning about and facing ones tormentor in order to obtain the knowledge of exactly who or what it is that brings us such unreasonable trepidation. Accordingly, since knowledge is power, understanding the source of our misgivings may aid in the eventual vanquishing of their authority over our psychological mind. (*see* Attack)

CHERUB: In dreams, a Cherub symbolizes child-like innocence and a slight mischievousness. The cherub may be a clear symbol that we need to take life a little less seriously. Conversely, it may serve as gentle reminder of a recent dishonest or manipulative action which we now feel guilty about committing. Perhaps we acted hastily in our impish and mischievous behavior and harmed someone close to us. Accordingly, the child's face and adult mind of this unique being, serves as a kind of reverse reflection of our adult face, and at times childish behavior.

CHEST: In many ways a Chest symbolizes our hidden truths and our ignored history. Furthermore, as it may contain dark, secret mysteries about ourselves and our past, the chest or trunk may represent endless movement and a fugitive outlook upon life. If then, in our dream, we find ourselves searching through the trunk, we may be looking to recapture something from our past. In this sense, we may be expressing an unconscious desire to stop this business of running and hiding from others and ourselves. Accordingly, the unconscious may be preparing the dreamer to reveal something about themselves with the full realization of the possible harsh and intolerant judgment of respective peers.

CHILD: To dream of a Child may involve a personal regression into ones past, back when the little dream boy or girl 'assumed' almost no responsibility whatsoever, simply because all needs were fundamentally fulfilled. The dreamer may be expressing the anxiety of a 'high-pressure' adulthood, where people must answer for their actions, create and reinforce their own support systems and reach old age. Alternatively, the dream child may be symbolic of the renewal of life found in spiritual conversion or any profound worldly awakening. For interpretation, the dreamer needs to analyze the activity, facial expressions and dress of the child to better understand its allegorical presence alongside the other components found within the dreams' entire landscape.

CHILDBIRTH: There are numerous recorded cases where men dream of giving birth to a child. In this context, a dreamer may be expressing a complicated message concerning the fear inherent in the expression of paradoxical emotional needs. For example, there may be a need for a caring mother figure which clashes with the need for an alluring, seductive and desirable woman. If, as in these cases, the dream image of the birth of a child is experienced as a painful sacrificing of ones own life, professional guidance may be necessary to work the dreamer through a difficult period in their life. On the other hand, a dreamer may be experiencing the symbolic miracle of birth as an illustration from the unconscious 'announcing' a new hope including a newly acquired and completely unexpected relationship.

CHIMNEY: In a dream, a Chimney represents warmth, family life and the removal of harmful spirits. When the chimney outside is discharging heavy plumes of smoke, the family inside the home is warm, healthy and presumably content. Furthermore, because of its connection with the fireplace and the warming of bones and flesh, the chimney is intimately linked with the union and celebration of love, including the affectionate memory of loved ones. However, if we spot old Santa Claus on the chimney, we may be expressing a longing for the innocence and faithful belief of childhood. Moreover, we may yearn for a charitable gift from an outside force. This could range from a simple raise of salary in our paycheck, to spiritual inspiration which could change the course of our lives.

CHORUS: In a dream, when we sing in a Chorus, it may well be a representation of our 'performance' within the society of our friends, family and co-workers. Naturally, if our dream voice is boisterous and entirely out of key with the rest of the singers, we may be expressing enthusiasm for the group's ideology, but a lack of faith in our own intimacy within the group. We may be experiencing feelings of self-doubt which can certainly lead to a deep anxiety about our personal acceptance within the sphere of their activities.

CHRIST: The Christ archetype is very complex and conveys multi-dimensional psychological and emotional parameters depending primarily on our feelings about the Jesus figure or super-real image. A religious person who views the dream Christ, may be experiencing moral confusion and/or guilt about recent behavior. In this context, the actions or admonishments portrayed by the Christ image should be fully analyzed. On the contrary, a non-religious person may be expressing biblical Christian symbolism, for instance, the deep pain and worldly alienation of personal sacrifice. Yet another biblical symbol of the Christ figure, is personal temptation, replete with anxiety about falling under the influence of a 'less than desirable' individual (devil) or equally demonic organization. In all cases, the movements, direction and facial mannerisms of the Christ figure need to be fully interpreted within the entirety of this conscientious dream landscape.

CHURCH: The house of worship, or Church, involves two direct representational figures. The first is a house, which reflects our psychological perception of self and the second is a ceremonial place, which involves the devotion necessary for spiritual transition. As such, we must examine the direct psychological effects of our ethical beliefs and moral integrity. We may harbor doubts about our worthiness to step foot into this sanctified place. Conversely, we may view the church as an organizational evil which forcefully and figuratively (hard stone and high steeples) impedes upon our tangible freedom. Moreover, the social aspect of religious unity, whether it is perceived as good or bad, by the individual dreamer, carries great strength and enormous influence. In full realization of this consideration, our unconscious may provide visual clues, in and around the church which clarify our relative aspirations and/or trepidations. For example, if we repaint, refurbish and bring in many and varied new members, we may be displaying an increase of our internal belief system, which may have become stagnant. Conversely, if the church looms high and dark over our horizon and seems to be full of fervent zealots who are angry with our behavior, we may be signaling oppression against our perhaps naturalistic style of life. (see Abbey)(see Ceremony)(see Christ)

CIGARETTE: In a dream, a Cigarette may represent a relaxed state of mind concerning ones social environment. Conversely, the act of smoking may indicate a necessity for stress release. Naturally, our feelings concerning cigarettes need to be placed firmly into the interpretation of their symbolic presence. For example, if the dreamer finds cigarettes distasteful and obnoxious in waking life, the dream image of interacting with a co-worker who happens to be deeply inhaling on his cigarette and then blowing out plumes of thick smoke (especially if the co-worker is NOT a smoker in waking life), may be a lucid indication of real (and perhaps repressed) feelings of hostility toward that person. Accordingly therefore, to obtain our unconscious message, we must combine our feelings about cigarettes, our feelings about WHO smokes the cigarettes, what conditions may be causing that person to smoke, and lastly, how that individual physically displays the action of smoking. Is it casual (social ease) or frantic (stress or anxiety)?

CIRCLE: In dreams, a Circle primarily represents the infinity of our perception. The archetypical image of the Mandela, which is a square inside a circle, represents the transcendence of man inside his cosmos. It illustrates a moment in time when physical man completes himself into the infinity of being. In so doing, man and his universe become one 'happening' greater than the sum of both parts. Accordingly, a circle in the dream sense, may indicate the deepest truths of ones own unconscious, which is itself infinite (both perceptually and conceptually speaking). Therefore, it is crucial to determine what other symbols the circle may encompass in the dream's ultimate panorama. (*see* Mandela)(*see* Round Table)

CLAIRVOYANCE: In dream life, as well as waking life, there are concerns we all share about the safety and good health of our loved ones. In this sense, we sometimes visualize in dreams, futuristic occurrences, both negative and positive, involving the people we love. These dreams may seem Clairvoyant to the reality of the waking world, but most dream researchers agree, this is not necessarily the case. However, since our unconscious may be keyed into an infinite source of mind (*see* Collective Unconscious), which may not be bound by individual human restrictions, including and especially the singular understanding of linear time (past-present-future), their may in fact be a legitimate argument concerning the ability of 'seeing' into the future, on a plane not yet understood or conceptualized by our awake (yet still learning) conscious mind. (*see* Telepathy)

CLAW: In waking life, we witness animals (and sometimes humans) using Claws as an instrument of aggression, primarily for hunting and\or self-defense. In this sense, we may visualize the claw in our dreams as hazardous to our well-being, especially our skin, eyes and flesh in general. Since our flesh represents how we 'sense' the world around us, the attack of our flesh by claws, which scratch or puncture the skin, may well refer to a violent incursion upon our normal worldly perception. We may be experiencing the forced 'bleeding' of emotional or spiritual suffering which accompanies a radical change in our private or professional life. To this end, we need to examine the symbolism associated with the animal which strikes out against us and determine why this dream figure effects our waking reality.

CLAY: Clay can be compared to the 'shaping' creativity of our quite extraordinary data bank of perceptions. We can 'shape' and 'mold' the decisions we make in life. As living creatures, possessing mind, we are far from being static. We are fluid, flexible and entirely transient. Therefore, in the dream sense, we must examine the clay form which we deem to lay our hands upon in order to fine-tune, mutate or ultimately destroy. In this context we must ask ourselves, is the clay form a projection of our own selves or personal characteristics? Ultimately, the interpretation of the clay dream may involve an internal concern about the power we possess over others and our willingness (or unwillingness) to use that authority, or outright psychological force.

CLEANING: In dreams, Cleaning generally refers to the wiping away of negative feelings. In the material sense, we are attempting to make ourselves lighter and therefore more spiritual. We may be symbolically removing the weight of mortal existence which seeks to bring us down into the reality of worldly particulars. For instance, and in the contrary sense, to dream a vision of a bloody hand, which cannot be wiped clean regardless of how many times we scrub it, may well refer to a guilty conscious which the psyche refuses to simply wash away. We may need to 'come clean' before we can erase the stain of 'blood on our hands.'

CLOCK: In the dream sense, a clock refers to a concern about time. This could involve a deadline or a more broad and abstract worry about growing old. To properly analyze the clock symbol, one must analyze the time 'shown' on the clock itself, the type of clock and any and all dream character's reaction to the clock. Moreover, we need to determine personal feelings about time in general. Do we live 'hurried' lives, or are we usually bored. Primarily, changes in ones physical schedule in life will bring about the clock reference within a new dream landscape; but there can be many other complicated, time-related variations on this symbols' conclusive meaning. (see Time)

CLOWN: A Clown represents a complex figure including the archetypes of mask, fool and performer. As such, its dream appearance may denote a psychological revelation about a dreamer who pretends to be happy in waking life, while actually experiencing melancholy and is attempting to 'cry out' for professional guidance. On the other hand, the clown figure may simply represent mockery (the fool), and its respective buffoonery, may act out a form of personal hostility toward the behavior of another, or conversely, a chastisement of our own actions.

COCK: The image of the rooster, or Cock, represents a strong will and persistent determination. Unlike a tiger for example, who's power is obvious, the cock is resilient, quick and single-minded. In this he can achieve far greater results than a mightier animal who lacks focus, boldness and above all, conviction. In the Chinese zodiac, the cock stands for fierce individuality and a deep understanding of the self. In this, the 'cock' personality hates to fail and rarely does. Therefore, taken together in the dream sense, we may be implying a steadfastness in our goals, desires and/or specific plans about the future.

COFFIN: In a dream, a Coffin may well represent preparation for a profound change, a kind of 'emotional' rebirth. In this sense, the coffin symbolizes a dip into the unconscious, and otherwise unknown. Naturally, there is an assumption that a coffin symbolizes death, however, it must be recalled that parting itself is symbolic of change, and given the spiritual beliefs on the afterlife, that change can either be very enjoyable, very discomforting or somewhere in between. Regardless, there may be change, and that change may be a major modification in ones life. The unconscious may well be telling us to be prepared for this junction in the journey of our lives.

COLLECTIVE UNCONSCIOUS: Carl Jung postulated that human consciousness is linked into a great symbiotic pool that each human being (since the first human being) is intimately connected. The implications of this doctrine are extremely far-reaching and have been the center of much debate since its very onset. Jung's theory of the Collective Unconscious explains why human beings throughout history and diverse cultures, possess familiar understanding of the extraordinarily similar archetypical images found in their mind's eye. Cave paintings, ancient carvings and modern textbooks all reveal the continuity of our major human 'themes.'

COLOR: Different Colors have disparate symbology. (*see* Green, Red, Blue, White, Black, Yellow and Purple)

CONTRACT: In a dream, a Contract may refer to anxiety about keeping ones word, or, if the contract is torn, guilt about having already broken a promise involving 'sensitive' secrets. A contract may also refer to financial concerns. To interpret the dream properly the dreamer must consider the writing on the contract, who delivers (or signs) the contract and what agreements may the contract be binding us (or our loved ones) into.

CORN: In a dream sense, fields of Corn (stalks) can be remarkably intimidating because of their lofty height and sheer number. In a dream landscape, we may find ourselves lost in a corn field which drastically reduces our normal human 'overview' on things and people in general. We may be experiencing feelings of inadequacy in life, or a real loss in our personal direction. On the other hand, a clean and delicious looking kernel of corn, which is very bright in its yellow color, may be symbolic of hopeful events yet to come, or a 'good' feeling about recently occurring and perhaps creative situations in ones life.

COSTUME: In dreams, Costumes represent the identity of oneself. Therefore, our unconscious may be illustrating how we appear to others. If we 'desire' to show people this simple or elaborate portrayal of ourselves, we may need to analyze why this is the case. The dream landscape itself may yield some unique and enlightening answers to this type of self-questioning. If we find that the costume we wear, is concealing our true nature, we may be expressing a fear about 'revealing' ourselves to the outside world. This self-doubt may be extremely counter-productive in our social and professional relationships. If our costume is distasteful, strange and unfamiliar, even to our own sensibility, we may be experiencing alienation from the norms of the group with whom we surround ourselves.

COUNCIL: In dreams, a representation of an authoritative society of our peers, generally refers to our feelings about how waking associates will 'accept' our recent actions, including job decisions and job performance, as well as our overall behavior. In the dream sense, we are being tested and appraised by a force greater than ourselves.

COWS: In a dream, a Cow may represent fecundity, stability and an overall maternal state of being. The cow gives milk freely and abundantly and she is content with fresh grass and clean water. In this sense, she is nearly, even in the western mind, a spiritual being. Therefore, in a dream, the cow may symbolize spiritual or emotional events, such as the birth of a child, reunion of old friends or a brand new love-filled relationship in ones life.

CRASH: In the dream sense, a Crash is symbolic of the impact of two separate forces colliding together. We may be experiencing anxiety about keeping separate influences in our life apart from each other. This is often the case with an unfaithful husband or a teenager who must show one face to his friends and quite another face to his family. Alternatively, the crash dream may wholly illustrate the terrible outcome of a high-speed and otherwise stressful life. Therefore, the dreamer needs to analyze his own life decisions and resolve what revelation is found in the crash image itself. (see Accident)

CROSS: To a religious person, the Cross or crucifix may refer to moral guilt. To a non-religious person, it may refer to intolerable sacrifices which have already been made, or need to be taken immediately. In this, we find a reference to the crossroads in ones life. We often need to choose a path in life. The course we take not only effects ourselves, but also the whole society of man, which we are very much a reflective part. As such, the archetype of the cross transcends even Christianity and represents the struggle between the physical and spiritual world. In order to be Christ-like, we must superimpose spirituality into the material world and as such, bridge the seeming infinite gap between spirit and matter. (see Christ)

CROW: In a dream, the Crow archetype may symbolize an angry or restless spirit. Since it is a scavenger, the crow symbolizes the soul which stays on the earth, mingling with mortals preoccupied with the secrets of death and immortality. In the dream sense, visualizing the crow may be a revelation of our own distraught and hungry soul in search of greater knowledge and greater experience.

CRYSTAL: The Crystal is a complex dream image in that it simultaneously represents clarity, balance and a reflection of light (or meaning). As such, while it may not be precognitive, the crystal dream may in fact demonstrate an accurate understanding (on our part) regarding a person or situation in our waking life. Following this line of thinking, the unconscious may be raising this question. Are we able to accept the truth of our own insight?

CUT: In a dream, Cutting may represent disconnecting and dividing something which is whole, thereby releasing its inner potency. Moreover, this efficacious liberation may symbolically effect the ritualistic transfiguration of the emancipator, in other words the person or persons which cuts. This liberation of blood from a wound has deep archetypal connections in cultures worldwide. However, the entity or organism itself, which is gashed or severed in the dream landscape, may provide more clues to the dream interpretation, than merely the relative vitality which is lost from it. The victim, either animate or inanimate, may possess an overwhelming source of materiality which may be painful to the dreamer in an emotional and/or psychological sense. This is why the dreamer often finds him or herself, the victim of the cutting, at times even self-inflicted. In this, we find a release of overbearing suffering (or distress) in ones daily waking experience. As such, the agony of the wound seems to expel, via disengagement, the agony of being. (see Bleed)(see Sacrifice)(see Ritual)

DAISY: In the dream sense, freshly cut daisies involve purity, innocence and the new and fragile beauty of youth. This is why a person dead and buried is said to be 'pushing up the daisies.' The implication is that a person's passing on, allows for a fresh new beginning of life. In this context, when we dream of walking through fields of daisies or if we confront unknown children carrying daisies, we may be referring to new beginnings in our life. Redemption and hope highlight this archetype in our dreaming experience.

DANCING: Our 'working' union with another person is symbolically expressed as a Dance. Are we in step or out of step with this individual? Since there is a rhythm of life, we need to analyze the full spectrum of our wide and quite unique dances with the separate people who surround us in waking life. For example, If in our dream, we are stepping on the toes of a particular partner and causing his or her feet to bleed, we may need to analyze why we are interfering with the progress of that individual and why we feel the need to draw blood (symbolic of deep emotions) from this person.

DEATH: In a dream, to witness the image of ones own corpse, may be a very extreme, yet entirely effective, unconscious illustration of deep and personal loss. However, this termination or loss is not necessarily negative. In life, a person may 'lose' a dependency, such as drug addiction. Similarly, a person may 'lose' a narcissistic point of view, or a person may 'lose' prejudice. The point simply being, many characteristics which define a person, quite frankly, can afford to be lost. Hence, a vision of personal death simply portrays the decisive end of one state of mind, either psychological or emotional, which may allow for the emergence of a new and perhaps wiser waking understanding of oneself. On the other hand, witnessing the corpse of a loved one who is still alive, may reflect a complicated feeling of 'loss' in the understanding, awareness or familiarity shared with that person.

DECEPTION: In a dream, a 'performance' of Deception, may well illustrate our own mastery for misleading members of the inner circle of our own life. We may be experiencing the inherent guilt involved in deceiving our own friends and family, naturally more than our co-workers or acquaintances. On the other hand, we may be experiencing the pain of our own folly with a full realization that we have been 'fooling ourselves' concerning the integrity of our own words and actions. Conversely, our unconscious may be warning us about the deceptive actions of someone new in our life, perhaps a recently acquired boyfriend or girlfriend.

DEEP: The symbolism of Deep generally refers to the infinite depths of our unconscious. Emotions or concepts which are difficult to accept are generally repressed into this dark region. Accordingly, when we experience confusion in our decision making, due to arduous situations in our life, we may feel a desire to repress all our emotions. In so doing, we 'sink' ourselves into the secret depth, overcoming the fear of our personal unknown, only with the silent hope to emerge renewed.

DEER: In a dream, a lone Deer depicts innocence, frailty and natural beauty. In the symbolic sense, the unconscious may be illustrating a dire need to protect a precious quality in ourselves or someone close to us. If however, the deer is a large stag with great pointed horns, the representation is one of freedom, independence and virility. In all cases the dreamer must analyze his or her interaction with the deer, if any, and the dream landscape surrounding the animal.

DELICATE: If we find a recurring object in our dreams, which is exceedingly Delicate, we must analyze what that object represents to us. Accordingly, we need to interpret why this symbol seems so fragile, exquisite or downright breakable. Often in dreams, an inanimate object is symbolic of a psychological state, therefore, the 'delicate' illustration of some object, may be a warning about a specific psychological frailty.

DELTA WAVES: Brain waves are measured on a sophisticated piece of equipment known as an electroencephalograph or EEG. These EEGs measure electrical energy released by the brain in terms of Amplitude (or width) and Frequency (or speed). As opposed to Alpha waves, Delta waves occur during deep sleep and are characterized by high amplitude and very slow frequency, in the range of 1-2 cycles per second. One could conceivably view Delta waves as large sweeping electrical scans of our entire neural region. Alpha waves, on the other hand, occur when a person is awake (A-1) or meditating (A-2) and expose lower amplitude and much higher frequencies, in the range of 8-12 cycles per second. As such, Alpha waves may be compared to sharp and focused neural activity, which bring the wide neural view into extreme close-up, where in fact, accuracy may be needed. For example, hunting for food, or a high-powered job interview, are two activities accomplished much more effectively, while wide awake. There are those who would argue that corporate executives have convincingly demonstrated how alpha waves are no longer really necessary, once the job is acquired. (*see* Alpha waves)

DEMAGOGUE: Hitler was a Demagogue. If we view ourselves as a Demagogue, leading great masses of people by stirring up their prejudices, we may be experiencing deep, unconsoled feelings of personal hatred, which need to be addressed. We may feel cornered by our fears and emotions of anger and seek help (in the form of dream characters) to aid us in our personal struggle. On the other hand, if the demagogue is a person known, a dreamer may be expressing anxiety concerning ignorance or prejudice found in his or her social sphere, especially intolerance directed against the dreamer's own nation, race or creed.

DEMON: In dreams, Demons may represent the seemingly paradoxical embodiment of our fears and desires. As such, demons are voices from deep inside ourselves, which appear in our consciousness when we are faced with moral decisions. These decisions usually involve the consequences of personal ethics. The struggle between a person's symbolic demons and angels is a normal part of the checks and balances found within that person's psyche. Moreover, theorists have put forth the hypothesis which claims, to be 'wholly' influenced by either good intentions (religious fanatic), or evil intentions, may imply an unbalanced and abnormal psychological grounding.

DEN: In a dream, The Den image may refer to a hideout. On the surface, the dream seems to be an indication of personal fear for oneself or ones family. However, the idea of hiding out in the earth itself may be symbolic of returning to the safety of the womb. To this end, we may require an analysis of the need to 'wrap' our own skin (which senses the outside world), within the protective body and sanctuary of the mother figure. The regression into pre-birth itself, may imply a paralyzing social or personal fear which has reached its absolute zenith in our daily waking life. Moreover, an examination of the symbolism of the animal (if any) which chases us into our dream den, may be necessary to elaborate further on the meaning of the dream itself.

DEPOT: The symbolism of a Depot carries within its parameters all three archetypes of poverty, isolation and the reconstruction of life. If in the dream, we find ourselves sitting motionless in a bus depot, we may be experiencing a total loss of direction in waking life. A desire to change major aspects in our life is certainly apparent. However, the anxiety centered around the 'confusion' of choosing this new destination in our life is equally displayed. On the other hand, if we find ourselves arriving in a bus depot, we may be experiencing a mild fear pertaining to a new situation 'approaching' our waking life. In all cases, we need to interpret the color of the depot and any and all characters within the entire dream landscape.

DEVIL: The Devil in our dreams may refer to decision making which directly involves our moral basis of reality. We must ask ourselves whether we are seduced by this demon or terrified by him. Based on this, we may be able to determine the direction our unconscious may lean. Do we need to open up to our dangerous, frivolous self, or find purity in our denial of all temptation. In either case, a transition in our life is clearly illustrated which may need to be resolved. (see Demon)(see Temptation)(see Tarot Major Arcana: Devil (15))

DESERT: In a dream, the Desert landscape may symbolize a cessation of psychological or emotional growth. The difficulty of desert travel, replete with intense heat, uneven terrain and lack of water are key signs of emotional stagnation. We may feel dry and incomplete in a one-sided relationship where our sentiments of love (heat) are not reciprocated. In the psychological sense, we may feel lost in the vastness of the desert plain which fails to reveal the best path to the 'better world' outside its limits. Yet, in another sense, the desert may imply ardent spiritual sacrifice experienced upon the entry into a new and moral way of life.

DIARRHEA: The symbolism of Diarrhea is roughly comparable to vomiting, which is yet another form of sickness associated with ones internal system. In this sense, our stomach is entirely representative of our feelings and attitudes about ingested or 'accepted' realities. As such, our diarrhea may represent the immobilization involved with a peculiar, or set of meticulous, realities. These may include relationships or simply complex situations which make us feel sick in the clearest, most articulate, of metaphorical fashions. (*see* Feces)(*see* Regurgitation)(*see* Stomach)

DIG: In a dream, the action of Digging may symbolize a search into ones unconscious. The removal of layer after layer of earth (representing our psychological consciousness and physical body) moves us closer to the 'depth' of our true and perhaps 'primal' selves. In this sense, we may be searching for the 'treasure' of our collective human wisdom. Conversely, there remains a conjecture which asserts our own personal knowledge was buried not too long ago in the ferocious storm of our upbringing or systematic socialization. Taken together, the digging dream may imply the psychological preparation necessary for a new and radical 'understanding' found in our waking lives.

DINNER: A Dinner in ones dream landscape may symbolize a personal taste and/or hunger for life and how this characteristic may effect ones interpersonal relationships. In waking life, a dinner usually consists of a group of people, perhaps a family, who 'share' a meal. In so doing, the entire group absorbs the shared human experiences of gathering, sustenance and equality. Accordingly, if in a dream scenario, any of these practices is missing in the dinner itself, the same qualities may be void in waking life. For example, if a dreamer views him or herself hoarding as much food as possible at a dinner table, personal greed or suspicion of ones business associates, perhaps in a recent transaction, may be illustrated.

DIRT: In dreams, a Dirty face may symbolize angry social defiance or conversely, repugnant emotions which need to be 'washed away.' However, finding in hand, dirt or soil which provides the rich 'environment' necessary to nourish a seedling to full growth, maybe symbolic of ones cultivating or parenting skills. Therefore, how and where we view dirt plays a significant part on its ultimate dream interpretation. (*see* Water)(*see* Cleaning)

DISAPPEAR: When we fear losing someone or something, their absolute form may vanish in our dream. If we find our own body disappearing, we may be experiencing a feeling of personal insignificance in our own waking relationships. In both cases, it is naturally crucial to examine all characters and symbols to determine the source of these negative motivations.

DISTANCE: Although a Distant city may suggest hope, the overall perception of distance implies a separation from ones goals. The interpretation of a dream landscape involving distance may be dependent on the speed and direction we travel toward or away from that distant location. If we move rapidly toward some welcoming object (home, oasis etc.), we may be expressing desire and emotional anticipation involving an upcoming event (marriage, birth of a child etc.). However, if we slowly move away from some beckoning object or person, we may be experiencing guilt and remorse concerning a past episode or relationship in our life. Consequently, in order to best understand this dream imagery, the dreamer needs to determine his or her 'feeling' about the distant 'object' and compare this awareness with the direction and speed away or toward that same article.

DIVA: The recurring dream symbol of a Diva may demonstrate deep wish-fulfillment on the part of the dreamer to be loved and cherished by all. The diva symbol further presupposes 'perfection' in performance, consequently, a dreamer may be expressing anxiety over his or her lack of self-discipline or natural ability, which is 'compensated' in this captivating and irresistible dream of effortlessly reaching out to the world in song and natural beauty.

DIVER: The Diver dream may be a visual representation of the link between the unconscious and conscious mind. A diver retains air by holding his or her breath, or by utilizing the proper scuba equipment or breathing apparatus. The air in this sense embodies the surface or conscious world which 'remains' with us submerged in the dark, mysterious and enigmatic unconscious. As such, the diver dream may illustrate a dreamer searching for a 'rational' solution to a riddle which is out of his or her day to day experience or understanding. Moreover, if in the dream, the diver faces difficulties or danger, all the factors therein should be analyzed for their waking ramifications.

DOCK: A Dock is primarily symbolic of transitional states of emotion. A dreamer might be experiencing a welcome return from the stormy sea of a recent and perplexing relationship. On the other hand, the dock may represent the psychological preparation necessary for an emotional 'outing.' In both cases, the condition of ones boat, all characters surrounding the dock and the dock itself, should be analyzed for peculiar significance.

DOG: In a dream, a Dog may represent a number of complex emotions, including fear, friendship, loyalty and obedience. A dreamer needs to completely determine the color, demeanor and intentions of the dog and compare these characteristics with ourselves and the landscape encircling the animal. For example, if a big, yellow dog seems friendly and leads us away from a particular location or situation, we may need to analyze the 'hidden shadows' and/or deceptions involved in the place or circumstance itself. In this example, a dog may reveal our own apprehensions, which we have foolishly, chose to ignore. In yet another symbolic association, that being the Chinese zodiac; the dog represents honesty and generosity, in short, a straight forward companion with no ulterior motives except unification and bonding trust.

DOLL: A Doll may represent wish-fulfillment on the part of the dreamer who wishes to gain a doll-like (flawless) appearance, and lifestyle (doll house). A variation of this symbolism, finds the image of a disfigured doll, which represents the psychological and emotional body of the dreamer. The doll reflects the 'pure' body which is 'torn' by life's struggles. In this context, we need to analyze the dream doll's symbolic deformities (missing arms, scratched face etc.) and how they might relate to the dreamers current outlook on life.

DOLPHIN: The Dolphin represents emotional trust combined with psychological freedom. This marriage of ideal states borderlines a spiritual 'feeling' of love and 'highest' human being. Therefore, to ride a dolphin in a dream may represent 'floating' on ones own crystalline optimism, personal faith and social altruism.

DOOR: Since a Door is both an exit and an entrance, and can deny passage as well as welcome a person through its threshold, its symbolism is entirely dependent on its working status. Is the dreamer locked out, and refused therefore, passage into potential change; or are doors opening automatically, simply because of the fervor and zeal of the dreamer's self-confidence? Therefore, we need to analyze our relative position to the door and any and all characters (or objects) which appear on either side of the door, for the legitimate meaning of our shifting state of mind.

DOUBLE: Seeing Double refers to personal confusion and/or paradoxical viewpoints upon a certain individual or situation. If we behold ourselves in this split mirror of consciousness, we may be experiencing self-doubt, guilt, or personal wavering involving our private or professional 'roles'.

DOUBLE-JOINTED: The conceptualization of the Double-Jointed individual illuminates potential and possibility far beyond the naturalistic norm. Our dream may be alluding to the length and strength of our being, which may not be apparent, yet burns with full intensity in the due course of our expression. In other words, if we can bend our reality beyond its typical or standard perception, we may find that our truth can be every bit as infinite as our own imaginative potential. Is this then, the catalyst for the miraculous? Perhaps, the dream may reveal an answer.

DRAGON: In the Eastern (and especially Chinese) tradition, a Dragon symbolized hope, love and energetic spiritual flight. While on the other hand and rather quite conversely, in the Western tradition, the Dragon represented lust, aggression and a haphazard ruin of sensible order. Taken together, it is easy to see how the overall archetypical dragon, today represents the extreme coordinates of an infinitely emotional unconscious. In the modern world, our giant, fire-breathing lizard may easily step in and out of these diverse 'worlds' of expression. However, because of its snake-like movements, flying ability and mouth of fire, the dragon is predominantly associated with the specifics of flagrant and passionate love, replete with all its sublime consequences.

DRAIN: In a dream, a Drain essentially represents a funneling and depletion of emotion, especially those associated with loss and heartache. However, this drain may remind us of cleansing and purification, which has taken away harsh impurities, which seem intent to cling to us in every day life. (see Basin)(see Unclean)

DRAPES: The image of dark colored, material-rich Drapes symbolize a multi-layered emotional state which shuts out the light of day (conscious awareness, rational thought). For example, in a dream, red and black velvet and lace drapes, may represent a painful conflict (red vs. black) in ones relationship. This conflict may be resolved if the dreamer allows in the light of day (reason), which may reveal the means wherein strife may return to unity.

DRIP: In the dream sense, a Drip may represent a slow, yet relentless loss of ones spiritual will. The unconscious may be illustrating a 'gradual' deprivation in a specific area of ones waking life. For instance, if we fear losing a job, or if a loved one, sustains prolonged illness, the effect of the disturbing condition may be slowly devitalizing our life force and real, tangible aspirations.

DROWN: When we sink into the deep waters of our heightened emotions, we may experience a desperate feeling of Drowning. In the symbolic sense, we need to avoid fear (panic) and swim calmly to the surface and dry land of reason. In an ideal sense, we may need to bond our psychological and emotional consciousness, in order to float safely on the periphery of both plains.

DRUM: Perhaps the most ancient human archetype is the visual and auditory beating of drums, reflective of our own heart beat and emotional rhythm of life. As such, the dream beat may represent the scope of the complete human experience, entailing love and sex (birth), life and standards (faith), and the death struggle (war). A need to analyze the 'meaning' of the beat to the dreamer, may be necessary to understand its position in the visionary landscape.

DRUG: The need for a 'quick fix' promised by both legal and illegal Drugs may be revealed to us by our unconscious. We may desire a potentially harmful, wish-fulfillment in the form of an 'instant' escape from our problems. It is crucial to analyze the escapist dream landscape for evidence pointing to what may motivate our demand to escape reality, and conversely, how may we liberate ourselves from the consolation of its personal deception?

DRY: As opposed to water, which symbolizes deep emotion, Dryness may refer to an exhaustion of feelings and moreover, an alienation from human sensitivity. At times, this removal from interaction may serve as a necessary component for psychological readjustment to complex situations in our waking life. However, if the dream is a recurring one, we may be displaying feelings of isolation and perhaps a general and gradual fracturing of self. This imagery may involve our consciousness reminding us to return, to the rain and torrents of an unpredictable, yet life enhancing, world of emotions. (*see* Desert)

DUMB: In the dream sense, Deaf and Dumbness may refer to a lack of communication in ones private or professional life. We may 'feel' our worth is ignored, or perhaps our knowledge is silenced by our own self-doubt. On the other hand, if we find a loved one or associate, dumb in a dream, we may need to consider our own failure in 'listening' to this person, an individual who may just be crying out for help.

DWARF: The archetype of tiny magical people appears in virtually all cultures to a greater or lesser degree. The child-like adult combines the lure of innocence, with the spirit of cleverness. Therefore, in the dream sense, the dwarf, or child-spirit represents the heart's inner being, the head's inner being, and the soul's innermost being. We need to listen to these tiny magical voices which together pattern the complex fusion of self.

DYBBUK: (see Vampire)

EAGLE: The ancient Eagle archetype embodies flying alone in ones spiritual awareness of strength, freedom and purity. Consequently, the symbol is, and has been, used to motivate great warriors, tribes and nations (including the USA). In a dream image, we may be expressing a need to fly above our temptations and worldly aspirations, to enter instead, into the transfiguration of being. To this end, we need to observe the eagle and the path of its eternal and effortless flight.

EARTH: The soil of our birth and the clay of our formal existence, only partially reveal the symbol of mother Earth. The earth beneath our feet and towering above us in mountain ranges represents the entire cradle, running field and closing haven of humanity. In the dream sense we must constantly analyze the earth and our position relative to its living landscape. To this end, we must continually decide whether the earth accepts or rejects our behavior. Does the earth offer a cave's shelter or a rich field to harvest, or does she rumble in quakes and burn our flesh on her barren fields and uneven rocks?

EAT: What we Eat (and/or desire to eat) is intimately linked to our choices in life and our general perception of reality. As such, the amount of food, color of the food and how we go about consuming the food (fast, slow, sexually, methodically, reluctantly etc.) reveal certain aspects about our acceptance and tolerance of the world around us. To say that one has a hearty appetite for life, implies that this same individual relishes the flavor and taking in of life. Naturally, WHO we happen to be dining with, is as crucial as how we happen to be dining. The internalization of a social situation, whether pleasant or unpleasant, may be illustrated in this rather heavy handed metaphorical montage of consumption. (see Cannibalism)(see Dinner)(see Stomach)(see Regurgitate)

ECLIPSE: The meeting of two levels of awareness, one negating the other, may be symbolically expressed in the Eclipse image. The unconscious may be warning us that we have shut out some person or situation in favor of another, without thinking about the repercussion of our selective behavior. For instance, in the symbolism of the moon covering the sun, we may have blocked reason in the name of passion and exposed ourselves for emotional regret and anguish.

ECZEMA: Since skin is representative of how we sense the world, experiencing Eczema in a dream, may symbolically reveal a complication in how we sense our emotional or psychological world. Conversely, we may be externally expressing an internal anxiety, concerning how we ourselves are perceived by others. In either case, we may need to look beyond our superficial beliefs and the shallow assumption of others, in order to find the 'sensitive' truth in life, about ourselves, and the society of individuals around us.

EDEN: The image of Eden has a dual symbolism of natural beauty and the unnatural 'temptation' to own or consume that beauty. In the dream sense, the unconscious may be warning us to allow certain objects, places or people, their privacy and individual sanctity. If we seek to 'physically' possess an 'abstract' emotion, such as love, we may be hurting others in ways we can scarcely imagine. Conversely, we may be expressing a personal loss of paradise due to our own foolish, unthinking or greedy behavior. (see Apple)

EGG: The Egg can be symbolic of birth, creative potential or fragile perfection. As such, the egg is an extremely complex dream figure. Accordingly, we need to analyze the size, shape and color of the egg, as well as its position relative to ourselves or other dream characters. Moreover, we need to decide if the egg is in danger of breaking, or is a hatchling emerging from its glowing shell? For instance, if at the beach, the tide washes in a sole egg and we decide to pick it up and carefully allow it to dry (incubate) in the warm sun, it may be the expression of an 'idea', which is 'delivered' from our unconscious, and now needs to be clearly analyzed and brought into life.

EGO: According to Sigmund Freud, the Ego represents our moral consciousness or 'highest' self. It is the component of the psyche which keeps social order via personal restraint. As such, the ego is the opposite of the Id, which desires immediate gratification without considering any consequences of its actions. However, in another sense, we may simply be referring to egomaniacal behavior as it appears in our dream landscape. Naturally, this involves self-love taken to a (perhaps) socially unacceptable level, dependent that is, on the relative pretentiousness of the social group in question. In any case, when this behavior is demonstrated in our dream and is not natural in terms of our normal day to day deportment, our unconscious may be illustrating either one of two things. First, we may be grossly overcompensating for a general lack of self-esteem in our waking experience, or conversely, we may be illustrating a call to be heard and recognized for our unique talent and/or abilities. As such, the dreamer may need to make an honest assessment of their own personal accomplishments and how they relate to his or her own peer groups. Our unconscious may be indicating an imbalance in the inner self versus the projected self. (see Image)(see Self)

EIGHT: Since a box consists of Eight corners, and an octave in western music returns to a 'home' note, we consider eight to represent the completeness of oneself. Moreover, since an octagon is the closest straight-line geometrical equivalent to a circle, in the visual sense, we must consider its representational strength and rotary grace. Appropriately then, in a dream, the number eight refers to psychological balance and a sound foundation in new enterprises and/or vocations.

ELECTRIC: The force of an Electric current can create or destroy, depending on how it is utilized. In Greek mythology, the supreme god called Zeus used bolts of lightning to vanquish his enemies, or anybody who basically angered him. In Victorian fiction, Mary Shelly placed the power of electricity into the hands of Victor Von Frankenstein, to bring a conglomeration of corpses back to life in the form of one man (if only for a short time). Naturally, in today's world, we have grown quite dependent on the energy of electricity, yet even so, we still fear its potential violence. In this sense, electricity is the modern man's living fire. Taking all this into account, we need to examine the context in which electricity is placed within the dream landscape. Does the electricity merge with the energy of our own central nervous system, aiding our living processes of breathing, sensing and autonomous healing, or does it act as an agent of destruction? If the force is creative, we need to interpret the electric symbolism as potential vitality introduced into our life. If the force is destructive, we may need to be cautious in our waking outlook on certain situations in our life.

ELEMENT: The Elements refer to the structure and materiality of nature. In this order we find grand diversity blended in an inspired symmetry which defies all human comprehension. Naturally, this unavoidable submission of man to the elements and mother nature which cradles his existence, is paramount in his ongoing perception of reality. He must learn to respect and work with his environment otherwise, the natural elements may cause a swift an unceremonious demise. Accordingly, in the dream sense, when we refer to elements, we may be alluding to a creation of balanced harmony with our outside world of experience, especially in the material sense of a physical planet. In the ancient world, the four elements which ruled temporal existence were respectively: Fire, Air, Earth and Water. Every aspect of each of these four elements were meant to be honored and even worshipped equally and with great humility. For it was understood, then as now, that man is subservient to nature (and/or God) and subsequently must thank her (Him) each and every day for her (His) extraordinary gifts which comprise the totality of life.

ELEPHANT: The Elephant is symbolic of power, single-minded determination and exaggerated memory. As such in the extreme sense, the elephant may represent the blind rage of vengeance, enacted as retaliation for some 'past' insult or injury. However, in a dream, an elephant primarily epitomizes will-power and fierce tenacity. The elephant, despite its size, is rarely a threatening force, moreover, the long ivory tusks of this animal are symbolic of long-life and sexual vitality. Unfortunately, this latter symbolism has caused man to dwindle their species by destroying thousands of males for their tusks. Man needs to understand that symbols are meant for the heart, mind and soul, not the mantle piece. (*see* Eden)

ELEVATOR: In the dream sense, an Elevator may represent emotional instability. In an elevator, we are carried up or down to a particular destination. Accordingly, an elevator which descends us deeper and deeper into the bowels of the earth represents being 'locked' in an emotional depression. On the other hand, if an elevator carries us to a 'higher' level, and then opens its doors welcoming us to that level, we may be expressing the exhilaration of a new found relationship, faith or personal transcendence. Taken together, the elevator which travels up and down repeatedly, symbolizes very dramatically, an emotional unsteadiness.

EMACIATE: The archetype of an Emaciated person or animal centers around the fear of lacking life's nourishment. However, this 'nourishment' does not merely symbolize food, but the entire spectrum of human needs. In this sense, it is crucial to understand the symbolism of the individual or animal which is emaciated and the nature of the landscape which fails to 'nourish' them. For example, if we spot our children looking frail and sleeping curled up in the chair of our work desk, we may be ignoring their other 'real' needs in our single-minded obsession to earn money for their future.

EMBROIDERY The symbolism of Embroidery involves balance, creativity and social union. We weave together the disparate emotions and beliefs of others in this complex illustration of cohesive humanity. In the dream sense, we may be preparing ourselves for an upcoming event or union where our creativity and community skill may be called upon.

EMPTY: The symbol of Emptiness represents a loss of potential. In the dream sense, a person may be expressing a lack of vital 'feelings' in the absence of fluid (emotions or spirit) in a vessel indicative of a body. (*see* Disappear)

ENGRAVE The symbol of Engraving represents permanence. In the dream sense, we may be communicating a desire to make our 'mark' upon the world. This need to 'exist' forever, may stem from a fragile perception of self, a self which seems to fade into the context of day to day reality. To further understand the engraving symbiology in our dream landscape, we must analyze exactly who's name is carved, or what illustration is chiseled.

EPILEPSY: The symbolism of the epileptic fit refers to a loss of control. In the dream sense, this physiological limitation primarily indicates psychological confusion in the 'method' of our actions. We may be expressing paralysis in our decision making and/or anxiety in our ability to perform both personally and professionally. However, we nevertheless may need to evaluate the energy involved in this debilitating indecisiveness. Our unconscious may be signaling that our energy level and enthusiasm is too high to swing in alternate and quite separate directions. In this, our dream may be illustrating that we instead aim our potential at one dynamic, yet fixed, goal.

EQUATION: In a dream sense, an equation may represent the parameters of a waking riddle in life. Primarily, we may be searching for new connections in our interpersonal relationships. On the other hand, we may seek innovative plans geared toward making our life more productive. In any case, the nature of an equation is twofold, either you have a question which searches for an answer OR, you have an answer in search of a question. Accordingly, in a dream interpretation of an Equation symbol, we need to determine, what questions do we have which need to be answered, or, what answers do we possess which need to be questioned.

EQUESTRIAN: A running and leaping thoroughbred may represent grace, sexuality and natural beauty. As such, how we ride a horse in a dream may be indicative of our personal self-confidence. For instance, if we fear falling off a horse who gracefully and skillfully leaps from obstacle to obstacle, we may be expressing sexual anxiety and/or difficulty in our relationships. Conversely, a smooth, eloquent ride epitomizes physical assurance in our undivided connection of mind, body and spirit.

ERECT: The framework of our psychological self is dramatically illustrated in the architecture of an upright structure. The sexual implications of this erected monument cannot be ignored, however, the entire perception of the persona unquestionably dominates the interpretation of the dream figure. In the solid edifice we may find the very qualities, or flaws, which define our personality structure. For example, if our own personal 'dream' building appears forbidding, shaky and extremely unsafe, we may be illustrating our incapacity to welcome people into our life. On the other hand, if our building appears to display sharp edges, we may unknowingly in the waking world, appear harsh and tumultuous to the people around us.

ERUPTION: In the dream sense, an Eruption may stand for a harsh revelation of oneself. Moreover, the symbolism of skin or land erupting substrata involves rapid and/or drastic changes in ones life. The 'rumbling' or 'irritation' of the surface plain may represent a psychological outlook and personal sensitivity scanning the outside world. The burning substance below the surface which 'bursts' through, may represent the hidden and repressed components of our anger, fear and anxiety. In the dream sense, we may be expressing the sudden discharge of one of these emotions, involving a dire change in our life, which may have built up gradually over time. This dream landscape refers to the 'boiling point' of our tolerance and its message may need to be addressed by a professional therapist.

ESCAPE: To Escape in ones dream implies anxiety about a waking situation which refuses to go away. In turn, the dreamer elects to run away from the circumstance, however, problems in waking life, cannot be avoided forever, and sooner or later the dreamer must 'return' to face his or her difficult predicament.

ESP: There exists a rather large ongoing record of study focusing on Dream Telepathy which has yielded promising results. The successful percentage for planting rational suggestions into the mind of dreaming individuals would suggest the mind in REM has the ability to become highly receptive in the collection of brain waves (see Alpha & Delta). Whether this synopsis of research supports Carl Jung's theory of the Collective Unconscious or a similar physiological communication (or memory) inherent in DNA information codes, is speculative. Notwithstanding, and in the dream sense, an episode involving ESP, may refer to an intimate connection with another individual. For instance, if in our dream a young person becomes lost in the forest, we may be concerned about the 'natural' curiosities growing within this adolescent and fear for their well-being and overall safety. (see Clairvoyance)

ETERNITY: The dream of life Eternal, may involve a witnessing of life in transition, especially the life of others. This may imply that we are either stuck or stolid in our worldly perception. Accordingly, we need to determine our reactions and responses to eternity or being eternal. Moreover, is the eternity found on earth, or on some other-worldly or heavenly plain? In short, do we find contentment in an eternal plain? If not, our unconscious may be illustrating that our fixed and unshakable point of view may be alienating us from the fluid and ever changing world around us. Moreover, the safety of our opinion, has left us unscathed by life, but at the same time, unaffected at the same time. As such, the living of life may only be valid in the experiencing of that life. Conversely, if we find contentment in an eternal plain, we may be alluding to spiritual peace, which we have achieved by the merits and pointed conviction of our daily life. (see Heaven)(see Tarot Major Arcana: Judgment (20) and The World (21))

ETHEREAL: The Ethereal body which floats above our sleeping and very physical body symbolizes a 'spiritual' overview on material life. In the philosophical sense, all human qualities are invisible to the naked eye. For instance, our emotions, faith, life-force, even the thought constructs, 'formulated' inside our brain, are all abstract, immaterial entities or 'components' of the human machine. Appropriately, the ethereal body may be perceived as the embodiment of our invisible, yet 'highest' gifts. In the dream sense, this spirit body may be 'watching over' our primal, physical selves, a kind of archetypal 'astral guide' to a fully realized life.

EUCHARIST: The taking in of a supernatural body has ancient sacrificial symbolism. When we ingest the figurative flesh of a deity or demigod, we become 'purified' in the name of that holy personage. Therefore, in the dream sense, we may be experiencing a deep 'taking in' of spiritual wisdom. (see also Cannibalism)

EUNUCH: In the dream sense, a Eunuch represents a lack of drive, sexual or otherwise. He is the embodiment of false contentment. We may be expressing in this dream symbol a rather complex form of sexual alienation as well as disaffection with life. Accordingly, we need to analyze the behavior of the eunuch and understand fully in which way (if at all) he seems to resemble ourselves.

EVERGREEN: The primary symbolism of the Evergreen is everlasting life. The strong scent and hard resilience of pine needles echo this revitalizing nature. In dreams, evergreens may represent highest human potential in life's endeavors. When we 'push' ourselves and strive for our greatest possible performance, we may dream of sprinting up an immense mountainside, opulent with tall and thick evergreens.

EXCAVATE: To remove something (or someone) from the earth itself, implies revealing a hidden aspect of oneself. Since the earth is symbolic of mother and womb, we may be referring to a deeply repressed instinct which became buried from the symbolic light of day. (see Dig)

EXCREMENT: The waste we leave behind is primarily linked to situations which we desire to see removed from our living experience. However, given the recycling and regenerative nature of Excrement, we may be alluding to a transition and reworking of a particular situation, perhaps even, a relationship. (see Feces)

EXPLOSION: In the dream sense, an Explosion rather dramatically represents a fear of personal destruction or painful disruptive changes in ones life. The key element to this dream imagery is sudden and unexpected 'jolts' in ones fragile construct of reality. For example, should a ten year old boy visualize himself walking through a mine field in his school's auditorium, he may be expressing anxiety pertaining to how his classmates will discern his actions or ability.

EXTRATERRESTRIAL: The aboriginal people of Australia believe that Extraterrestrials came to earth in the 'Dreamtime' and transformed themselves into all 'life' on the planet as we know it. Moreover, the aborigines maintain that 'one day' the Dreamtime will return and the extraterrestrials will mutate into new and reanimated life forms which will remarkably complete their dream cycle and return into the heavens. Appropriately, in the dream sense, the ET or alien archetype refers to help from an 'outside' force, in other words, hope for mankind, or conversely, a sole individual. For instance, to dream of being captured and analyzed by aliens may strongly represent a personal need to be heard and understood. In this context, the aliens may illustrate a 'wiser' social power whom 'recognize' our true worth and incomparable ability.

EXTROVERT: In our dreams, we sometime illustrate personal 'masquerades' which display wish-fulfillment or reveal passions of guilt. In this sense, a dreamer must examine his or her own 'feelings' about personal Extroverted behavior which appears in dreams. Conversely, and rather hypocritically, if an 'associate' or 'family member' emerges overly 'outgoing' in a dream land-scape, our unconscious may be depicting particular apprehen-sion, concerning aberrations in this individual's recent behav-ior.

EYES: In the dream sense, Eyes symbolize being observed or ana-lyzed and causing insecurity or fear. Consequently, they lose the humanity of the 'head' in which they function. As such, they be-come simple and focused embodiments of our paranoia. We may need to 'stare down' our unconscious and perhaps volatile eye, to bring back the predominance of our clear mind and faith-ful spirit.

FABLE: A Fable is a complex tale replete with symbols which em-brace a moral message or universal truth. Accordingly, a fable-like atmosphere in a dream landscape, may be the unconscious way of 'highlighting' its intended bulletin and central idea. As such, we need to pay special attention to dream fables which de-liver a continuous gift of wisdom, designed upon our own per-sonal psyche.

FABRIC: In a dream sense, we must analyze the color and respec-tive 'feel' of Fabrics upon our skin. For example, wool may rep-resent warmth or hot irritation, while silk consistently symbol-izes cool, comfortable sensuality. On the other end of the spec-trum, polyester garments mark artificial environments and constricting personal experience.

FACTORY: The image of a pollution-creating, pitiless fortress which 'constructs' thousands of identical products on an essen-tially dehumanizing assembly line, may certainly be representa-tive of a modern world, a world separated from nature and the true nature of creative man. In the dream sense, the factory rep-resents personal alienation from our 'connectedness' with our spirit (greed), our neighbors (competition and contempt), and the land beneath our feet (contamination). On the other hand, the factory dream vision, may be a warning concerning poor health conditions, which may need to be 'cleaned up' immediately.

FALLING: When our emotional or psychological balance is thrown off, because of recent and drastic changes in our life, we may experience a falling away from 'ourselves', into unknown and therefore, terrifying horrors. However, the point of these dreams seems to emerge from their present operation or performance. In other words, we have not fallen, yet we are in the act of falling, the implication being that we are at the crossroads betwixt regaining our balance, or falling flat on our face. Therefore, in a dream, our unconscious may offer a symbolic support beam, which needs to be interpreted. Hence, in clarifying our waking emotional dilemma, in the model of an accurate dream explication, we may be prevented from falling unnecessarily.

FAMILY: Our Family represents our closest ties and 'immediate' social safety net. As such, we carry a responsibility to guide and protect this group as well as gaining support and protection from within its gregarious confines. Appropriately then, in dreams, any small group which we 'feel' an instinctive need to protect, may be representative of our family. Therefore, we need to analyze in our dream environment, the needs of this small collection of people (or animals), and conversely, any personal message or warning they may collectively or individually convey to our dreaming selves.

FARM: A Farm represents health, harvest and the honest work necessary to successfully achieve them both. Naturally then, any aberrations in this symbolism, for instance, barren fields, sick livestock, or sluggish farm hands, may represent a cessation in personal growth, health and individual ambition. Along these lines, we need to analyze all the 'effecting' factors and characters in the farm landscape to interpret the impetus for our waking regression and degeneration.

FAT: The symbolic imagery of obesity varies from jovial or 'jolly' old souls, to high-powered, cigar smoking bosses of industry. The similarity in both examples is centered around 'excessive' behavior. The reality of obesity is much more complex and involves in many cases, physiological and social imbalances, which have little (if any) to do with the choices or behavior of the individuals themselves. Nevertheless, and unfortunately, in the symbolic sense, 'overweight' persons are thought of as weak willed, obsessive or lethargic. Hence in the dream sense, viewing oneself as extremely corpulent, may involve feelings of guilt about excessive, self-fulfilling behavior. In the sexual sense, viewing ourselves as obese may imply a repression of our own eroticism and desire. As such, we may be placing a layer of cellulite around ourselves to protect us from the difficulties of courting, romance and relationships in general.

FATHER: In many ways, a Father represents the masculine and authoritative natures within ourselves. Appropriately, how we view the behavior of the father figure in a dream, may be reflective of personal feelings about our 'recent' behavior effecting the society of individuals around us. This is especially true of persons believed to be subordinate to us, for instance children, employees or service laborers.

FATIGUE: In the dream sense, Fatigue may represent emotional or psychological exhaustion. As such, our unconscious may be illustrating a necessary surrender concerning a difficult personal situation. We may need to stand away from the living experience of our emotional or psychological realities, in order to readjust ourselves to their complex intricacies.

FEAST: Primarily, Feasting involves a joyous absorption of life. In this, we see a fulfillment of our waking experience, both physical and spiritual. However, a primal factor of hunger and the reality of the food as life force may also be implied. In other words, the feast image in our dream may involve the conclusion of any survivalist behavior. As such, the feast may involve sexuality or relationships in general which have flourished before us and moreover, because of our personal actions. (*see* Eat)(*see* Celebration)

FEATHER: Because of its 'lighter than air', fragile, beauty, the archetype of the Feather indicates wisdom, freedom and peace. As opposed to the collection of feathers which make up a bird's wings and aids in flight, the single feather 'floats' up 'spirit-like' into the breeze, and remains airborne in the perfection of its developed form. This is why we write down our 'wisdom' with a quill, and why a 'feather in ones cap' is credit for a great and nearly divine achievement. In the Egyptian Book of the Dead, a deceased man's heart, or Ba/Ab, was weighed against a feather, which the ancients represented as divine order, to determine whether or not that particular individual was worthy of eternity. If the person's heart was weighed down by the immoral nature of his worldly character and behavior, the feather would deny his entrance into the infinite afterlife. (*see* Tarot Major Arcana: The World (21) arcana.)

FECES: In a dream, Feces may represent the purging of unwanted feelings or situations intruding in ones life. For example, we may be experiencing regret or guilt pertaining to our pugnacious behavior toward someone once close to us. Alternatively, we may feel violated by a person who refuses to keep his or her distance. In our dream, we may be symbolically removing this person from our immediate lives.

FERRY BOAT: In the dream sense, a Ferry boat symbolizes a slow emotional transition toward a new 'state' of being. Moreover, in medieval Europe, and further back into ancient Egypt, it was believed that a 'ferryman' paddled individuals from the death plain, into the netherworld. Taking all this into account, we may interpret a ferry boat journey, as a voyage with poignant consequences and deep meaning in our waking lives. The relative roughness (or tranquillity) of the 'river crossed' may need to be analyzed for the dreams complete interpretation.

FETAL POSITION: To find oneself in the Fetal position, reminiscent of womb warmth, safety and nurturing, may dramatically symbolize hiding within oneself. We may be expressing an emotional or psychological regression into a dark and silent past where ALL of our needs were provided for. In the dream sense, we may be expressing difficulty in our 'adult' roles replete with the complex anxieties of personal and/or family responsibilities. (*see* Womb)

FETISH: A precious Fetish (hope) which is clutched in a person's hand, may be representative of harnessing ones own strength and personal 'magic.' Moreover, we empower ourselves via the 'force' of this image or idol held in our hand or placed under our pillow at night. Therefore, in the dream imagery, the possession of a fetish represents deep faith in our ability to succeed when 'set' under the guiding light of our loyal spirit familiars. Accordingly, we need to analyze where the fetish is found (or positioned) and determine how the symbolism of that particular fetish offsets our waking psyche and any personal dilemma we may be working through.

FEVER: The body temperature which is raised in the heat of Fever, may symbolize a complex mixture of passion, aggression and fear. Appropriately in a dream, our unconscious may be revealing a physiological change effected by a hot emotional situation which needs to be immediately resolved. To further interpret this symbolism, we need to analyze all physical changes represented in the body, and study the separate meaning of these respective body components, relative to passion, aggression and perhaps, internal anxieties.

FILM: Some of the best selling points behind photography and video tapes in general, have always revolved around the concept of 'capturing' life's joy. Conversely, many primitive people feared photography, believing that images captured were the parallel of souls stolen, or 'possessed', in our 'modern world' terminology. In both cases, the key is a detailed attempt at 'capturing' and holding 'life' as we know it. This very well may represent the starting point of Film symbolism in the dreaming sense. Since dreams can recreate individuals or places 'at will', one needs to question why 'pictures' or 'reproductions' of characters or places are displayed by our unconscious at all. The answer may lie in the imagery of a 'missing person' photo, and our frozen memory of that particular person. Our unconscious, like a private investigator, seems to say, where is this person (or place)? Why is he or she no longer involved in our active relations? Moreover, have we done anything to harm or push this person away? These are questions which must be addressed in order to interpret these unique dream revelations.

FINGERS: Equipped with opposable thumbs, our human hands manipulate our immediate environment like no other creature on earth. Our Fingers coordinate to perform complex operations and intricate (even astounding) procedures which, by and large, we take for granted. Therefore, when these fingers appear in dreams, we need to examine their message which may regard health, ability or our multifarious sexuality. For instance, should our fingers appear injured and immovable, our unconscious may be illustrating an anxiety involving our ability to function or execute demanding tasks in our professional arena. Conversely, a hand which incessantly runs fingers over curved and smooth (or silky) surfaces, may be communicating a desire for sexual contact and erotic wish-fulfillment.

FIRE: In each case of intense emotion, we seem to find a reference concerning Fire. In yet another sense, fire refers to civilization in the form of protection from a cold, wild and decidedly inhuman landscape. Capturing and utilizing this fire demonstrates power over our own fears and subsequently opens a door to our own creative potential. In a rather peculiar, yet poetic twist, much of the creative invention which hones our modern existence becomes forged by fire (laser, electric etc.) itself. (see Ablaze)

FISH: Fish swim in lakes, rivers and oceans, each of which is symbolic of separate states of emotion. Accordingly, we need to analyze where a fish swims, its color, species and behavior, to determine its significance in our emotional paradigm. For instance, if a school of hungry shark swim in a river under a narrow bridge which we happen to be crossing, we may well be depicting an intense fear concerning a present relationship AND the course of action necessary to change this painful relationship. On the other hand, if a school of Angel fish appear in our in-ground swimming pool and circle our bodies, we may be illustrating a new emotional or spiritual love in our waking life. (see Dolphin)(see Shark)

FIT: In our dream, when something Fits well, we generally imply a feeling of unity and cohesiveness with certain aspects of our reality. On the other hand, if another person's things (clothing, car etc.) seem to fit us well, we may be referring to a desire to become like that person. In this case, we usually desire opposite attributes or possessions, from our own. However, our unconscious may be telling us, we can never know a man or woman's perceived reality, until we have walked in his or her shoes. Good fit or not, we may be in for a few unexpected revelations.

FIT: The Fit primarily involves indecisiveness and the frustrated reality of behaving in two or more worlds. Moreover, in a symbolic sense we witness the energy which the body transports fluidly and with great symmetry throughout the body from brain to spine, suddenly finding reason to impede or cut off from normal patterns of regulation. As such, we may need to examine the relationship between mind and body in the waking experience of the dreamer. Our thoughts in certain situations entirely removed from our behavior, and if so, why. In the fit imagery, we have many deep and probing questions to ask ourselves. However, the presence of the dream itself, may illustrate a healthy key toward a balanced individual. (see Epilepsy)

FIVE: In the Tarot deck, and in folklore 'magic' in general, the number Five is symbolic of 'man' equipped with two arms, two legs and a head. Notwithstanding, a pentagram is often thought of as a Satanic symbol, while its actual representation is of 'man', (the five-sided star), inside the infinity of being, (the circle). Another example of this ancient archetype is the Pentagon in Washington DC, representational of the power and order-keeping ability of man. Taking all this into account, the number five appearing in a dream may refer to 'marks' and directives meant specifically for the dreamer's waking awareness and strength.

FLAG: A Flag is symbolic of a nation or social movement. Therefore, a flag may represent an action taken for what we believe is the 'greater good' of the 'people.' As such, a flag is a powerful symbol of unity and order. It embodies the axis which a nation (or society) radiates out from. In our dream, our unconscious may be calling us to action, or warning us about our demagogue-like social behavior. We may need to analyze whether we 'lead' or 'follow' our social group and whether we believe in the motivations and goals of our assembly.

FLOAT: When we obtain the inner-faith of self-confidence and its accompanying psychological quiet, we may 'experience' a temporary freedom from the weight of life's problems. In this peaceful state of mind, we may encounter the ability to Float in the heavens, at one with our 'higher' qualities of spirit, love and elation. Comparatively, if we float on a tranquil sea, our unconscious may be signifying a profound 'emotional calm.' However, if we perceive our sea becoming stormy and our body floating too far away from land, we may be depicting anxiety and panic over our good sensations coming to an end, as we realize we've moved too far into the unknown and immeasurable depths of our own psyche.

FLOWER: Flowers symbolize the highest, yet most fragile, human receptions of love, union and death. As such, we need to interpret the color, type and number (bouquet?) of flowers observed in the dream, and our specific and detailed 'feelings' about their presence. (see Daisy, Rose, Wreath)

FLY: As opposed to floating, Flying represents psychological and emotional power, direction and control. In a dream sense, if we are able to 'steer' ourselves through our dream horizon and landscape, we are indicating successful management over the actions we take in waking life. On the other hand, if we are flying out of control, our unconscious may be warning us that we have gained too much force and momentum too quickly, and we may not be ready to 'fly over' all of life's obstacles.

FLY (insect): The Fly has many connections with demonic or immoral fears. In fact, the name Beelzebub literally means Lord of the flies. The reason for this allusion to evil forces involves the living condition and behavior of the tiny and relatively harmless bug. The fly is annoying, persistent, resilient, fast and its young are brought forth from putrescence. As such, our dream implies that our irritating and persistent condition of reality, may involve the passivity of our own actions. Perhaps we sit with our guilt when the moral aspect of our psyche feels we should be undoing our wrongs and purifying our reality. Moreover, we may be envisioning a hot and sweltering place, which may allude to a torrid situation involving iniquitous, even profane, behavior. (see Unclean)

FOG: In the dream sense, a Fog may represent a fear of the unknown. Furthermore, it may symbolize a difficulty in understanding the exact boundaries and/or 'heading', or direction, of a particular waking situation. We need to analyze therefore, why we harbor such personal fear and uncertainty, regarding certain conditions or circumstances in our life. Moreover, we need to interpret any and all objects which literally appear in our field of vision, regardless of the dense fog. These objects, or characters, may represent agents of 'clarity' which may in fact, throw light upon our (perhaps irrational) foreboding.

FOREIGNER: The complex image of a Foreigner includes exotic behavior, far away lands (themselves symbolic of promise), and a strange new experience. Nevertheless, while we are inevitably 'drawn' toward the unknown, we also may fear its actuality. Appropriately, we need to interpret emotions 'felt' upon meeting this particular character in our dream landscape. Yet another way of comprehending this dream figure regards the dreamer. The foreigner may be a representation of changes found in ourselves. We may be indicating that we are no longer recognizable to our friends, our family, even to ourselves. The latter example may necessitate professional counseling, unless we are absolutely and unequivocally certain why we appear 'foreign' to our own natures. For example, if we formulate changes in our life which are unique to us, solely to appease our loved ones, we may experience ambiguity and strangeness in our normal self-perception.

FOREST: The archetype of the Forest resides deep in our species memory. The symbolism of the landscape 'rich' with utterly wild plant and animal life-forms beckons to our immeasurable unconscious conceptualizations upon fear, aggression, desire and spirit magic. In fact, the mythological journey into the forest has often represented the sacred and necessary trip into our deepest selves. We realize in this archetype a rather balanced perception of personal light and darkness, good and evil, if you will. The successful journey through the forest primarily involves a total acceptance of the thicket itself, in other words, a surrender of human control. Accordingly, in the dream sense, we are welcomed into the unconscious when we leave our 'static' view of the world behind us, back in the light of day and waking consciousness.

FORESIGHT There is a great ongoing debate between neurologists, philosophers, psychologists, metaphysicists and almost anyone else you can think of, about the true nature of time and our relative perception of it. To grossly oversimplify the matter, time may be looked at as linear or arrow-like, leaving a past behind and heading into an uncertain future, or conversely, as a circular or spiral matrix which overlaps itself and doing so, creates a continuum of space and time which may be theoretically crossed. Furthermore, theories involving the collective unconscious demonstrate an infinite web of knowledge, which each living being possesses and programs into personal and evolutionary existence. Naturally, this being an infinite substance, it is thought to transcend any and all limitations and restrictions which time sets upon us. Therefore, taking all this into account, we may dismiss a dream involving Foresight in which a loved one is injured as a projection of our own worries. However, it is not out the realm of possibilities and the dreamer should not feel stupid in making calls providing reassurance. (*see* Clairvoyant)(*see* Time)(*see* Collective Unconscious)(*see* Jung)

FORGE: The symbolism of Forging creations with mallet and fire, may be representative of 'shaping' ones future with the fortitude of passion. While this masculine imagery may seem healthy and vital, the reality may be a bit more complex. For example, a condition of intense emotion, as in a loving relationship, may revolve around a 'giving up' of oneself. Consequently, personal strength may be necessary to surrender the guard around oneself. However, anger and aggression, which seeks to break down a person's barriers before they are ready to be broken (if at all), may be extremely dangerous for both parties, and should be avoided at all cost. As such, we need to analyze the nature of the creation which we forge into shape with all our hot pounding. In this sense, we need to 'see' if the forger completes his or her creation and then cools its red- hot metal in water, or simply and endlessly pounds the shapeless object throughout the duration of the dream. Lastly, we need to interpret the metal sculpture forged and its 'effect' upon our emotional perception in waking life.

FORM: Disparate Forms possess extremely different and diverse meanings. For example, a circle may represent infinity, God, and the universe, while a square represents a person's body and four-cornered psychological approach on reality in general. Two shapes in juxtaposition may represent conflict or an engagement into unification, while parallel lines infinitely mirror, yet never fuse together to form any affiliation. That assignment belongs to the archetype of the cross, or intersecting lines, which carry the responsibility of psychological, emotional and spiritual balance and unity.

FOUNDATION: The Foundation on which we create and build, clearly symbolizes our psychological and physiological strength, balance and creative potential. If our foundation is solid, well thought out and resistant to destructive outside forces, we may be prepared to erect a poignant edifice reflective and thankful of our place in the cosmos, and in context with the society of our fellow human beings. On the other hand, a shaky foundation represents anxiety concerning our ability to grow, either psychologically or emotionally. We need to interpret why a particular dream foundation is not too sturdy, and look for ways of improving the buttress, columns, supports and entire substructure of our psyche, in the witnessed location of the dream scene itself.

FOUNTAIN: A Fountain equipped with high spraying jets of water and brightly colored lights is symbolic of emotional joy and elation. In a dream sense, a fountain may represent a deep and entirely unrestrained outpouring of sensitivity involving a new relationship in waking life. Conversely, if the fountain runs dry, we may be experiencing the intense sadness of 'coming down' from the delicate euphoria and exhilaration found in a full and passionate life. In another sense, a fountain is often representative of the gushing, internal human soul. In this imagery, we fruitfully combine the separate interpretations of light and water to signify a swelling metaphoric enlightenment.

FOUR: The number Four symbolizes the balance and entirety of being, including the compass points: north, south, east and west and the ancient elements: air, earth, fire and water. Furthermore, all intersections of perfect balance create four perfect and all-encompassing segments of reality. In the dream sense, the number four symbolizes the finite parameters of the material world and our psychological place within that world. (see Square)(see Tarot Major Arcana: The Emperor (4) arcana)

FOWL A Fowl is a bird which cackles, lays eggs and leaves the serious flying to other birds. As such, it is a bird attached to mother earth. Symbolically, a Fowl is sole representative of the maternal wisdom of reproduction. Accordingly, in a dream sense, viewing ourselves with chickens may imply wish-fulfillment concerning the bearing of children. On the other hand, we may be depicting ourselves as cacophonous hens in order to reveal guilt over spreading rumors, or simply gossiping a bit too much.

FREEZE The action of Freezing involves alienation, isolation and an utter stagnation of self. This hesitation involves a slow process of restriction and a subsequent hardening of fluid, yet uncontrollable, emotion. (see Antarctica) (see Water)

FREUD, SIGMUND: Dr. Sigmund Freud, born in Vienna, Austria 1856-1939, is considered to be the father of modern psychanalysis. His early research involved intense dream analysis which centered around the belief that phrases and ideas which 'slipped' into the consciousness of dreaming subjects (and patients involved in word associations) revealed truths repressed in the unconscious. However, his theoretical concern with the unconscious shifted gears when he developed his own three-tier system of human consciousness, namely the ID, Ego and Superego, each of which supported a level of human development from infant wish-fulfillment (ID), to moral restraint (Superego). In limiting dream consciousness to the confines of the individual's mind, Freud differed from his student Carl G. Jung, who believed in the infinite temporal and spatial reach of the collective unconscious and its revealing archetypes.

FROG: In the dream sense, the complex symbiology of a Frog may represent sacred riddles, elusive truths and hidden beauty. Yet another aspect of the frog is its squatting ease, floating on a lily pad, which may be representational of spiritual tranquillity and emotional wisdom. In our dream, we need to pinpoint which facet or behavior of the frog is highlighted. If the frog calmly disappears into the murky pond, we may be witnessing a figurative trip into our own unconscious. On the other hand, a frog which swims and frolics with grace and beauty may symbolize inner resplendence in ourselves or some other persons in our social environment. As such, we may need to pay extra attention to our slippery friend the frog.

FRY: The dream of Frying may involve a longing for home and the good, hot emotion of its pointed resolve to feed, nourish and protect. In this sense, we see the frying as a completion of love and family which we take into ourself. On the other hand, frying may refer to being caught and beginning the process of being burnt to a crisp. Accordingly, we need to determine the intent of the frying which is nevertheless, and in either case, a pointed, poignant and emotionally driven metaphor.

FUMES: The dream involving Fumes may indicate a fear of silent, creeping evil intent which threatens to build up and eventually devastate our waking existence. We may need to wake up and check our gas lines! However, if the dream is symbolic, we may need to evaluate whether or not our fears are based on realistic observation or simply paranoid distrust. The working mechanism in this dream landscape is the invisibility of fumes. As such, we need to determine exactly how we detected the presence of the vapor. The reference of smelling or feeling 'evil', may indicate an internal predisposition about a situation or a group. We may need to explore our prejudices versus our actual experiences.

FUNERAL: The image of a Funeral may be symbolic of preparing oneself for the change of renewal. Buried into the womb of the earth, our bodies depict the seed which bursts and allows new life to enter the world. The funeral procession and the flower wreaths all signify the social blessing of our parting, replete with memory and love enshrouding our resting place. In the dream sense, we may be expressing division from our group and absolute renewal in our waking environment. Conversely, if we attend a funeral of another person, we may be indicating that this person is figuratively 'dead' to us. In other words, we have become disassociated with this individual. All characters in the funeral dreamscape should be analyzed in terms of their relation to us. Have they motivated our need for transition, or do we miss their presence and overview on our life and crucial decision making process?

FUNGUS: Fungus thrives and grows rich away from direct sunlight and drenched in a moist environment. As such, a fungus may flawlessly symbolize strange, and perhaps dark, emotions 'hidden under the surface' of our day to day consciousness. Moreover, a mushroom is a fungus with deep archetypal significance elucidating 'visions' and 'hallucinations' from the deepest part of our own psyche. A number of ancient cultures employed the sacred mushroom in ceremonial rituals. The visionary or 'medicine man' consumed the mushroom, or peyote buttons, to 'bring' him into the world of spirits (unconscious), where he hoped to learn the 'brightest path' for his people, and the answers to their tribal concerns, including the cures for all their various forms of illness. Accordingly, in a dream sense, we need to analyze who locates the fungus (if not ourselves), and furthermore, in what secret place is that same fungus discovered. We then may need to decide how this place and/or person correlates with our undisclosed emotions.

FUR: In the dream sense, the archetype of Fur may symbolize 'protection' from the outside world of sensations. Our unconscious may be revealing an ancient memory of harsher, colder times when we certainly required thicker 'coating' upon our hide. Appropriately, in a dream incarnation, the vision of possessing, or hiding under, fur, may allude to an outside person or place which alarms our human fragility. It must be noted that dream fur may only be significant if it materializes in a place, or on a person, where it would not 'commonly' appear. For instance, if we dream about a bear, it is only natural that it should have a thick coat of fur and we should instead gear our interpretation toward the animal itself and not its pelt.

FUTURISTIC: The vision of a Futuristic world in our dreams may represent wish fulfillment, or, an intense fear of the immediate future, dependent on whether the fantasy is crystalline, bright and inviting, or conversely, torturous, dreadful and dehumanizing. In either case, we may be expressing an unconscious projection of reality, based upon our repressed desires or repulsions. As such, we need to clearly interpret these futuristic worlds as the visceral landscapes of our emotional psyche. All colors, shapes, characters and numbered layouts, need to be cross-correlated to provide us with this significant understanding of self.

GADGET: The image of a useful Gadget in our dream may be representative of a rudimentary procedure or skill necessary to realize a difficult, yet desired goal. We may need to analyze the exact use of this device and ascertain our skill in using it. For instance, if our skillful use of a dream gadget, opens locked doors, we may be reflecting on a new found personal ease in staging (formally difficult) transitions in our life. On the other hand, if our gadget looks fancy and complicated, yet is totally useless, we may be illustrating personal ineffectiveness in certain situations in our waking life. As such, the gadget is symbolic of our own competence, or lack of the same.

GALLERY: The dream landscape of a Gallery or exposition is representative of an unveiling of personal creativity and novel imagery. In our dream display we may find images alien to our immediate experience which our unconscious deems to be explored. Conversely, we may find portraits which echo memories deeply embedded in our psyche which perhaps need to re-enter our living day to day actualization. Taken together, the gallery environment may be a revelation of symbolic windows opening out into the vast expanses of our perception.

GAME: In the dream sense, a Game represents psychological and/or physiological competition with another individual or group. Accordingly, we need to interpret what sort of game we are engaged in, how do we perform within that game and what are the 'stakes' involved in 'winning' this game. Naturally, as it contains so many separate symbols, the game imagery can be indeed complex. However, The key aspect remains in the 'challenge' itself. As such, we need to interpret our relationship with our respective competitor. Having done so, the complex symbiology of the game may become clearer and point toward an understanding involving this perhaps confrontational relationship.

GARBAGE: The dream symbolism of Garbage is highly dependent on what we do with that refuse. For example, if we push heaps of trash into another room and lock the door, we may be expressing difficulty in letting go of someone or something which may be harmful or distasteful to our living experience. On the other hand, if we burn our garbage, we may be illustrating a passionate consummation of a difficult past experience or relationship. Consequently, we find the significance in both these dreams is not merely the garbage, but how we 'deal' with the garbage.

GARDEN: In the dream sense, a Garden is symbolic of growth, beauty and nurturing. Because we refer to a garden and not simply a 'field' of flowers, we imply the labor, toiling and love involved in cultivating such resplendence. As such, a garden may be representative of how we view ourselves and moreover, the 'fruits' of our labor. Accordingly, we need to analyze the condition of the garden. Is it laid out creatively and lush and magnificent, or is it covered with weeds and wilting flowers? We may need to interpret the specific flowers as well as the geometrical layout of the garden for more detailed symbolism. (see Eden) (see Apple)

GARGOYLE: The image of the horrible, winged Gargoyle which guards our dwelling, may well be representative of our human recognition of a shadow unconscious. As such, we assert and reveal a part of ourselves which may be considered 'evil', in order to fend off the greater evil inherent in an unbalanced psyche. Furthermore, on roofs of buildings, we find that gargoyles are primarily designed as rain-spouts. Viewing this in the symbolic sense, we observe a commanding imagery of 'channeling' the flooding rains of our more fervent emotions, which otherwise could prove disastrous.

GARLIC: In the conception of Garlic, we find a potent, absolving agent, which literally conquers anything in its path (including nostrils). As such, ancient men and women hung cloves of garlic on their door to ward off disease and other evils of an unknown, unclean environment. Accordingly, in the dream sense, the use of garlic may represent a cautious attitude involving a corrupt or contemptible situation in our waking life. On the other hand, if we fear garlic in our dream, we may be expressing guilt about our own poisonous behavior, including perhaps, social vanity. Lastly, since garlic's potent odor is able to revive an individual who has fallen unconscious, we may be indicating a necessary awakening from a charm or enchantment which is damaging our better judgment.

GATE: The symbolism of the Gate involves entrance into a visible world. However, while this world or place is discernible, we nevertheless must be welcomed into its confines. As such, we need to prove the merit of our worthiness to gain passage. However, we may come to realize that gates so eagerly crossed, may close behind us and subsequently trap us in the forceful world of our own deepest aspirations and desires. These wishes, once realized, may prove to be entirely destructive to our own nature. (see Door)

GELATIN : In the dream sense, Gelatin may refer to sweet and easy, hence, immediate gratification. As such, gelatin may indicate the desired fulfillment of child-like needs and/or wishes. However, these aspirations are not primarily infantile, and may involve a complex craving to complete oneself through relentless sexual behavior. In the dream interpretation, we may need to explore several aspects of the gelatin such as color, taste, movement, place where we find the gelatin, and who serves us the gelatin. Taken together, these aspects and characters, may reveal the exact nature of our need for immediate gratification.

GENITALIA: In the dream sense, Genitalia may not merely imply carnal knowledge, but an elaborate expression of joy (or anxiety) concerning procreation. In the symbiotic sense, the human body illustrates aspects of our own personality. Appropriately, genitalia refers to 'conscious' masculinity and potential, hence we may need to interpret the condition of the genitals and explore the activity of the procreative function for signs of atypical behavior.

GEOGRAPHY: The physical extremes and real elements displayed in a dream image figure prominently in its psychological interpretation. As such, the enormous mountain may be seen as an obstacle to overcome and once surmounted, a revelation of ones personal triumph. Conversely, a harsh, flat wasteland may be viewed as emotional isolationism. (see Water)(see Desert)(see Landscape)

GESTALT THERAPY: Therapist, Frederick (Fritz) Perls, developed a technique for dream interpretation which involved a re-enactment of the dream itself with active participation from the dreamer as well as other individuals acting as the 'supporting' characters in the dream scene. The word Gestalt comes from the German tradition and suggests an entirety so complete that it cannot possibly be obtained from the sum of its parts. Accordingly, Gestalt Therapy searches for whole 'segments' of self and personality which cannot be reduced further. For example, a dreamer may act out a dream sequence where she is in a hospital bed surrounded by young girls who are healthy and vivacious (played by the support group), and after a short time she finds herself suddenly angry and hostile toward these girls. When the girls (support group) ask her why she is angry, she may in that instant gain the entire realization that she is furious at them because they reveal herself and her own unfeeling treatment of her mother, who has recently passed away. We see in this example, a clear example of guilt which cannot be easily discounted.

GHOST: In the dream sense, the complex symbiology of a Ghost, involving memory, guilt, fear or repression, seems highly dependent on the 'personage' of the apparition itself. For example, if the ghost is a deceased friend or relative who appears sad or disheartened, we may be expressing guilt concerning our past relationship with this person. Conversely, if the deceased specter seems warm and friendly, our unconscious may be illustrating support for a recent action enacted by the dreamer whose moral basis may be rooted in a history with the departed individual. On the other hand, if the apparition is unknown to us, we may be depicting a complex symbol of our own repressed fears. Appropriately, we may need to face the face of our fears, by interpreting the full expression, and any verbal message possibly conveyed, by our ghostly guest.

GIANT: The archetype of the Giant may involve a testimony of the human struggle against nature and his other competitors, a battle which was 'won' with man's use of 'brains over brawn.' As such, a number of cultures, including and especially, the ancient Greeks, incorporated giants into the core of their mythology. Greek mythology relates the tale of a world ruled by giants for a 'thousand years' until the Gods and 'man' defeated their numbers and assumed 'rightful' control. In the Biblical tradition, fragile and young, yet cunning David slays Goliath the giant and becomes leader and king of his people. In today's world, where man has significantly dominated his environment, symbolic giants are no longer feared and are readily embraced in myth. Hence, figures like Paul Bunyon, Babe the Ox and the Jolly Green Giant, are but a few of our gargantuan allies. Accordingly, in dreams, we either encounter angry giants which may indicate physical fear and personal insecurity and a need to 'think' our way beyond their apparent ferocity, or friendly giants which remind us of our human potential and far-reaching capacity of kindness and warmth.

GIBBERISH: In the dream sense, Gibberish may represent personal confusion. As such, we need to interpret our 'correlation' with the person who chatters the unintelligible language. Conversely, should the dreamer find him or herself speaking gibberish, it may be an indication of frustration concerning the dreamer's ability to communicate ideas, or perhaps, self-worth.

GIFT: The meaning or purpose of Gifts exchanged remain expressions of mutual joy and intimate acknowledgment. As such, a gift given or received in a dream landscape, may represent a 'reward' for hard work or personal achievement. However, if the gift turns out to be something unwanted and loathsome, we may be embodying preposterous fanfare around a false hope.

GLASS: The transparent image of Glass may refer to a desired object or person 'behind the glass' which is within view, yet firmly out of reach. Moreover, the reflective quality of glass may represent varying 'feelings' which accompany our separation from the object or person behind that glass. Appropriately, we need to analyze three distinct aspects of the glass imagery in our dream landscape. First, the shape or form of the glass (see Form), second, the image and/or color reflected upon the glass, and third, and most importantly, the image 'seen' through the glass itself. Taken together, these three components of the dream vision may uncover the impetus for any 'transparent' barriers we may suffer in waking life.

GLUE: The image of Glue may refer to a fear of being trapped and the subsequent permanence of this entanglement. We may be referring to the cautiousness necessary to maintain freedom of movement. However, a fear of partnership or commitment may also imply a distrust of people around us in waking life.

Conversely, our unconscious may be implying the creation of a cohesion of elements in our reality. As such, we may be formulating a collage of experience. Perhaps, this unity of perception may aid us in the balancing of our psyche and the desired anchoring of our fundamental self.

GNARLED: The image of a Gnarled face may imply knowledge and wisdom gained from experience. The wrinkles of age may also illustrate the worries and concerns of a complex reality which must be endured before gaining its appropriate lessons. In another variation, spiritual idealism may be represented in the surrender of ones smooth, unblemished facade, which may be viewed as superficial and as such, motivated only by material concerns.

GOAT: In the dream sense, a Goat may symbolize excessive or mindless behavior. As such, the goat in our dream landscape may be an expression of guilt concerning our greedy and/or 'obsessive' actions in the recent past, or planned immediate future. Moreover, the raw quality of a goat's manner may carry a sexual indication which cannot be ignored. Accordingly, we need to analyze the location where the goat is seen, and observe all his habits, especially 'material' chewed and swallowed.

GOD/GODDESS: Contrary to popular contemplations on the old, white haired, Caucasian look of the 'supreme being', the image of God varies dramatically according to culture. However, there are certain common denominators in the universal figures of Gods and Goddesses. Perhaps the most 'central' aspect of these supreme beings is their 'separation' from man. In order to get around this factor, gods and goddesses utilize messengers, prophets, angels and spiritual envoys (including their own sons and daughters). Hence, in the dream sense, the image of a god or goddess usually symbolizes an untouchable, unreachable perfection which we hope sheds a figurative 'light' and 'protection' upon our mortal, physical and very vulnerable selves. Moreover, we may be illustrating wish-fulfillment in our projection of ourselves in conjunction and synergy with such a perfect, unblemished being.

GRAB:: The concept of Grabbing in the dream sense refers to the moment of capture. We may be expressing insecurity in our waking life involving a situation which has recently ensnared us, or plans to do the same. Accordingly, we need to interpret the person, animal or plant which 'seizes' us. We also may need to analyze which part of our body is clenched in the formal act of the apprehension. For example, if our arm is grabbed by an authority figure, we may be indicating an anxiety concerning an older person (perhaps a father) who seems to usurp our strength, by treating us as a subordinate, rather than an equal.

GRASS: The lush green 'covering' of Grass may be representative of rich and ample living. Hence, we need to analyze the relative condition of 'our' dream grass and the location of its appearance. For example, if the grass is patchy in our own backyard, we may be expressing concerns about the 'togetherness' or general health of our family and/or significant others. Conversely, if the grass in our backyard is tall, wild and unkempt, we may be depicting a lifestyle which is too rich and lazy. In this case, we may need to wake up and push our symbolic lawn mowers over the excess swelling of our personal creature comforts and create instead a streamlined, balanced and well organized blueprint for our waking lives.

GREEN: The color Green symbolizes life and growth. Therefore, when a focused object in our dream appears bright green, we may be referring to an enhancement in the significance of that object. In essence, it has 'grown' in importance. Green may also be representational of envy or the immaturity of a novice. It is no coincidence that in both cases the conceptualization of 'potential' (revenge or completion) is decisively suggested.

GRIFFIN: The mythical creature called a Griffin possessed the body of a lion and the head and wings of an eagle. Its presence referred to protection of a great 'treasure', designating it as a glorified 'guard dog' of sorts. The combined symbolism of the 'spirit' of the eagle, and 'strength' of the lion, implied the moral fortitude necessary to resist greed and temptation (symbolized by the treasure). Accordingly, our unconscious may be demonstrating a caution to exercise moral restraint in a waking situation. As such, we need to analyze exactly 'what' the griffin protects, and from 'whom'(if not ourselves).

GROW: In a dream, the image of Growth is as complex as the phenomenon itself. The conceptualization of an increase in size and strength based upon an internal DNA/RNA program of potential is fully reflective of life on the whole. Life, or reality, is rooted in the repeated material realization of its understood design potential. Whether or not this 'plan' is previously laid out, or learned through time, is a matter of great philosophical debate. Nevertheless, the fact remains of a blueprint and the fulfillment, via physical manifestation, of that basic plan. However, since exact growth may vary according to behavior, we witness how this design is rooted in variable probabilities and possibilities. As such, the dream may reveal various aspects of potential, either previously achieved or probable, and then again, merely possible. Furthermore, we need to interpret the position of growth, rate of growth and whether or not the growth is desired. Therefore, if a particular body part or unique object grows, we need to analyze its individual symbolism and determine how the factor of increase may directly effect it and our overall relation to it, especially concerning our waking talent and future promise.

GUARD: In the dream sense, a Guard may symbolize a denial of entry. As such, we may need to interpret the meaning of the location or entrance which is respectively shielded. We may find our unconscious is illustrating a barrier or block (repression) against our own wishes or desires. For further information, analyze the color and clothing of the dream guard or sentinel. (*see* Bull)

GUMBO SOUP: In the dream sense, the image of Gumbo Soup is one of fusion, or the placing together of separate entities and their emotional 'flavors' if you will. Consequently, we need to examine social gatherings and/or collections of diverse incidents which seem to be merging or colliding in waking life. Moreover, we need to interpret our relative position in this 'coming together' of disparate, and perhaps esoteric, souls.

GUT: We may refer to the removal of essential living materials in the Gutting dream. As such, our unconscious may be illustrating a reduction, or elimination, of ones basic humanity. Furthermore, to cut into an animal's vital body, we may represent the absorption and taking in, of that creature's particular strength and/or skills. Unfortunately, this acquisition is symbolically obtained at the expense of that living being. Hence, we need to interpret the direct effect of our lust upon our opponents' well being. Is our forward progress dependent on the failure of others? If so, we may be displaying an insecurity about our own ability to succeed by our own talent and/or merit. In all case, we need to ask ourselves, is accomplishment ever worth the loss of humanity?(*see* Abdomen)

GYMNASTICS: In a dream, the action of Gymnastics involves the solo performance of an individual in tune with his or herself. Moreover, the conceptualization of human potential is clearly presented in this powerful, yet fluid display of physical movement. As such, the balance achieved by the gymnast reflects all the merits of a symmetric psychological and physiological union. Consequently, in the dream sense, we may be referring to our relative performance and poise in waking life. (*see* Balance)(*see* Ballerina)

GYPSY: The Gypsy represents movement, freedom and magic. Accordingly, we may be depicting a need to escape from the rigors of waking life. Moreover, because of the magic and carnivalesque life-styles of the free-spirited gypsies, we may be indicating a need for psychological and/or physical challenges in our life. We may need to analyze whom the gypsies represent (if anyone) in our waking life, and discover how these individuals figure into our personal freedom.

HADES: As opposed to a Christian conceptualization of hell, which is an eternal landscape of misery, constructed only for evil men and women, the ancient Greeks viewed the land of eternal death for ALL human beings and named it Hades. As such, no deceased person returns from Hades, ever, no exceptions. (Unless you're in very special favor of the gods and ask for a momentary visit). In any case, this harsh eternal plain of the dead, may symbolize more than straight forward moral concerns. The dreamer may be implying a stagnant, exhausted and lifeless existence which reveals no change or hope of escape. As such, the dreamer may need to critically analyze and interpret all the characters in the Hades landscape. In this regard, the unconscious may reveal the individual/s (especially ourselves and our own actions) and situation/s which have caused this feeling of existing in a death-like trance. In a psychological sense, a series of repressions and/or depressive behavior, may cause an individual to sink into this comatose state of reality perception. In such extreme cases, the dreamer must come to realize (via therapy and/or continual social support) that he or she IS in very special favor of the gods (self), and may return to the quality of life and the land of the living, any time he or she pleases. Moreover, this LIFE is where they belong and fully deserve to be. (*see* Hell)

HAIL: In the Hail landscape we witness a slow, painful and obstacle-ridden movement or experience. Since hail is primarily frozen rain, emotional difficulty or hardship may be involved. Accordingly, we may interpret the hail dream as an expression of anxiety concerning difficult emotional situations or misgivings concerning psychological metamorphosis. For further information, we need to analyze the symbolic location of the falling hail and its physical effect upon our material body.

HAIR: In the dream sense, Hair implies virility, strength and sensual ease. Accordingly, we need to analyze the color, texture, length and relative fullness of the hair revealed in the dream imagery. For example, long flowing red hair may symbolize fiery passion while unending black hair may symbolize mystery and extreme sensuality. On the other hand, short hair may imply aggression and swiftness, in other words, 'purpose' and 'freedom' in movement and action. Conversely, a loss of hair primarily indicates insecurity about sexual performance, age or other aspects of low self-esteem. However, the act of having ones hair forcibly cut off may indicate an attack on ones vigor or potency by an aggressive or otherwise intimidating outside force. (compare Baldness)

HALLOWEEN: Their are two separate representations of the Halloween imagery in our dream landscape, which are nevertheless fundamentally connected. The first concerns our childhood ability to fulfill role playing in the form of costumes and disguises. As such, the child is able to become someone other than him or herself. Moreover, the child is allowed to become anonymous (unknown) and in this pretense, is allowed to throw off the shackles of responsibility and pointed consequence. In this sense, the children become akin to wandering spirits who cannot be directly blamed for their deceit. Hence, the game and the playing of the game become one in the same. The second representation involves the adult regression into childhood, which itself implies a disguise used to avoid the natural obligation and accountability of adulthood. So we see an adult disguised as a child disguised as an imposter, who becomes an invisible or ghost-like force. Hence, in a very elaborate illustration of continually transcending bodies, we witness the revelation of a repressed desire for unlimited freedom. Perhaps this is why we allow for the democratic release of candies and other sweets to quench the passionate thirst of a newly realized autonomy and its subsequent and outright powerful existence. If only for a day. (*see* Mask)

HALO: The symbolic image a Halo, or spiritual light, which radiates from a person's body and head, refers to unearthly intervention in the 'purpose' or 'motivation' of that human being. As such, these individuals emanate 'divine' or 'spiritual' integrity. In the dream sense, an illuminated person or entity may be drawing us into its experience of love, happiness and/or glory. (*see* Aura)(*see* Circle)(*see* Ring)

HAMMER: The ancient Nordic symbolism of the Hammer of Thor, referred to the powerful and instantaneous 'order' inherent in total authority. In the modern world, judges bang their gavel upon the gavel plate to indicate a verdict ruled and therefore finalized. Accordingly, in the dream sense, a hammer which pounds once with great authority may refer to a conclusion in a waking situation. Conversely, an incessant pounding of hammers may refer to the pounding of our heart (emotion) or in our head (psychological). As such, we need to interpret the nature of the 'hammering' which pounds upon our psyche.

HANDS: Hands represent ones absolute manipulation of the world around them. In fact, the Latin root of the word manipulation is 'movement of hands.' Moreover, a person 'handles' situations, which means THAT person either fixes or copes with the problem at 'hand.' Naturally, we see how hands are fundamental archetypes of our overall behavior, both psychologically as well as physiologically. In the spiritual plain, the movement of fingers represents magic as well as music. The hand, in the archaic sense, became the map of our entire life, allowing palm readers, otherwise known as palmists, to read the future of our love, health, family and creative disposition. The hand became so prominent in our historic and psychological expression of self, that rings (made specifically for fingers) and scepters (made especially for hands) were chosen as the instruments fully indicative of 'divine' royalty and 'holy' matrimony. Taking all this into account, we need to examine the use and intent of all hands which figure into our overall dream landscape. (*see* Fingers)(*see* Tarot Major Arcana: The Wheel of Fortune (10) arcana)

HANG: The symbolism of Hanging refers to being forced or 'choked' out of our normal existence. As such, we may need to analyze which aspect of our waking behavior has become restricted and otherwise cut off. Moreover, we need to interpret why this conduct or internal mental construct has left us 'dangling' and powerless. Once we have discovered the grounds for our symbolic hanging, we may begin the process of forgiving ourselves and returning to the natural 'flow' of our lives. However, if the hung person fights against his or her fate, our unconscious may be signaling a warning to resist any limitation which may prove to contain disastrous long term consequences. Consequently, we need to determine the exact 'feelings' of the individual being executed upon the dream gallows and the nature of the 'crime' which has brought them here. (*see* Tarot Major Arcana: The Hanged Man (12) arcana)

HARBOR: In the dream sense, a Harbor represents a home or haven for our deeper emotions. Appropriately, we need to analyze the calmness of the waters in the harbor and the condition of the vessels anchored in that close proximity. If the crafts are safe and well kept in sunny smooth bay waters, we may be depicting 'comfort' in our family relationships. Conversely, a rough harbor which tosses around neglected ships may imply a deep anxiety about our affiliations not so close to home.

HARVEST: The symbolism of the Harvest is highly dependent on the weather found in the season. A cold spring and summer may leave hard soil and feeble growth, representative of sickness and cold, distant emotionalism. On the other hand, a hot, wet season may bring forth a sturdy and robust harvest indicating good health, a considerable sex drive, or perhaps, the birth of a child. Accordingly, we need to examine the symbolic contents of the harvest, as well as, the representative climate of the harvest season itself.

HAUNT: The concept of Haunting revolves around ones own fears. The unstoppable figure of a ghost or demon may reflect our unconscious and its long list of repressed realities. As such, we need to determine why we are haunted in the dream and what harm, if any, can befall us. A majority of psychoanalysts believe that a dreamer, under normal conditions (i.e. not suffering from psychosis) should challenge the spectral image which does the haunting and question its intentions. In this manner, the dreamer may come to understand the symbolic meaning of this nightmarish figure. Especially, if it answers!(*see* Ghost)

HAWK: The Hawk is known for its precise eyesight, soaring speed and keen instincts. As such, a hawk may symbolize accurate judgements and/or keen decision making. Furthermore, flying high above the landscape akin to the eagle, the hawk possesses spiritual insight and divine affectations. In ancient Egypt, the ruling messiah Horus, the son of the sovereign gods Osiris and Isis, possessed the head of a hawk and the respective body of a pharaoh. As such, he symbolized the 'ideal' visionary ruler of mankind.

HEAD: The Head possesses six crucial characterizations, one being the mind, the second the face, and the last four being the individual eyes, ears, nose and mouth. Appropriately, we need to determine which aspect of the head is pinpointed in the dream imagery and examine the symbolism of that respective 'part.' However, if the entire head is focused upon, we need to turn to the psychological structure of the dreamer's self-image and perception of the world experienced. For example, if in a dream, our own head was screaming on the 'chop block' of an ax-toting executioner, who looked remarkably like ourself, we may be rather dramatically illustrating how our own personal actions have 'severed' our own personality and life-style. Case in point, our unconscious may be demonstrating how we have needlessly cut ourselves off from society by adopting radical new methods of existence with no social merit whatsoever.

HEADDRESS: The ancient practice of adorning a shaman or temple priest's head with an ornamental Headdress, symbolized an invitation to the spirits into the tribal psyche. In ancient Egypt, and later in Greece, individuals wore similar headdresses within the chambers of dream incubation temples to encourage the entry of guiding dream spirits. Hence, in the dream sense, the vision of an ornamental veil worn by a dreamer, may represent an enticement to outside forces to influence or enlighten ones waking life. Conversely, if an individual other than the dreamer wears the headdress, evidence of personal guidance may be presented in the form of that person.

HEALTH: Health may concern an acknowledgment of ones strengths and/or limitations. As such, we need to determine the symbolism of certain parts of ourselves which may appear unhealthy and otherwise dysfunctional. Conversely, if the body part appears healthy, our unconscious may be signaling us to call upon its metaphoric specialization, right here and right now in our waking life.

HEARTH: The image of Hearth in general terms, may refer to a feeling of overall contentment, stability and peacefulness in ones life. This tranquillity may come with the wisdom of age, which teaches to slow down, plan and foster caring, mutual and therefore ongoing, relationships. (see fire)(see Warmth)

HEAVEN: In the dream sense, the Heaven landscape, or perfect bliss, primarily symbolizes compensation, and consequently escape, from our imperfect and harsh reality. However, every so often, a dreamer may be depicting harmony and fluid movement in his or her actual waking experience. Dreams often serve as reflections of our more passionate moods, as such, heaven may be perceived as absolute joy. In order to determine on which side of the emotional line we stand, we may need to honestly assess our waking life and compare its relative 'bliss' to our dream's visual jubilation. If they seem to represent an utter contradiction, we may need to address our escapist behavior by seeking professional counseling.

HEEL: The connotation of the Heel involves power and subservience. In the sense of the foot which crashes down with authority, we see control (of mother, primarily). In this sense, we witness a correlation to sexual command and domination in general. Hence, to be placed underfoot seems to symbolize ultimate submission. Conversely, in the sense of our Achilles heel, we see vulnerability and metaphoric pain which never leaves us. Accordingly, we need to determine the position and intent of the heel in its particular dream orientation. (see Achilles Heel)

HELL: The archetypal image of a world of pain and punishment, sometimes labeled Hell, represents expressions of personal torture and guilt. Accordingly, when our emotions and passions painfully smoulder within our psyche, we may need to create the landscape of our suffering in the form of a hell-like spectacle. Providing our deeper emotions a location, may enable us to move, react (and, in the case of self-guilt), 'accept' its relentless castigation. (see Hades)

HEMP: The ritual smoking of Hemp, in order to propel into the enigmatic world of our unconscious, may be representative of hiding from ones commonplace, monotonous, or thoroughly onerous reality matrix. As such, we may need to analyze the location of our hemp experience and any and all visual or hallucinatory signs revealed. This way we may better understand wishes which remain unfulfilled in waking life and may need to be compensated for.

HERMAPHRODITE: In ancient times, a significant number of tribes exalted Hermaphrodites into sacred social status because of their unique possession of both male and female reproductive organs. In the modern world, people are beginning to understand the necessity of a balance in their masculine and feminine attributes. As such, the combination of strength and sensitivity is considered futuristic and ideal in our social and personal behavior. Accordingly, the hermaphrodite dream image, may refer to a completeness and balance in our gender-related characteristics. For example, a woman who controls a corporation with fierce (and sometimes harsh) executive power, while tenderly raising three children at home, may well dream herself into the body of a hermaphrodite. As in ancient times, this dream imagery remains normal, powerful and self-advancing.

HERO: The archetype of a Hero/ine refers to an outside force which has the ability to save us from evil. The hero/ine provides physical and psychological courage in place of our own mortal vulnerability. In the dream sense, we may be supplanting our own responsibilities into the hands of another. As such, we may be exemplifying detrimental forms of personal regression and escapism. On the other hand, if we ourselves are heroic in dreams, we may be declaring personal strength and the ability to move beyond our own limitations.

HEX: The feeling of a curse placed upon us by some person dabbling in black magic, may symbolize a fear of our own powers and/or harmful intentions, which have come full circle and now return to us in a devastating manner. This is primarily because a curse, or Hex, involves revenge or a unique blend of retaliation for some grotesque act of disrespect. In this, we may witness a fear concerning our own impertinence toward certain or all tenets of magic or witchcraft itself. These may include naturalism, feminine instincts concerning their bodies and free sexuality, elemental forces and otherworldly spiritual influences, or all of the above. In any case, our dream indicates that we have crossed, or annoyed in some way, a force which is perceived to be, greater than ourselves. In this, we explore a form of abstract domination over our individual being. In the psychological sense, this control is projected from the self, back toward the self, in the most horrendous, fearful form imaginable, (naturally, by the self). Furthermore, counter-magic, or the protection of self, can only occur when the plagued victim harnesses enough personal strength and force of will to match and neutralize the initial self-inflicted negative force embodied in the shape of our tormentors. Herein, we witness how black magic is similar to other practices. Its strength lies in the force of our belief and faith in its words of truth, or conversely, under its spells of potential disaster. (*see* Witchcraft)

HIDE, ANIMAL: In the Native American and otherwise aboriginal sense, to be covered in the Hide of a dead animal, symbolizes taking on its medicinal and spiritual properties. As such, what we wear, becomes who we are and moreover, who we are able to become.

HIEROGLYPHICS: In the dream sense, Hieroglyphics may symbolize an unknown language or knowledge which may need to be deciphered. Hence, we may be alluding to desired information which has eluded our immediate understanding. Moreover, the historical significance and rarity of hieroglyphics may demonstrate a form of dream information which is indicative of absolute truth and/or wisdom. Taken together, we find our dream imagery may in fact symbolize a quest for truth and/or unique knowledge which may expose the wisdom of our own elaborate and ancient unconscious.

HIGHWAY TRAVEL: In the dream sense, Highway Travel symbolizes speed, movement and sexual freedom. Moreover, since a highway stretches across the landscape moving us from old locations to new locations, we may be depicting fast and exhilarating psychological changes. Plainly, the concept of potential is inherent in this far-reaching dream landscape. However, if our dream highway is loaded with traffic, potholes and illegible road signs, we may be expressing difficulty in movement, or a dull, routine waking life, which seems to be heading nowhere.

HOAX: In the dream sense, a Hoax or chicanery, may symbolize a fear of deception in some formality in our waking life. Our unconscious may be issuing a warning about being misled in our beliefs or planned actions. Accordingly, we may need to determine the nature of the subterfuge, or joke, played upon us, and the motivation of the trickster. Moreover, do we know this person, or group of people, who deceive us, and what exactly is our working or personal relationship with them?

HOLE: The concept of a Hole, or absence of space, involves the double-sided reality of the unknown. As such, a hole may be something we fall through, or conversely, a hole may be a void which allows us to see another landscape of reality, other than the one in which we are fixed. In another sense, the circular nature of a hole implies a relation to rings and provides a physical space for the insertion of an axis or center pole. As such, spiraling electro-magnetic energy creates, and at the same time, centers around, a hole, or absence of space. This hole is oriented neither north nor south, west nor east, it is merely a circular vortex of potential. Accordingly, physical manifestations of living creatures allow for holes, or cavities of plausible growth. Human Beings possess eye, ear, nostril and pelvic sockets, each of which allot for the development of the specialization of human adaptation. In the dream sense, we may need to determine the possibility of the hole. Will we fall through its drafty abyss, or will it harness our psyche into a multifarious wonderland of twisting promise. (*see* Ring)(*see* Circle)(*see* Den)

HOLSTEIN (*see* Cow)

HOME: As opposed to a house, which represents our psychological make-up and overall characteristics, a Home symbolizes our emotional stability. As such, the home is a far less fixed concept. In fact, the feeling of home may change from day to day, even minute by minute, dependent on our relationship with others and our sanctity of self. In laymen terms, the house is in our head, while the home is in our heart. Moreover, in a symbolic gender sense, it is the father figure who creates the house and mother figure, the home. Accordingly, disorientation of home may involve difficulty in ones feminine aspect. This is why a shy recluse, who hides from masculinity and outside relationships, may be thought of as 'homely.' The term has little to do with appearance and rather centers around a rather basic imbalance of masculine and feminine principles. (*see* House)

HOOD: In a dream sense, the Hood implies the undoing of the head and all its neurological senses, both symbolic and material. As such, the hood erases our psyche and therefore, our unique individuality. This being the case, we may feel anonymous in society at large. Moreover, we may seem dangerous to others in the diminishing of our responsibility and furthermore, levels of sensitivity. In the realm of this conceptualization, the Grim Reaper represents the insensitive, anonymity of death which steals away life regardless of individual status. Illustrating this idea one step further, we find the covering of heads executed and the jacketing of corpses and their faces, in general, primarily to reveal their introduction into the unknown ranks of the dead. Accordingly, in a dream, we may need to understand who wears the hood and for what purpose. The death of our own individuality is usually a paramount factor.

HORIZON: A Horizon symbolizes the parameter of our landscape, a celebrated beginning or somber conclusion. Furthermore, the horizon represents our goal or future, it is the product of a world in absolute transition. As such, it represents continual rebirth and regeneration. In our dream, we may need to analyze the terrain leading toward the distant horizon and the colors and mood of the skyline itself. It may also be critical to interpret any person or creature which moves or interacts within this imagery. For instance, a high flying hawk soaring across a brilliant sunrise may indicate a direct and positive outlook on the future.

HORNS: Primarily, Horns indicate fertility and productivity. However, the action and relative condition of the horns translate their inherent meaning. For example, horns on a charging animal may symbolize speed and steadfastness in purpose, while a broken horn on a caged beast may represent a departure from course or sexual interest. On the other hand, when horns present a dream threat, there may be an indication of repressed passion and an inability to let go of oneself. Interestingly, within the unconscious terror of being pierced through, exists the very real possibility of self revelation. (*see* Bull)

HORSE: In the Chinese zodiac, the symbolism of the Horse individual involves independent natures, attractiveness and enormous popularity, combined with a cheerful intelligence. The horse itself has always implied powerful freedom in the grace of gallop, majesty of leap and outright force of kick. Man naturally feels a connection with the mighty horse because the animal is willing to work and merge its regal energy with the balance and skill of a rider/provider. The mutual benefit of man and horse raises to another level of relationship where freedom, power and grace is blended with discipline, balance and artistry. As such, we have come to love our four legged friend, every bit as much as our own self. (*see* Equestrian)

HOUSE: In the dream sense, a House may represent the structure of our entire psychological self-perception. As such, separate rooms within the house symbolize diverse characteristics. For example, a bedroom may imply marriage or sexual relationships, while the bathroom may represent feelings of cleanliness and purification. Following along this train of thought, we find the kitchen representing family togetherness and/or bodily sustenance and the living room expressing life-styles and general psychological perceptions (TV,VCR,LIBRARY etc.). As such, we need to interpret the relative condition, shape or state of each of the rooms which comprise our house and determine which idiosyncratic room of our self may need repair or reorganization.

HUNCHBACK: The symbolism of strength, loyalty and determination, all tempered with a humble submissiveness represents the Hunchback figure in our dream landscape. It is crucial to understand the symbolic disfigurement of the hunchback allows for his endearing humility and faithfulness. Accordingly, we may be revealing a personal or perceived distortion of self, either physical or psychological, which renders us eternally compliant to our peers. Perhaps our unconscious is indicating that we should use the strength of the hunchback to finally free ourselves from the subservience of our peer group and regain our personal freedom.

HUNT: The archetypal symbolism of the Hunt, refers to the struggle of survival. Consequently, the lone predator, whether it be a man or a hungry lioness, must outperform and out-think the desired prey. In order to live another day, either the predator or the prey, must emerge victorious. In the social sense, a group of hunters may represent a dreamer's ability to work with others toward a common goal. In addition, this band of trackers may refer to the dreamer's family or coworkers. Conversely, the notion of being hunted oneself, may represent feelings of being stalked by life's challenges. In other words, our fearful struggle for survival may be wearing us down and we desperately may covet a halt in the excruciating pace. Accordingly, we may need to analyze the landscape of the hunt, the hunter/s themselves, and the motivation behind the hunt. In the latter example, we may need to determine exactly what or whom wants to destroy us, and why. In most cases, the dreamer is hunted or pursued by his own fears, which need to be faced and categorized in the waking psyche.

HYBRID: The concept of two or more beings which are combined to form a new model of living creature through genetics or metaphysics is known as a Hybrid. In a dream, these hybrids, man or animal, while existing as unique life forms, nevertheless possess traits and behavior of all (its) ancestors and/or ingredients. As such, we need to examine the symbolism of the separate components which comprise the hybrid itself. Once knowing this, we may determine if these aspects negate each other, or combine to form a kind of super-being. For example, crossing a wolf and a human creates a fearful, yet tortured creature, who is more powerful than we may care to think about. Conversely, a wolf and a dove may combine to form an animal with powerful spiritual influence, nearly angelic in the determination of its composure. Accordingly, these hybrids may reflect internal struggles which either strengthen us, weaken us, or render us completely immobile in our waking behavior. (*see* Animus)(*see* Transmutation)(*see* Zoomorphism)

HYGIENE: The act of meticulously cleaning oneself, may involve guilt about ones actions. In this, we witness the dream illustration of purifying oneself from influences of negativity. In the archaic sense, evil is nearly always equated with unclean objects and persons. This is why the name Beelzebub is translated 'Lord of the flies', as we know flies are inexorably drawn toward refuse and bacterial substances. Moreover, we find a slight variation of this cleaning involving the wishes of mother and home life. If we cleansed ourselves, we were rewarded with love and attention. Naturally, girls relished in this behavior, formulating deep relationships of equality with mother, while boys struggled with independence from mother and closeness to mother, simultaneously. In this sense, we find an allusion to sexuality, especially in males, who may find themselves concerned about love of mother, and in a parallel discernment, a socially unapproachable love of the feminine aspect within themselves. (*see* Cleaning)(*see* Baptism)(*see* Unclean)

HYPNOSIS: In the dream sense, Hypnosis may refer to an uncontrollable psychological suggestion which may become an obsession. Our unconscious may be revealing our folly in being reined in by an individual or group. Conversely, if we hypnotize another dream character, we may be illustrating self-guilt involving the personal manipulation of a friend or relation in waking life. Moreover, the symbolism of hypnosis seems to contradict the powerful conceptualization of autonomy altogether. As such, we may find ourselves invoking a call to freedom or emancipation from some outside force which seems to possess an extraordinary influence over us.

ICE: The symbolism of Ice in the dream landscape, refers to frozen or paralyzed emotional states. However, melting ice, may imply a re-entry into the warmth of spring, romantic love and the welcoming, yet sometimes wild, world of nature. Along those lines, dislodged icebergs symbolize the slow, yet gigantic movement of emotional passage into sexual or psychological maturity. We need to interpret where the ice settles in the dream and what cold and alienating event may compel its continued existence. (*see* Antarctica)

ICEBERG: The Iceberg defines an enormous amount of emotional strength in the vastness of its cold landscape, or conversely, the intensity of its hot dislocation from an even larger mass. In either case, the potential of the ice mass is unfathomable and may cause major devastation if underestimated. Hence, the Titanic's eternal reminder of human fallibility. In this larger sense, the iceberg is symbolic of man's ultimate subordination to nature. Accordingly, a dreamer may need to contemplate the wisdom of his or her forward progress against nature, or natural forces; which may be far greater than they appear to the naked senses.

ICON: The dream of an Icon perhaps suggests a personal bridge between an image and the spiritual reality which that image conveys. In other words, our unconscious may be presenting a physical metaphoric reality (representational painting or sculpture) and asking us to discover the abstract reality behind and beyond that symbol. In so doing, we may come to realize that genuine steps into deeper and truer reality become more apparent and more tangible. In the icon example, we find first a painting (object), then a representation (or symbol), and finally a meaning (or significance). Accordingly, the dream icon may represent the process of gaining deeper understanding of the visual world around us each and every day.

IGUANA: In the dream sense, the archetypal Iguana may epitomize cold, fierce and above all, inhuman poise. The iguana represents an ancient time when the world was sweltering, harsh and hostile toward animal life (including human beings). However, in this unforgiving terrain, the iguana stood motionless, without fear, and arguably noble, almost surreal. Taken together, the Iguana in the dreamscape may represent an almost unstoppable, inhuman (yet very human) determination, which we may find appalling and terrifying, yet nonetheless, awe-inspiring. Appropriately, we may need to determine if the iguana represents a certain individual or group in our waking life whose behavior has us frightened and/or spellbound.

ILLNESS: In ancient incubation temples in Greece (see Aesculapius), patients were encouraged to search their dreaming mind for possible remedies and cures for their various illnesses. Conversely, in modern dream interpretation, we find the physical imagery of illness, representational of a psychological or emotional breakdown in the dreamer. Accordingly, we need to analyze the severity of the illness and which part of the body it primarily effects. For example, a painful stomach affliction such as an ulcer, may indicate greed in procurement or the acceptance of bad or inappropriate psychological nourishment, in other words, bad food for thought.

IMAGE: A dream which reveals a person, place or thing as a direct Image, either on a screen, or in 'thin' air, may be focusing on the meaning of the form of that particular manifestation. This conceptualization of a 'meaningful' shape, may seem strange in this contextual sense. However, each and every day we create and modify a particular 'look' which we hope speaks volumes about our character, or active characteristics, which we would like to be associated with, either directly or indirectly. In other words, we present an image of self, roughly matching our internal hopes, passions and drives. This rule does not simply hold true for persons who dress well or fashionably, but also to casual, traditional or simply uninterested styles of appearance. Every appearance, like it or not, is appraised by society, along with physical mannerisms and articulation, or slang, of speech. Being aware of this basic tenet, our speech, manner and dress usually conform to one another, creating a basic image of self. Accordingly, in a dream, a viewed image reveals the psychological meaning within that person. As such, our unconscious may be referring to the connection between our inner self and our exposed social self. Are the two coinciding, or are we disguised and therefore hiding from our own beliefs and/or desires, in other words, ourselves. Conversely, if the image uncovers a person known to us, we may need to compare this image with the clear image we know of that person. The dream image may represent our own desires placed upon the form and subsequently, psyche of that person. In this sense, we may be recreating this individual to fit into our own perception of reality. Moreover, this reworking of another, may reflect a desire for that particular human being, to become more involved in our own life style and/or life on the whole.

IMBRUE: The symbolism of Imbruement, which entails a physical staining of the body with blood, refers to forced spirituality or a sacrificial ritual which brings one closer to the sensation or presence of God. In the biblical story of Exodus, Moses covers his people (the Hebrews) doors with sheep's blood to protect them from God's wrath against the first born (male) children of Egypt. In this sense, the stained doors drew in the reality of God, just enough to placate his essence, yet send it off in the direction of the Egyptians. In ancient warrior traditions (universally), the blood of the warrior's victim, man or animal, ended up smeared upon the face or body of that warrior. As such, the blood became a sign and justification of the sanctity of the spirit released in battle. Hence, in a dream landscape, the staining of blood refers to the sacrificial embodiment of spirit to flesh, soul to reason.

IMITATION: In the dream sense, Imitation refers to flattery and idolatry. As such, it is crucial to note if the dreamer is the imitator, or the person imitated. If the dreamer finds him or herself imitated by another person, an expression of intrusion may be indicated. Plainly, we may feel our creativity or style has been wrongfully stolen and used unjustly by a competitor. Conversely, if we imitate someone else, we may desire someone or something which that person possesses. While appearing harmless, this escapist dream mimicking represents a difficulty in accepting oneself and may lead to a detrimental self-catharsis.

IMMERSION: The archetypal symbolism of Immersion comprises

the ritualistic preparation for thorough, and perhaps absolute, change. Accordingly, the nature of that transformation is dependent upon the representational medium in which one is immersed. For example, to be immersed in a foul, trash-like substance, may be an illustration of anxiety, involving a forced entry into a suffocating, unpleasant and perhaps, immoral situation (or new position) in our personal occupation. Conversely, to be immersed in a hot, liquid medium may involve a dreamers surrender and complete consummation into physical libidinous reality. On the other end of the spectrum, immersion into cold liquid, may symbolize harsh celibacy and a purifying act of regeneration and rebirth into the solitary self. Lastly, we examine immersion into blood, which may represent the dreamer coming to terms and fully realizing his internal needs, honest desires and soulful direction.

IMPALE: To be run through, or Impaled, symbolizes a violent or passionate release of ones own repressed and sequestered emotions. In other words, a person is symbolically set free from the physical limitations of their own psyche. Furthermore, because the lance or sword remains intact in our body, that weapon's own symbolism, including directness, aggression and sexuality come into immediate play. Appropriately, we need to analyze which part of the body, including vital organs, is penetrated in the symbolic impalement.

INCENSE: In the dream sense, Incense is symbolic of spiritual warmth, sanctity and inner peace. The burning flame or ember, which originates the incense plume, is representative of the radiating source of love which permeates our being. To whom we offer this inner devotion is entirely up to our own personal sense of purpose. Accordingly, in the dream landscape, we may need to determine the location of the incense and decide why this location is consecrated, or needs to be anointed in our waking experience.

INCEST: The conceptualization of Incest may involve a restriction of outside influences and experiences. To find ourselves drawn toward a reflection of ourselves, in the embodiment of relatives, signifies a fear of strange new desires, passions and emotions. To respond only to that which is familiar, may be reflective of a deep and unhealthy sexual repression. Moreover, a lopsided narcissism (as in ancient royalty) may be overcoming our natural craving and physical sensibilities. As such, in our dream landscape, the witnessing, or participation in incest, may reveal a limitation in our openness to the outside world of experience, and perhaps an escapist egomania, which could in fact, prove harmful.

INCONTINENT: This dream may illustrate a fear involving a personal loss of control. The management of ones own body is critical in our symbolic understanding of mind and spirit. Therefore, when our bodies act on their own, we fear the demise of our own powerful soul and hence, our basic humanity. This dream seems to illustrate more than a fear of old age, but rather a phobia about our strength as an individual. As such, persons suffering from psychological anxieties may question their self and social worth. It is interesting to note that being out of control is not at all like being wild and destructive. While both examples display chaotic behavior, the anarchy of the latter is 'let loose' and therefore enjoyed in a mental release of all responsibility. While on the other hand, the anarchy of the former is 'pulled away from any and all command' and releases responsibility much to the individual's personal chagrin. In a strange sense, the former example may be a direct consequence of the long standing repression of the latter example.

INCUBUS: In medieval times, an Incubus was believed to be an evil spirit which descended upon a sleeping woman and performed sexual intercourse with her. This convenient belief explained sexual explorations or passions which may have overcome a sleeping woman in the course of her dreams. Naturally, this incubus reflected the sexual repression of an entire society. It was far easier to believe an evil spirit possessed the body of a sleeping righteous woman, rather than accept the fact that this upstanding woman was still a sexual being. Nevertheless, these puritanical images remain with us, when we practice sexuality in dreams and abstinence in waking life. Our unconscious may be demonstrating a need to balance our feelings of desire with our absolutions of self purity.

INDIAN, NATIVE AMERICAN: In the dream sense, the Native American refers to honesty and quiet wisdom. Moreover, the culture of the American Indian is highly representative of personal power and a union with nature and all her elements. In this noble figure we find the perfect transcendence of earth and spiritual worlds, traveled freely back and forth by one human being. Appropriately, in this dream imagery, our unconscious may be alluding to personal dedication, or social situations in our life, which are graced with sublime inner peace and divine simplicity.

INDUSTRIAL: In a very real sense, Industry has become the unmatched nightmare in the world of man, and especially nature. The inhuman speed and sheer number of goods manufactured into the world has enabled society to quadruple in less than one hundred years. Society grows faster than the availability of land, and the flowering of natural sustenance, necessary to maintain that society. All this coupled with the reality of greed, which expands exponentially with the lack of resources, has created an angry an callous environment, in which we are forced to thrive as best as we can. Taken together, the Industrial dream, may indicate an individual life of mounting complexity which has caused the dreamer to lose spirit and the will to thrive in a progressive and naturalistic direction. We may feel ourselves becoming the inhuman offspring of a cold and unfeeling technology. This illusion is not only escapist, but defeatist as well, and needs to be addressed both socially and individually.

INFANT: The Infant dream, involves the reality of early life. In this life, all of our basic needs are provided and our stress and responsibility levels are nonexistent. In this sense, we may be expressing a form of regression into a simpler time where the absolute difficulty of adulthood is pretty much, nonexistent. However, if the infant is in danger, our unconscious may be illustrating our maternal and paternal instincts to protect the vulnerable side of our young, or conversely and more often the case, ourselves. In this, we find a connection between our fragile self, requiring attention and affection and our protective self, fearless in its dedicated resolve. Our unconscious may be telling us to quench our irrational fears with the sound strength of adult logic and reason. (see Baby)(see Womb)(see Child)

INFESTATION: The symbolism of Infestation involves a terrible intrusion upon oneself, both physically and psychologically. The idea of the body of self becoming host to parasites, may be indicative of mortal vulnerability and weakened defense mechanisms. Our unconscious may be warning us against individuals who seek to invade our autonomy with their influence and powerful presence. In order to stop this infestation, we may need to immerse our bodies into the cold water of purification and isolated retreat. Once we have regained our solitude and cloaked our bodies in self understanding, we may be able to withstand the encroachment of others upon our bared soul.

INFINITE: In the dream sense, Infinity refers to limitless potential. The landscape which goes on forever may be the living reflection of our unconscious. As such, we need to gain a detailed account of all objects, characters and layouts of the infinite panorama and decide which relative direction and/or figurative path we may need to follow in order to obtain our maximum creative facility and visionary goals.

INFLATE: The act of Inflating, may be representative of growing tension and stress-related anxiety. As we blow up our figurative balloon, we increase its relative force while decreasing our own. Plainly, we must reach a point where the balloon can no longer become inflated and finally bursts. This bursting is symbolic of our own mental breakdown into depression and listlessness. Accordingly, our unconscious may be warning us to inhale and release the hot air of our tension balloon. As such, we may need to liberate our pent-up anxiety and divide the previously inmost components of our daily concerns into rational compartments of achievable obligation.

INK: The image of Ink in our dream landscape, may refer to permanence, as in an unwanted stain. Moreover, since ink is used to convey language and subsequently thought and wisdom, we may be referring to a misunderstanding with long term consequences and/or a mistake in judgment, each time we witness spilled ink. Conversely, the coordination of mind and hand with ink and paper, may reflect the lasting and unchanging value of the written word, which gives form to content and otherwise manifests our abstract mental processes. This being the case, we should take great care in analyzing the position and form of all ink markings in our overall dream narrative and its determinate physical landscape.

INSECT: The relentless, exacting, nearly robotic activity of an Insect may be symbolic of an anxious psychological state of mind. However, the species of a specific insect and the focused action of that particular creature, may be extremely significant in the analysis of our own process of psychological exertion. (see Bug)

INSTRUMENT: Each Instrument has its own peculiar tone, ornate color and honed material, out of which it is constructed. Accordingly, we need to determine our own attachment to unique instruments and in a larger sense, melodies in general. Often music is associated with emotional experiences which must be released and reflected against the society of our peers. Our instrument is always reflective of ourself and moreover, our deepest internal passion. (*see* Accordion)(*see* Beat)(*see* Dance)

ISLAND: An Island is defined by its watery boundaries, as such, the effect of its geographic isolation offers a unique set of symbolic images. For example, odd and wonderful life forms flourish within the confines of an island and epitomize creative distinctiveness. Conversely, the circumstance of being on an island may refer to being lost or trapped, in which case the island becomes a symbol of alienation or solitude. Along those lines, if one is trapped with others upon a desolate island, our unconscious may be hinting at a lost cause within which, we may find ourselves ensnared. Whatever the particular circumstance, the dreamer should keep in mind, that ultimately, the island is a symbol of a tenacious, reliant, self-strength, and the propagation of unique, unrestrained creativity.

ITCH: Since our skin symbolizes how we sense the world, any complication or discomfort involving the skin, may imply psychological disarray. Accordingly, in the dream sense, an Itch may be representational of a painful psychological or emotional complexity which has become enmeshed in our daily realization of the world around us. Moreover, attempting to scratch the itch and rid ourselves of its pain, may cause distress upon healthy surrounding parts of our body (psyche). Our unconscious may be warning us to stop reacting and otherwise toil at the 'effects' of a particular problem. Instead, we may need to isolate the 'source' of our psychological or emotional wound, and purge it once and for all. In other words, we need to face our difficulties and determine a course of action to deal with them as effectively as possible. The itch dream illustrates the error in accepting or ignoring our quandaries, which instead of disappearing, tend to grow bigger, and far more irritating in our waking experience.

IVORY TOWER: The symbolism of the Ivory Tower refers to an intellectual retreat which heightens our awareness and stimulates our future aspirations. In the dream sense, the image of the pure, ivory edifice is both naturalistic and noble. Its wisdom is gained through shaped and honest virtue and not shadowy, abusive deceit. Consequently, an ivory tower would teach man to love and honor the great ivory-tusked bull elephant and never destroy its numbers. In a dream landscape, the ivory tower may epitomize a moral and honorable decision which may need to be made in the near future in order to assure the physical, psychological and emotional well being of ourselves and those around us.

JACKAL: The symbolism of the Jackal pertains to petty and unscrupulous, yet crafty, behavior. As such, in our dream landscape, we may be expressing guilt over devious actions perpetrated. On the other hand, since the jackal is primarily a forager, we may be illustrating an aimless search for something useful or challenging in our life. Consequently, we may be masking anxiety over a lackluster existence without practical goals.

JACKHAMMER: In the dream sense, a Jackhammer's pounding may represent breaking through deep foundations of reality. The fact that the unconscious uses a jackhammer, may be representational of forceful influences in our life who may be involved in this process of breaking or destroying elements of our psychological infrastructure. Consequently, we need to determine who operates this jackhammer (if not ourselves), and interpret this person's control in our awareness. If the jackhammer is operated by a stranger, or runs itself, we need to examine recent upheavals in our life which may be beyond our control.

JACOB'S LADDER: In the bible, Jacob had a dream vision consisting of a staircase which led up to paradise and God, upon which, angels ascended and descended freely. In biblical times, the fully believed interpretation of this dream, was the undeniable existence of an elevated path to heaven, which was open to all righteous souls. In today's world, the dream vision of Jacob's Ladder, may imply a spiritual hope, or wish, to raise oneself up and out of the sometimes cruel and harsh misery of an earthbound reality.

JAGGED EDGE: The symbolism of a Jagged Edge refers to a painful and otherwise unclean emotional transition. In the dream sense, we may be expressing difficulty in adjusting to a new and perplexing situation. Furthermore, this new situation may be reinstating old and painful, hence jagged, memories. Our unconscious may be warning us that in order to adjust properly, we may need to sharpen our senses by executing clean breaks and unequivocal entries in the pinpoint and detailed schemes of all our forward progressions.

JAR: In the dream sense, a Jar symbolizes a transparent enclosure in which we store psychological or emotional perceptions for an elongated period of time. As such, witnessed through the glass, we remain fully aware of our emotions, yet are unable to change them. In this isolated condition we find ourselves utterly powerless to alter any of their overall effects upon us. Accordingly, we must determine whether the emotional contents of the jar should remain preserved, until the proper time of their announcement, or whether the jar should be shattered in revelation of a more complete, and perhaps well-balanced, fulfillment of self.

JAW: The image of the powerful Jaws of an animal, which desires the tearing of our flesh, involves our fears about personal destruction and more exactly, the loss of our conceptual wholeness. This intact and unbroken sense of self, may involve any of a number of perceptive realities including economic status, spiritual tranquillity, or physical health, just to name a few. The sharp teeth which deem to penetrate and tear at our well being, absorbing in the process the core of what we are, may be reflective of influential realities which we deeply fear and mistrust. We need to determine who these forces are and what real or perceived control they hold over our waking life. Ironically, if the jaws belong to a pet dog, we may be referring to a reversal of trust and loyalty, or conversely, madness or mental illness which impedes on our daily life. (*see* Bite)(*see* Teeth)(*see* Penetrate)(*see* Cut)(*see* Bleed)

JAZZ: The single and unique feature of Jazz as a musical style, involves its open range of improvisational expression. In this sense, jazz demonstrates an inordinate display of physical, spiritual and psychological dexterity and potential. Moreover, since music expresses ones passions, we find in the jazz dream a rather intense range of emotional latitude. Perhaps in this interpretive sense, we begin to see the magnitude of this musical style and its metaphoric reassurance of our own free and unique individualism.

JELLYFISH: In the dream sense, a single Jellyfish may refer to cowardice, while a school of jelly fish, may refer to barely visible, or altogether unseen danger. The connection of these two representations is not coincidental. The danger presented in social cowardice, or individuals who refuse to act, is indeed invisible. Appropriately, our unconscious may be projecting a jellyfish into our dream awareness to remind us about our own stagnant, and otherwise fearful, behavior. Furthermore, this dream symbol may be a clear indication of a personal need to assert ourselves more in the communal spectrum of our waking experience, including our home, occupational and social fields.

JESUS: The dream image of Jesus, or any deity which we fully believe in, may involve our feelings of guilt, or conversely, our feelings of spiritual joy. Naturally, this depends upon our self perception of moral ethics and moral behavior, and how they correlate to each other. Accordingly, an evil person may fear Jesus, while a pious person may cherish and adore his presence in a dream. However, the dream may reveal hidden truth, wherein, the devout person realizes hypocrisy in his deportment and is guilt-ridden under this lord figure, while the criminal person finds love, or compassion within him or herself and changes the course of their life. In any case, the dream is extremely subjective and equally effectual. (see Christ)

JOB: Our place of business, or the location where we perform our occupational duties, may be symbolic of the perception of our own self-worth and self-reliance. Accordingly, in a Job related dream, we need to interpret the circumstance involved, any and all characters present, and the physical condition of the work place itself. For example, if everything seems to be functioning normally in our occupational landscape, yet we are not present, we may be experiencing a feeling of uselessness in our own job environment. Conversely, if we find ourselves working exceptionally hard, while our coworkers sleep peacefully, our unconscious may be revealing a bad workaholic habit which may be threatening our overall well being.

JOKER: A Joker symbolizes a sly, yet powerful character. In the dream sense, the joker may refer to a sudden change of luck, either good or bad. Accordingly, we may need to interpret the moment of the joker's appearance, and what cards we held prior to this riveting entrance. Was the Joker wild?(*see* Clown)

JOSHUA TREE: The image of the Joshua Tree, with its limbs spread out in prayer, is one of complete and unshakable faith. Additionally, the plant's upright stature and green and white flowers epitomize purity and natural achievement. Plainly, in our dream vision we gaze upon spiritual life. At this point, we need to determine our relationship with the metaphysical plant in our dream landscape. Does the Joshua Tree provide us with strength and courage, or are we crooked and ashamed beneath its boughs?

JOURNAL: The act of recording the events of our life in a Journal may be representative of saving and otherwise encoding those events and incidents into our permanent memory and/or family history. As such, in a dream scenario, we may be illustrating a need or desire to engrave recent endeavors permanently into our recollection. However, our unconscious may be hinting at the possibility of rewriting history, or inventing history, to satisfy our own vanity and conceit. Accordingly, we need to interpret the clear recorded message in the journal and compare it, to the best of our memory, with the actual events experienced (if any).

JOURNEY: The mythical Journey is fully representational of a voyage into the unknown regions of an infinite human consciousness. As such, the journey through our dream landscape may be seen as a search for new and unconditionally unique experiences. At the same time, the voyage into a new world of reason is entirely reflective of an escape from another world, an old world of hardship and personal pain. Hence, we may need to determine the symbolic similarities between our waking reality and our dream expedition. If we find ourselves incessantly fleeing from familiar terrain, we may need to address our escapist behavior which offers no real solution to our waking obstacles. In an ideal sense, the journey into the unknown pertains to a collection of experiences, each new experience expanding upon our limitless reality base. As such, instead of escaping from our past, we are able to build a sturdy bridge which transgresses our past, present and future into a single moment of fully realized existence.

JUGGLER: The image of the Juggler may involve the balancing of many situations and/or social relationships in the scope of our waking life. As such, we need to observe the relative skill of the performer. If the juggler is adept at what he or she does and displays flare and passion, our unconscious may be revealing a steady and relentless balance in our life. In such a case, we need to determine to what end the juggler performs. Is the execution for oneself, or others, perhaps peers? Examining this in a real sense, is this all necessary? Only the dreamer can know the relative worth of his or her balanced load of reality. Conversely, if the juggler is failing at his or her craft and balls are flying in every chaotic direction, our dream may be assuring us that our hands are full. (*see* Acrobat)

JUNCTION: A Junction in the road may refer to choice which needs to be made in our waking life. The severity of this decision is demonstrated in the long term future derived from this particular choosing. In another interpretation, our unconscious in the junction dream, may be implying that our decisions in life may be too extreme and that in waking reality, some roads run parallel or occasionally weave in and out of each other. In either case, we need to determine the reason for our confrontation with our decision or decision making in general.

JUNG, C.G.: The Austrian, Carl G. Jung, began his career as a protégé of Sigmund Freud. Eventually however, Freud and Jung parted company with a divergence of fundamental points of view. (*see* Freud). Jung, disagreeing with Freud's theoretical approach to the human unconscious and utilizing his own studies and observations, theorized that the entire population of humanity shared a universal or collective unconscious. Furthermore, Jung believed the human unconscious contained the entire primordial memory of human existence and revealed this ancient wisdom through archetypal or universal symbols. He believed and eloquently explained in the course of his life time how these archetypes were innately understood by all men and women of every race, creed and geographical locality, and in turn taught and transcribed to their people via diverse and infinitely varied forms of expression.

JUNGLE: In the dream sense, the Jungle archetype symbolizes the wild and untamed side of our unconscious nature. In the primordial jungle, man operates exclusively via his instinctual drives and desires. Therefore, any impulse which carries us into activity without the express consultation of reason, may refer to this unrestrained component of the psyche. Accordingly, the jungle dream, may involve feelings of passionate drives which may have been repressed in our unconscious, but may finally need to emerge. Hence, it is crucial to interpret which features of the jungle landscape we are drawn toward, and which facets we fear.

KANGAROO: In the dream sense, a Kangaroo may symbolize a complex connection of maternal and paternal protection and an otherwise balanced psychological development. Since the female kangaroo carries her young in a physiological pouch, we may be expressing the mothering and decisively female aspect of our own nature. Conversely, the marsupials' reputation for fighting with fists, legs and tail, clearly represent the aggressive, masculine component of that same psyche. Taken together, the dream image of the exotic kangaroo, may refer to the creativity needed to enable naturalistic and well-balanced decision making in both ones personal and professional life.

KAYAK: In the dream sense, a Kayak may represent an isolated and individual struggle against our own emotions. Accordingly, if the Kayak spins out of control in rough breakers, we may be expressing a difficulty or confusion in handling our deeper fears and/or emotional desires. Conversely, a solitary kayak operating smoothly and efficiently on course with rapid flowing river, may illustrate the heightened experience of our singular sensation of the world within. (*see* Boat).

KEY, SKELETON: The Skeleton Key is symbolic of both potential freedom and personal accessibility to previously unreachable goals. In either case, the dream key illustrates a hopeful future and a new position to gain the benefits offered in that future. Accordingly, we need to interpret where we find the key, which specific locks can be opened and which thresholds are subsequently crossed. However, if our key fails to open any locks at all, our unconscious may be revealing false hope discovered in a transient waking situation.

KILL: The act of Killing in a dream is primarily a straight forward symbolic reference to change and drastic transition in life. Therefore, we need to understand the full metaphoric allusion involved in the context of who or what is killed. If we ourselves are killed, we need to determine who kills us and exactly how we die. This disclosure will hold clues to aspects within our-selves which may need to be concluded in order to move on in new and healthy directions. There is a common MYTH which holds that if a dreamer dreams of death, he or she will die. Naturally, the dead do not (normally) speak, and so, do not relay their dreams before dying. Moreover, millions of individuals dream of their own death each day and night and live to tell about it, time and time again. In fact, death in ones dream is quite similar to death in the Tarot deck, which is looked at as a sign of change in ones experience. In the devout or religious sense, we may think of dying as the physical transfiguration from bodily or worldly life, into the intangible life of ones holy spirit. (*see* Death)

KINDLING: The symbolism of Kindling wood involves a psycho-logical breaking down of our problems into their smallest parts. Naturally, this systematic fragmenting is done in order to ren-der the whole riddle compliant to our relative experience. Moreover, the representation of the burning wood may involve passion or an otherwise emotional undertaking, including mar-riage and the raising of family. The long, dedicated work of chopping the 'log' into its kindling may be itself symbolic of child rearing and parenthood. (*see* Ablaze)(*see* Hearth)(*see* Wood)

KING: In the dream sense, a King may be representational of abso-lute authority and the apex of social order. As opposed to tyrants or dictators, who lead their respective empires by force and the conquering passion of lust and desire, the heralded king assures tranquillity and a code of morality in the ranks of his own do-minion. Accordingly, in a dream, the image of a king may refer to taking charge of a particular situation or mediating a dispute with organizational, ethical and spiritual wisdom.

KITCHEN: In a dream, a Kitchen refers to both physiological and emotional nourishment. As such, we may be expressing con-cern for the needs of our family and/or significant others. For example, the image of a clean and well-stocked kitchen may il-lustrate personal health, or a caring, loving family. Conversely, a dirty, rancid kitchen, lacking food or drink, may clearly indi-cate a depressed and needy emotional status. In either setting, we need to analyze our acceptance, or dissatisfaction, within the dream imagery.

KNEECAP: In a dream, a kneecap may refer to ones physical pain in symbolic, hence spiritual, traveling, or similarly, the exertion involved in making psychological leaps. Moreover, the kneecap may indicate ones ability to stand up straight, once again symbolic of moral integrity and furthermore, self-confidence. In a rather complex interpretation, we may also examine the injury of water on the knee. In this dream imagery, we may witness emotional realities (water), which interfere with our own forward progress and ability to hike into higher realms of social and personal existence.

KNIFE: The symbolism of the Knife refers to psychological or emotional separation. As such, the meaning of the knife image is highly dependent upon the action and placement of the sharp instrument itself. Appropriately, a kitchen knife which slices a loaf of bread, may be representative of sharing, equality and community; while a dagger, hidden in the pocket of a stranger's jacket, may represent potential and very real danger. (see Jagged Edge).

KNIGHT: In a dream, a Knight may represent chivalry, courage and honor. In this sense, we find the embodiment of the spiritual warrior, an individual who gathers strength to battle the relentless forces of evil. Therefore, he is able to love and honor a fair maiden, but unable to perform sexual union with the poor girl, for that base carnal act would prove him hypocritical to his spiritual cause. Hence, we may be expressing moral and spiritual strength, including chastity, in our dream vision of the mythical Knight. (*see* Castle)(*see* Dragon).

KNOCK: The sound of Knocking in a dream usually refers to expectations either welcome, or conversely dreaded, with deep and perhaps even repressed, consternation. In this sense we understand the allusion of opportunity knocking on our front door, and of course on the other hand, death, who also comes knocking on our front door. We need to note the extremity of good or bad fortune which this representational outside force desires to bring into our life. However, interestingly, the house (i.e. the door), represents the psyche of self. In this, we begin to see how this knocking force must nevertheless, in spite of all its power, yield to our human will, in the form of our choice to allow or deny its entrance. In clinical studies involving the terminally ill, practitioners find, time after time, that death only comes when the patient has DECIDED to let go of life. In this sense, we witness the metaphysical testament of the human mind. There-fore, in a dream, we need to fearlessly determine the source of the knocking and once found out, choose to permit or deny its influence over our waking reality. (*see* Beat)

KNOT: In the dream sense, a Knot may be representational of an emotional or psychological entanglement. We may find our-selves unable to move or free ourselves from a predicament in our waking life. Accordingly, in our dream, we may need to in-terpret the physical location of the knot, the character who tied the knot and any attempts to loosen the knot. Plainly, the na-ture of a knot causes it to tighten as we pull and tug attempting to escape. Hence, we may need to stop and calmly reason our way out of the intricate overlapping bonds of our symbolic en-tanglement.

KNOWLEDGE: In finding a loss of Knowledge in our dream, we may fear the ability to properly express our skill and wisdom. As such, our presentation, or image, of self, may be involved in this dream interpretation. We may be nervous about an inter-view or social situation in which our relative intelligence, as perceived by another party, may effect our future. Conversely, an increased knowledge in our dream, may involve repression of ideas and opinions due to social intolerance. Therefore, women all over the world are still taught to speak with their eyes instead of their mouths. The romantic allusion to 'know-ing eyes' however, fails to cover the limitation and repression of an individualized self.

LABORER: The image of the Laborer may involve our feelings about work and alternatively, tasks which we may need to com-plete. In the sense of the creative laborer, who builds something which functions as more than the sum of its parts, our dream may be illustrating the potential of our hard earned efforts. However, if the laborer is trapped in a mindless, repetitive ac-tivity, with little chance of change or transfiguration, we may be indicating our own feelings of personal obscurity and mundane achievement in our daily existence. The essential difference may be located in the desire to work and achieve, versus, being forced to work to maintain humble survival. In a forced situation, we are rarely able to express our full potential and feel therefore, entirely stagnated by the entire enterprise. In this sense, our entire life may become a laborious effort and it may become increasingly difficult to maintain normal social and interpersonal relationships. On the other hand, when our work thrives, our sense of self thrives, and therein lies a major component of a well-balanced and self actualized individual.

LABYRINTH: The complex symbolism of the Labyrinth involves the dead ends and open passage ways towards life's goals. As such, we find ourselves driven toward an unseen purpose. The dream may be illustrating the necessary obstacles and pointless roads which we must traverse in order to find the fulfillment of our own wisdom. In the mythological sense, the labyrinth's goal is guarded by the Minotaur who represents the last bastion of our own repression. In order to overcome his base influence and aggressive behavior we must place our spiritual quest above our mortal fear. Accordingly, the labyrinth dreamscape may illustrate the complex and obstacle ridden path explored faithfully by the guiding enlightenment of our deepest emotional, psychological and spiritual conviction.

LACE: The symbolism of fine Lace is reflective of the sensual and erotic qualities of our physiological and psychological selves. The frail fabric of lace depicts an almost vulnerable surface of visible carnal desire. As such, we need to analyze who wears the lace and what promise that person beckons. Furthermore, we need to interpret the condition of the fabric itself. Is it torn, tattered or otherwise affected in some strange and atypical fashion? Moreover, If the lace is worn or displayed on some specific part of the body, that body part's symbolism, may need to be interpreted as a crucial component in the dream's entire landscape.

LADDER: A Ladder in our dream landscape, may involve climbing to new heights of reality and/or perceptions, either psychologically or emotionally. The interesting facet of this particular dream image, involves the steep vertical ascent and conversely, descent, of the ladder itself. This physical reality may imply a rapid ascent into our new perception or emotion. At the same time, there may be an equally obvious risk of falling from these same exaggerated heights. As such, we may need to consider the relative soundness of each rung and what we perceptually find at that level. In any case, the ladder may imply a social, sexual, economic, or even spiritual, rise, which needs to be scaled very slowly and with extreme caution. (*see* Jacob's Ladder)

LADYBUG: The Ladybug represents beauty, innocence and mirth. The insect's tiny non-threatening size, combined with her bright red coloring and sudden bursts of flight, seem to epitomize unexpected pleasure and joy. As such, in a dream landscape, the ladybug appearance may symbolize a sudden and optimistic realization of self. Conversely, our unconscious may be illustrating a desire for creative and fluid spontaneity. Accordingly, it may be important to note the landscape where the ladybug emerges and any character she may unexpectedly land upon.

LAGOON: The image of the Lagoon reflects a warm, personal and creatively unique emotional state of being. Hence, in a dream landscape, we may be expressing the rare quality of our deeper sensitivities, including sexual and individual tastes. Moreover, the womb-like nature of the lagoon signals a rebirth in consciousness. In this sense, we may be indicating a new incarnation for ourselves which involves a purity in awareness.

LAMB: Today, as in historic times, the Lamb symbolizes peace, innocence and social tranquillity. Moreover, because of its wool coat and easy manners, the lamb has provided man with warmth, milk and various other forms of physiological sustenance. Traveling back to biblical times, the lamb's innocence and white fleece combine to serve as the ideal sacrificial animal to a mighty and benevolent God. Following this tradition, the early Christians called Jesus the Lamb of God, who suffered the sins of the world by sacrificing his own life in exchange for granting all of righteous humanity a place in heaven. Consequently, the lamb in the dream landscape may represent a form of self-sacrifice which ultimately strengthens the living society of our peers. However, an entirely opposite interpretation may be the case. Hence, our unconscious may be warning us against running with the herd and opting instead for the complete establishment of our own unique identity. Accordingly, we may need to fully analyze any and all symbolism found in the complex and rather peculiar, lamb dreamscape.

LAME: The conceptualization of Lameness may involve insecurity about ones mobility, or a fear of standing up for what one believes in. This is primarily because the dream image of our legs, represents our ability to choose whether we will charge, flee or 'dance' around our confronted obstacles. The dream likeness of our sudden lameness, involves the limitation of our overall potential. In this sense, we become frozen in fear, akin to a deer in the headlights. Our unconscious may be revealing on outside force in our waking life which has narrowed our decision making and subsequently hampers our creative fulfillment. The dream, like a messianic figure, may be telling up to get up and walk. It may hurt a little at first, but eventually, we will have learned the sturdy balance and potent forward progress of our own abilities. (*see* Ice)

LANCE: The projected rod, or Lance, symbolizes the aim of our intentions. The exertion with which we handle the lance may represent the resolve of our position. Moral concepts involving 'an aim which is true', are deeply imbedded in this dream imagery. Moreover, the natural metaphor of sexuality transforms into a value system of social relationships, including romance, marriage and inevitably, family. Accordingly, if the lance is broken, or launched without power and determination, we find a symbolic breakdown of ones faith in a chosen commitment. In a rather complex combination of the former and latter representations, we may witness a competition for sexual and mating rites of passage. As such, in demonstrating our physical and sexual potency, we display our ability to propagate the species, which is in fact, our evolutionary aim, via our hormones and unique, individuated DNA/RNA structures. In this revelation, we hope to gain the trust of potential mates. Furthermore, in human beings, both genders participate in this ritual of sexual projection and social posturing. (*see* Arrow)

LANDSCAPE: Its extensive use in dream interpretation demonstrates the significance of what is termed, the dream Landscape. In fact, the entire dream scene itself is referred to as the landscape or dreamscape of the psyche. Our environment defines us in a way that is understood on a plethora of representational levels from our physical, material and economic status to our enigmatic and diverse psychological development. Accordingly, the world presented in our unconscious is a visible icon of symbols which defines our singular, yet complex uniqueness in the world of human experience. In other words, a dream reveals our vital comprehension of self.

LANTERN: As a path is symbolic of a course taken in order to find our truest selves, a Lantern implies the enlightenment or spiritual guidance necessary to safely and accurately traverse the passage toward the inner most self. In the mythological sense, the hermit holds high his lantern of wisdom and spiritual truth. His pondering, cryptic figure accepts the darkness of the unconscious yet places trust and spiritual faith in the embers of his burning lantern. Appropriately, in the dream sense, the lantern may symbolize a moral quandary which may need to be addressed by the light of reason. Moreover, the lanterns presence within our dream may be indicative of a new and clear direction in our waking life. Should the lantern be snuffed out, our unconscious may be illustrating a loss of honorable principles, which may be affecting our heading in life's complex labyrinth.

LATE: The concept of being on time demonstrates accuracy in planning our affairs, adeptness at projecting allotted times necessary for each undertaking and a social responsibility to join parties at coordinated meeting times. Doing so, avoids any unnecessary interference with the group or individual's own sensitive schedule. As such, being Late may involve the exact reversal of any or all, of these dedicated social components. The most prominent weakness in this sense, entails insecurity about our ability to understand, organize and perform in a social setting. Therefore, we further isolate and alienate ourselves from the group by arriving late for the communal event or experience itself. This is known in psychological terms as Reaction Formation, or the self- creation of our own deepest fears. The flip side of this tardiness details our lack of concern for the social meeting altogether. This lack of responsibility illustrates expressions of emotional stagnation and a general disruption of our natural maturation process. In the clinical sense, this may include ongoing forms of regression experienced throughout ones life. However, the goal of personal freedom may be immersed in this complex participation of social organization. In this connotation, we need to examine how late we (or other individuals) appear in the dream itself. For example, we may find ourselves 'fashionably late', which in some circles, is considered a very good (social) thing. (see Self) (see Image)

LAUGHTER: In this dream image, we find a dualistic expression of extreme elation, or dire embarrassment, dependent upon which side of the Laughter one happens to fall. As such, we need to examine the impetus for this release of psychological or emotional control. In other words, what's so funny? Furthermore, we need to determine if the humor is good natured, or mean spirited and in that capacity, is it geared at a weakness, or an absurdity?

We may need to carefully search the dream for the source of the humor. Once discovered, we may analyze the symbolic reasoning for all the amusement. For example, we may be reacting in the form of compensation, to a very serious and solemn issue. Conversely, we may have linked social and personal absurdities in life which gratify us because they undermine the supposedly 'unshakable' order of humanity, and the great society etc. In any case, we need to find the appropriate analogy for an emotional outburst in our waking experience. Accordingly, the unconscious may be asking us not to take something too seriously, or warning us about not taking certain issues seriously enough. Moreover, we may find a representational connection to madness and unhinged behavior. If this is the case, we may need to examine the full range of our dream emotions and compare their diverse catalysts. The dream may illustrate the nature of our overall and focused perception and as such, reveal a great deal about our repressed desires and outright fears. Therapy may be recommended if this dream recurs and if the behavior of Inappropriate Affect begins to appear in ones daily life. Inappropriate Affect involves abnormal emotional responses; for example, laughing at a loved ones funeral, or becoming depressed after winning the lottery.

LAVA: The hot threatening liquid that emerges from the womb of the earth and covers our symbolic landscape may illustrate a flood of sensual emotions which dictates our waking behavior. As such, we may find ourselves tortured and paralyzed by our own repressed fears. The rumbling volcano which blows out the Lava may represent our unconscious which vents our hidden drives or desires. Conversely, the lava may be symbolic of female cycles and regenerative principles. Accordingly, in the dream landscape we may need to interpret the location of the lava flow, any and all characters effected by the lava and the full destructive capabilities of the lava itself.

LEAF: In the dream sense a Leaf may be symbolic of rich, swaying and delicately animated life. Moreover, the leaf represents the fragile mortality of nature which must return to its origin or source. Consequently, the leaf illustrates the potential of cyclical and eternal rebirth. Furthermore, a leaf may symbolize skin and the utter sensation of experienced life. Taken together, the dream image of a leaf, may indicate a fragile encounter in our waking life which may have ignited a personal transfiguration in our day to day existence.

LEAK: The image of Leaking represents a fear of loss. Since water is primarily the substance which is lost, we may be referring to an emotional loss which seems irreversible and irretrievable. Naturally, we need to determine the severity of the leak and compare it to the relative force of the catastrophe. In a rather interesting judgment, the slight leak of water, which falls in drips, has become an archetype linked with madness and the slow loss of ones mind. Strangely enough, wives commit husbands to psychotherapeutic hospitals, only after they can no longer tolerate their loved ones psychosis and otherwise abnormal behavior. They are routinely asked when the extraordinary behavior began. In most cases, they cannot pinpoint an exact event. In this we witness the gradual dripping sanity as it fights the ongoing obstacles found in everyday life. (*see* Basin)

LEATHER: The image of worn Leather elicits a tough, rugged hide and an otherwise thick and impenetrable psychological skin. The visual media has enhanced this perception by portraying erotic, anti-social and entirely untamed individuals sporting leather regalia, from cowboys to young street gangs to underground sado-masochistic sexual deviants. Appropriately, the dream image of leather symbolizes a complex conceptualization of extreme physicality which may lack a bit of emotional maturity and/or responsibility.

LEMONADE STAND: The image of the Lemonade Stand may imply another time and place where trust and simplicity were commonplace in small communities nationwide. Furthermore, this image may involve our earliest concepts of value and a sense of responsibility about fairness, hard work and the sacrificing of a present moment, for a later gain. These concepts are all very much a part of adulthood and social maturation. In fact, in a fair example of absolute symbolism, we find the lemon itself considered as an adult fruit. This conceptualization can be centered around its bitter taste which satisfies a thirst longer than any of its sweet counterparts, which crave the requirement of repeated intakes of their sweet sugar base. In this, we see long term gratification, rather than immediate, or in Freud terminology, Id gratification. As such, what better soft drink for the (Superego) instructional Stand, than good old lemonade?

LETTER: In a dream, a Letter may represent communication with, or feelings about, individuals outside our immediate experience. Furthermore, the symbolism of the love letter refers to a revelation of deepest emotion transcribed in hopes of capturing a significant love interest. As such, the idea of potential may be inherent in the letter imagery. This, of course, is supported by the reality of cover letters, query letters and resumes, all created in hope of some desired future fulfillment. Accordingly, the letter in our dreamscape, may refer to an unconscious longing to bring a distant reality into true fruition. Conversely, the image of a "Dear John" letter, may represent a preparation for separation in certain aspects of a waking relationship.

LIE: In a dream, dishonest behavior enacted by honest persons known to us in waking life, may be representational of growing feelings of distrust, or an otherwise lack of faith in that individual's recent actions. On the other hand, if we find ourselves engaged in Lies in the dream landscape, our unconscious may be revealing a personal deception. In other words, we may be involved in activities which are unnatural to our basic instincts or beliefs. In order interpret this dream properly, we need to analyze the exact nature and particulars of the lie/s perpetrated, determine who is being lied to and what precisely motivates this duplicity.

LIGHT: The complex symbolism of Light, may involve an intricate combination of illumination, warmth and hope. Examining the primary source of all light, the sun, we observe the full embodiment of representational images concerning light. For example, a shimmering and warm sunrise may refer to hope promise and furthermore, a fulfillment of personal aspirations. Conversely, a hot midday sun may refer to exposure, difficult labor and a relentless psychological or emotional struggle. Lastly, the brilliant and captivating western sunset may illustrate a feeling of deep reverence, personal enlightenment and the realization of a burning persistence of faith, which remains within us, regardless of the dark unknown future which lies ahead.

LIGHTHOUSE: A Lighthouse may represent a warning of impending hazard or outright danger. Moreover, since the lighthouse is situated near the sea, our dream may be implying an emotional adversity, which can and should be avoided. Naturally, the other side of this symbolism involves real hope in the face of perilous diversity. (see Water)(see Boat)(see Light)(see Lantern)

LIGHTNING: The archetypal symbolism of Lightning refers to God-like and otherwise superhuman power, and the reality of its threat. As such, mortal human beings are reminded of their ultimate submission to God and/or nature herself. However, in the dream sense, the massive electrical potential of lightning, may be indicative of a brilliant new idea or a powerful direction found in the high frequency spark of our radical brainstorm. Accordingly, we need to examine our emotional reaction to the lightning and the physical location upon which the bolt strikes its devastating, yet illuminating blow. (*see* Electricity)

LION: The ancient symbolism of the Lion combines two separate representational facets, that of the wild and powerful beast and the converse nobility of the ruling king. As such, the complex lion archetype represents the aggression, power and ferocious behavior necessary to rule ones own emotions and overcome the obstacles found in an otherwise competitive environment. Furthermore, the lion is intimidating enough to rule its own psyche and maintain significant influence throughout its pride, or society, without the use of destructive aggression. Accordingly, our unconscious may be indicating a need for honorable leadership in our own personal or social life, without petty anger or gratuitous and entirely unnecessary violence.

LIZARD: The Lizard is a cold and poised reminder of our primal instincts and predatory beginnings. Scientists often refer to the brain stem as the reptilian brain. This is because it enacts our basic functions, without which, we would cease to be. In as much, we begin to see the correlation between our 'automatic', or innately triggered, consciousness and the further evolved, decision making, consciousness. Accordingly, we witness the unconscious expression of our basic primal drives including sexuality, hunger, pleasure in and under sunlight and of course, fear. In short, the initial use and virgin examination of all of our five senses is explored in this age-old archetype. This dream involves experience over thought, excess over slow lingering deliberation. (*see* Iguana)

LOCK: The concept of the Locked door entails closing oneself off from the world, or conversely, having the symbolic doors of life slammed shut and locked in your face. In both cases, an internal mechanism of fear is implied by the unconscious. Appropriately, we need to examine our own trepidations or conversely, the doubt and suspicion we seem to inspire and bring forth in others. In other words, why is passage refused? Questions of our worthiness may be illustrated in this dream, as well as complex associations and alienation from respective nature or civilization. In the latter example, being inside a house and behind the locked door, may imply civilization and the manifestation of the Superego self. Conversely, being outside the locked door, may reveal our natural, yet anti-social and entirely Id, self. The dreamer needs to determine which side of the door he or she may be on, and what are the intentions for crossing over. Finally, we need to determine who has locked the door, if not ourselves, which is primarily and oddly enough, the implication of the unconscious which we observe prefers doors open and free access in general, into the entirety of our being and full potential. (see Door)(see Key)

LOCUST: Since Locust invade land and crops, we may symbolize them as an interruption to the union of man and nature. Locust, like tornadoes, indicate to man that nature, like man, has a bad side and that side may strike at any time and ruin our well being. In as much, the dream may illustrate the fallacy of permanence and indestructible methods and strategies concerning life. This forced realization of human vulnerability may have the dual purpose of keeping mankind humble, as well as, pushing him to strive for a better and more respectful confederation with nature and environment. In the Biblical tradition, when God became angry at the Pharaoh, he took the form of locust, to break the back and spirit of the Egyptian people. In this, we see the archetypal connection with god and nature. In fact, even today, a government relief claim, involving locust devastation, would certainly be considered in print, a justifiable 'act of God.' (see Infestation)

LOTUS: The Eastern symbolism of the white petaled Lotus, which indigenously occurs in low lying areas, involves an intricate collaboration of tranquillity, sensuality and metaphysical transcendence. Furthermore, its connection with calm pools of water illustrate emotional maturity and a serenely feminine union with nature's enlightened blueprint. Appropriately, the appearance of the lotus in our dream landscape, may depict emotional comfort and spiritual grace in our conceptualization of a certain situation, or perhaps, our entire perception of the world around us. Conversely, if the lotus is threatened, we may be expressing anxiety over a of loss of individual faith, which conceivably may involve a sinking emotional interrelationship.

LUCID DREAMING: Lucid dreaming entails a semi-consciousness within the framework of the dream itself, which enables the dreamer to manipulate his or her surroundings by force of imaginative will. In other words, the dreamer may decide a horse in his or her dream should instead become a Ferrari, and immediately this transformation occurs. Naturally, the concern here centers around the supposed elimination of the intended dream and therefore, unconscious message, which in this example, chose to picture a horse. So we say, we need that horse and its symbolic reality, to learn something about our intrinsic selves. Well, and good. However, an alternative argument is that the unconscious is fully aware of the individual who practices lucid dreaming and may present undesirable objects to create a direct negative pathway of imagery, which the dreamer may well follow in a personalized corrective succession. In this sense, the unconscious is actually pinpointing its intentions far more accurately than in a normal dream scenario. The debate continues. In any case, for those interested in the practice of lucid dreaming, let us say that perception and meaning are intertwined. Keeping this in mind, the dreamer may initially need to view his or her waking reality as a living dream, placing meaning on objects and intensifying these meanings until they (perceptively) transcend the objects themselves in the waking world. Doing so, the objects/meanings become the true 'language' of distinct, or lucid, memory. The dreamer must then learn to recognize this unique language as it appears and is utilized by the language of the unconscious. The awareness of self, provided through recognition, allows a fundamental entry into the deep and abstract layers of the dream. At this point, the lucid dreamer travels into the dream image itself, with comprehension, and moreover, a heightened sense of curiosity about the nature of the perceptive reality of overall dream symbolism. In this faculty, the lucid dreamer may come to witness that fact and comprehension are in this world, one in the same.

LUMBER: The symbolism of Lumber may refer to the natural construction and formulation of our psychological makeup. Accordingly, we need to determine the condition of the lumber and the soundness of our architectural layout. For example, sturdy oak planks criss-crossed to form a stable rustic cabin may be symbolic of a well-balanced psyche, replete with ancient, naturalistic and modern reason oriented sensibilities. On the other hand, termite ridden lumber, may represent psychological stagnation and a break down in our perception of self, including social cohesiveness, personal worth and moral integrity.

MADONNA: The archetype of the Madonna figure involves the mesmerizing combination of maternal nurturing and divine spiritual love. The madonna icon, or vision, illuminates a bridge between earth and sky, birth and transcendence, creation and the animation of life itself. In the dream sense, the imagery of an eternal mother, may imply trust, warmth and hope in an uncertain future. She is the guidance and care of the cradle of humanity.

MAGIC: The symbolism of Magic refers to illusions, surprise and impossible feats of reality. Accordingly, in a dream sense, a magic act may represent an enactment of the seemingly impossible. In other worlds, we may be expressing extreme self confidence or conversely, a delusional sense of superreal personal ability. In either case, we may be illustrating via compensation a basic fear of failure or an insecurity about being labeled ordinary. Appropriately, we may need to analyze the nature of the magic involved and all the characters effected by that respective magic.

MAILBOX: In the dream sense, a Mailbox may represent expectation, desire and hope. Furthermore, the mailbox may be compared to a womb which accepts the combination of procreative life and delivers that life into true fruition. Each day we explore the confines of the mailbox to find news which may change our reality and hence embody our physical, emotional and/or psychological rebirth. Accordingly, we need to interpret the color, condition and naturally, contents, of the dream mailbox. (*see* Letter).

MANDALA: The archetypal image of a Mandala, replete with a square within a circle, symbolizes the infinite radiance of micro cosm to macrocosm. Used in Hindu and Buddhist traditions to represent the foundation of universality, the mandala embodies the form (*see* Circle) of its own indicative meaning. Appropriately, in the dream sense, we may be referring to the limitless potential of our own unconscious; the infinite mind, within the finite body.

MARBLE: In the dream sense, articles constructed of Marble, may symbolize fragile beauty, inspired artistry and superhuman eternal adoration. As such, we need to determine the form and/or character depicted in the contour of the marble. If the sculpture is recognized as someone we know, we may be expressing an everlasting fondness for this individual, tinged nevertheless, with a personal estrangement from that person. Perhaps the person has grown larger than life in the grandiosity of his or her own self-perception and pretentious exploits, and hence negated our admiration. Conversely, if we ourselves become marble statues in a dream landscape, our unconscious may be illustrating a well-defined mockery of our own overblown ego. We may need to eradicate the image of ourselves and replace it with the proven operation and fulfillment of our meritorious goals and aspirations.

MARCH: A March may be symbolic of a political or spiritual cause which requires the impact of social unity to display the merit of its validity to all present. Accordingly, in a dream, a march may refer to a solid position or belief which we and our social group join together in strengthening. Conversely, the march scenario may indicate an insecurity regarding our own opinions, which may require organizational support in order to remain valid in our individual consciousness and belief system.

MARIJUANA: The conceptualization of drugs in general, may involve various forms of escapism. The longing to enter into the potential freedom of ones mind and its active imagination, has long characterized human kind. However, the social reality of Marijuana has created diverse limitations which are in direct contrast to personal freedom. Moreover, the use of hallucinogens by archaic cultures operated as forms of social ritual meant to bring together tribes in peaceful union. In today's world, the isolated use and underground culture of pot may separate individuals from family and other instrumental social organizations. As such, it operates as a rationalization for serious forms of alienation, which could in fact, effect personal development. In this, it loses its true archaic value of communal transcendence and symbolizes instead, a personal difficulty which has forged a path into a rather elaborate, yet nevertheless repressive, fantasy. (*see* Hemp)

MARIONETTE: The Marionette may refer to a loss of control in ones life. As such, we may feel like a puppet manipulated by the strings, or attachments, of the people around us. Accordingly, we need to analyze the suggestive movements and the style and color of the clothing worn by the marionette itself. This inter- pretation may reveal the reason for our suppression and subju- gation by certain individual/s in our life. However, if we ourselves are NOT depicted as the marionette/s, but rather sub- ordinates in our waking life, including spouses and children, our unconscious may be signaling our completely unnatural rule over these persons. (*see* Puppet)

MASK: The ancient symbolism of the mask used in divine rituals from the preparation of tribal warfare to the unification of mar- riage vows, refers to the spirit we present in the face of super- real events. Moreover, a majority of archaic civilizations, in- cluding Judaism, believed that supernatural forces entered into, and resided inside, the head and face of human beings. Conse- quently, a Mask worn over a face served as either a greeting to, or barrier against, spirit messengers. In the dream sense, the mask may represent the personal spirit and animated face we present in certain situations in our life. For example, a big, burly man, may become docile and remarkably tender in order to win the affections of a very feminine, young woman. As such, he may dream himself wearing the mask of a fragile and delicate child.

MASON: In a dream, a Mason may refer to the building of ones own psychological and social development. As such, the rela- tive skill and adeptness of the mason needs to be determined in the dream landscape. For example, a foolish and inept mason who builds a shabby log cabin on top of a lake, drastically depicts a psyche unable to handle, or otherwise deal with, ever-present emotional realities. Conversely, a master builder who crafts a sturdy chapel on top of an exalted elevation, may be indicative of growing spiritual, emotional and psychological strength and forbearance, which illuminates the entirety of self.

MAZE: The age-old symbolism of the Maze involves the closed pathways and open roads we traverse in order to find our deep- est desired goals. As such, we witness the trip through the Maze as the journey into self understanding. The overall con- ceptualization of the maze illustrates a layout which is prede- termined by some greater force who in turn, observes the choices made by the traveler within the elaborate puzzle. We may view the 'greater force' as God, but the symbolic reality may instead point to the lone traveler within the labyrinth, who begins dimly aware, but over time, through negative and positive (associations), begins to understand the distinct sequential paths necessary to arrive at desired goals. Accordingly, we need to ascertain our own forward progress (or lack of it) in the dream, determining precisely, what pushes us, or conversely, hold us back, in the day to day experience of our waking life. (see Labyrinth)(see Path)

MEAT: In the dream sense, the symbolism of Meat may refer to physical desires and/or cravings. Conversely, if the dreamer happens to be a vegetarian, the image of meat may refer to aggression, suffering and/or immoral behavior. In either case, if the meat appears rotten, our unconscious may be illustrating a degradation in our physical health or psychological drive.

MELODY: When a melody is repeated in a dream it may be symbolic of a particular feeling or time which is etched in our memory. The precise physical and mathematical beauty of a musical motif, may embody an otherwise fragmented, recollection of a significant event in our childhood. As such, in the dream sense, a melody may refer to a regressive state of mind, or an elaborate fear of a future, bearing momentous changes in our life. In the psychological sense, it is easier to remain in familiar territory, than venture into an alien unknown. A melody is symbolic of the accepted and intimate world of our past. (see Memory)

MEMORY: The conceptualization of Memory is crucial in the dream sense as it involves the infinite pool of the unconscious. Hence, the recollection of repressed memories, returned to waking consciousness, may reflect a growth in our human awareness. In theory, we instinctively and innately understand the universal balance of our own psyche. Accordingly, remembered dreams guide us in our ongoing experience of life. Moreover, dreams which leave a strong impression on us and are remembered in detail, are decisively more significant than forgotten dreams, whose recollections may not be important to our intimate sense of self.

MERMAID/MERMAN: In the dream sense, a Mermaid/Merman may be representational of ideal beauty, fluid emotions and unexpected wish-fulfillment. As such, we need to determine the symbolism of the location where the mermaid/merman is discovered, his or her intentions and motivations and our own behavior toward the zoomorphic dream figure. However, if a known person becomes a mermaid or merman in our dream, we may be illustrating an almost abnormal desire for the affections of that person. This sort of singular drive, based primarily on the physicality of an individual, may indicate a lack of personal self-esteem and an immature outlook on the affinity of 'real' persons involved in a loving relationship.

MERRY GO ROUND: Primarily, the Merry-Go-Round represents hypnotic, childish glee, and perhaps, the beginning stages of romantic love. However, the symbolism of the merry-go-round, may also involve a complex connection of regression, psychological stagnation and the fear of realizing an entirely unique path toward adulthood. Accordingly, we need to determine our personal feelings as we turn atop the carnival apparatus. Moreover, we need to analyze the look and pose of the imitation horses upon which we ride on the merry-go-round itself. If we feel alienated by the endlessly rotating ride, replete with toiling horses and infantile music, yet find ourselves too afraid to jump off, we may be expressing anxiety concerning the harsh transition from youth to adulthood. This dream may occur if we are nervous about forthcoming nuptials, or any other adjustment into adulthood and responsible behavior.

METAL: The archetypal symbol of Metal involves a hardness or coldness of emotion. In the dream sense, we may be depicting a shield or barrier against personal and entirely human pain. Moreover, in the image of cold metal, we observe the force and accuracy of man's mind and logic. However, if our dream reveals metal which is rusted, cracked or frayed, our unconscious may be illustrating a weakness in our personal meddle and intellectual refinement. On the other hand, any combination of metals and organic materials, may represent a healthy balance of intellect, emotion and spirituality. For example, the dreamscape of a glass and metal greenhouse thriving with life, may epitomize an articulate understanding of nature and all her fervent creation.

METAMORPHOSIS: In a dream, any and all acts of Metamorphosis, may be decisive in symbolic undertones. Conclusively, our unconscious illustrates transitions from one state of being, into other and nearly opposite, states of being. If the change is fluid and natural, we may be expressing a necessary modification in our formal awareness which may enhance our individual or social self. On the other hand, a complicated transformation into an unpleasant or unkind entity, may signal erroneous conduct in our life which may serve to harm ourselves and/or others. As such, we need to determine the nature of the change and any and all effects it causes in our overall dream landscape. (*see* Zoomorphism)

MILK: The symbolism of Milk refers to nurturing, maternal purity and emotional sustenance. As such, the image of milk in our dreamscape, may refer to an endearment and compassion for new acquaintances in our life. Moreover, the serving of milk may imply an aspiration to strengthen our relationship with these respective individuals. However, the vision of spilled milk may negate all these representations and symbolize instead a loss of faith, opportunity and trust. Nevertheless, if this same milk is spilled, and an unrecognized animal comes along and laps it up anyway, we may be epitomizing the loyalty of a friend, who unbeknownst to us, returns our love and care in a humble, yet naturalistic, fashion.

MIRROR: The Mirror pertains to the image of oneself and how that image may compare to the inner perception of oneself. Taken another step and in the social sense, our actions demonstrate our merit. Conversely, our image, by and large, always remains the same. Therefore, when we commit atrocities, or, if our life for whatever reason, begins spiraling into a veritable nightmare, we may find ourselves searching in the mirror for the familiarity of who we are, who we might have been and more importantly, being that person, how could this have happened to us in the first place? We seem to ask, is this face guilty, or innocent? The image in the glass offers a silent answer which is gravely understood. In a variation of this mirror reality, we examine the tenets of beauty. Can inner beauty be witnessed in the external reflection of the glass? In other words, can we reveal our psychological make-up in the symmetrical expressions of our face and soulful gaze. The answer, as any psychotherapist concerned with the psychology of Self knows, is absolutely, positively, yes. Therefore, beauty (as well as bitter ugliness) is anything but skin deep. (*see* Double)(*see* Self)(*see* Beauty)

MISSILE: In the dream sense, a Missile may represent the immanent and inevitable destruction caused by prejudice and directed aggression. When we practice a fixed and entirely intolerant ideology concerning others in a social group, it becomes predetermined that we will cross paths and lock symbolic horns. The image of the missile reflects this anger and/or vengeance we feel toward another individual. In another sense, a missile may represent the symbolic outburst inherent in new romantic encounters or loving relationships. As such, our feelings drop a 'bomb' on the world we once knew.

MIST: The notion of Mist revolves around mystery, enigma and the exotic lure of the unknown. Naturally, many dream landscapes seem to find themselves shrouded in these B-Movie clouds. In any case, the reality of mist is rising moisture, and as such, both representations of water and floating are rather dramatically presented. Accordingly, we need to examine the more comforting, yet fragile emotions, emotions which may lead us into danger. The big screen werewolf seemed to be plagued by mist because we needed to feel his eternal anguish and pain. Here was an individual who loved and who loved life, yet due to his misfortune, was now forced by the full moon (lust, madness etc.) and the bite (primal awareness) of a wolf (the loner), to devour and kill the very life he cherished. In this sense, large night clubs spray clouds of mist into large crowds to disguise the complex emotions of their exotic, 'wild' and largely hypnotized, behavior. (see Fog) (see Water) (see Float) (see Wolf) (see Bite) (see Hybrid)

MOAT: The Moat is symbolic of emotional barriers placed around oneself. In other words, we may display our harsher emotions such as anger and apprehension, to approaching strangers, who we fear may otherwise invade the inner sanctum of our fragile being. Accordingly, we need to determine on which side of the moat we appear in our dream, and furthermore, analyze the creatures which live in that moat and appropriately find the symbolism of these menacing emotional passions. If we find ourselves outside, trying to enter a precious castle, but are halted by a perilous moat, our unconscious may be warning us to honorably wait for the proper invitation of a drawbridge, before forcing ourselves upon the sanctity of others. (see Castle)

MONEY: The image of Money, as it appears in dreams, may refer to concepts of social status. However, the acquisition and our personal handling, of money, play a big part in the perception of our not so material, worth. Did we earn, steal or borrow our money? Are we used to handling (or seeing) this amount of money? Conversely, why do we have no money at all? Did we give our money away to the poor? Did we steal it from the poor and invest it in corporate share holding? Naturally, we begin to see how our behavior patterns and our complex self development prominently figure into our overall economic reality. (*see* Accountant)

MONGREL: The image of a Mongrel may concern inner feelings of social alienation, combined with low self-esteem. However, the unconscious may simultaneously be revealing the stealth, cunning and longevity of the mongrel, who survives against all odds with the commendable resolution of his place in the cosmos. As such, we need to interpret the mannerisms and direction of the wayward animal. (*see* Dog)

MONKEY: In the Chinese zodiac, a Monkey personality refers to practical and clever genius which generates popularity and in some cases, even fame. In the western sense, the natural coordination, intelligence and kindness of the monkey in general, is almost certainly symbolized in its deliberate dream imagery. Moreover, the wild nature of a primate is offset by its nearly human aptitude, including and especially, its communication skills. Therefore, we find in the monkey conception, a deep language of union entailing the attachment of our intellect and emotions. Thus, we find the genius of understanding what we feel. However, knowing our emotions, does not mean controlling them, or their effect. Knowing what we feel, merely transcends the meaning of who we are, and furthermore, illustrates how our unique personal life reflects and therefore, may co-exist, with universal being. (*see* Ape)

MOON: The symbolism of the moon pertains to romance and wild behavior. Moreover, the moon may be indicative of madness. These intense emotional patterns may occur because of the moon's effect upon oceanic tides. In the dream sense, we may need to determine the phase of the moon in order to ascertain its relative impact upon our psychological and emotional demeanor. As such, a new moon may represent young and virginal love, or a delicate transition into womanhood. Conversely, a half moon, waning or waxing, may be symbolic of psychological and emotional balance, a sort of physiological Yin/Yang. In concluding, the imagery of the full moon represents our extreme passion, the high tide of our entire psyche. Appropriately, In this last example, we need to interpret our personal motivation for howling at the big, bright moon with open heart and flaring teeth. (*see* Tarot Major Arcana: The Moon (19))

MOUNTAIN: In the dream sense, the mountain landscape symbolizes highest reason and spiritual truth. The seemingly infinite
vision found atop a mountain may be reflective of our dynamic
human potential and never ending quest for knowledge. However, if the oxygen is lacking in the dream altitude of our mountain, we may be indicating a delusion of grandeur which may
need to be confronted by a humble and low-lying reality base.

MUMMY: A Mummy may be symbolic of our unconscious and its
ancient unknown world of exotic and timeless beauty. Consequently, if the mummy chases us in a dream, we may fear the
archaic wisdom of our own consciousness. Conversely, the
mummy imagery may indicate a need to preserve and otherwise save, some rare aspect of ourselves. Furthermore, the quest
for eternal life which has daunted man from the beginning of
time, may be alluded to in this antediluvian Egyptian answer to
the riddle of life, death and immortality. As such, we may be expressing a concern about our own mortality and the lack of a
permanent and personal legacy left behind for our future descendants. However, in a general sense, we may simply seek to
safeguard a personal item or belief which is outwardly threatened by time, custom or novel fashion. (*see* Heaven)

NAIL: In the dream sense, a Nail may refer to an intimate bond or
connection of diverse symbols. In the portrayal of Jesus nailed to
the cross, we find a masterful nexus of flesh and wood, epitomizing an ephemeral and ethereal fusion, which satisfied mo-
nastic, as well as paganistic, sensibilities. Conversely, the nails
which seal a coffin, provide permanence to our coupling with
earth, maintaining the stillness and peace desired in dissolution. As such, in the dream, the driven nail may symbolize
a healthy, stable and permanent union of opposites and moreover, a forced alliance whose confederation, may illicit the fusion
of otherwise entirely conflicting principles. (*see* Wood) (*see*
Flesh) (*see* Skin) (*see* Impale) (*see* Bleeding)

NAKED: The symbolism of Nakedness in the dream sense, may
refer to a feeling of being exposed and consequently, vulnerable.

The protection offered by clothes in most cultural traditions, includes sexual concealment, economic assurance and social inclusion. As such, the absence of these clothes may represent a stripping of civilization's attire and the promise of safety which comes along with it, in the form of law. Accordingly, we need to interpret our own feelings concerning which aspects of ourselves have been exposed and/or lost in the moment of our nakedness. Conversely, the wild and primitive freedom offered by a baring of self, may be desired in our waking life and in turn, fully illustrated in our own unconscious. In this event, our nakedness may seem normal and healthy in our own perspective, while other characters in the dream, may express confusion and moral quandary.

NATURE: The conceptualization of Nature involves everything which is untouched by man and in this logic, virginal. Moreover, the wilderness which underscores our primal beginnings, illustrates the harshest truths of reality including survival of the fittest. Taken together, we find a representation of resilient integrity which fights and otherwise wards off, all forms of contamination. The question we ask ourselves is a simple one. Is our knowledge of self strong enough and dedicated enough to fend off civilization's contamination of this natural environment and consequently, our natural self, or are we part of the problem? Accordingly, we need to analyze our interaction and appreciation of the natural environment revealed in the dream landscape. Do we fear its unknown potential for danger, or do we welcome its delicate fruits and unspeakable miracles? (see Aboriginal) (see Elements) (see Seasons) (see Virgin) (see Kill)

NAZI: A Nazi soldier may represent the potential for our anger and aggression. Moreover, the blind passion of prejudice plays a major part of our overall dream symbolism. The third Reich itself was quite aware of the influence of symbols upon the human psyche. The movement utilized internal archetypes in well-programmed methods of propaganda which have been repeatedly used in political power plays throughout the world. In this sense, our dream may be warning us against being blinded by symbols which only represent singular distinctions about our waking reality. (see Demagogue)

NEEDLE: The concept of pinpoint accuracy symbolizes the Needle. Moreover, the tiny manifestation of the needle may be indicative of a minuscule difficulty, including a complicated solution, which cannot be discovered without exhaustive and nearly impossible exertion. Furthermore, the image of a needle and thread, may illustrate a deliberate weaving, or restoration, of torn emotional, or psychological, skin. Consequently, in the dream sense, we need to analyze the position and operation of the needle in order to determine its conceivably significant message.

NEST: In a dream, a Nest may refer to ones home and family. Consequently, we may need to determine the condition of the nest and the hatchlings inside its confines. For example, if we observe a little, red bird attempting to build a nest in a heavy rainstorm, we may be illustrating frustration concerning the emotional, psychological and economic difficulties involved in starting, or simply supporting, a family in today's world. (see Matriarch) (see House) (see Child) (see Falling)

NIGHT: The complex symbolism of Night involves mystery, danger and erotic seduction. Accordingly, when our dream landscape takes on a nighttime flavor, we may be alluding to darker and decisively concealed aspects of own nature. Hence, the image of night may allow for a smooth reappearance of repressed desires and impulses. Furthermore, this escape from the scrutiny and exposure of light, may reveal a creative faculty which has been ignored, or otherwise pushed aside, by the pressures of our day to day reality. Hence, in our dream, the star-filled skies of night, may provide a safe haven for our ancient and articulate passions, alive and well in the pool of our unconscious memory.

NINE: The archetypal symbolism of the number Nine, pertains to individual horizons, their subsequent finality and a preparation for rebirth. Furthermore, the end of numbers signifies the apex of understanding. Consequently, to move further, would entail a new beginning in another plain, or novel field, of cognizance. The cycles of life and learning, must possess points of entry and departure, the numbers 0 and 9 respectively, suggest these finite positions. Accordingly, the appearance of nine objects, or the numeral nine, may refer to a culmination or completion of plans, which allows for a fresh beginning in ones perceptual awareness. (see Tarot Major Arcana: The Hermit (9) arcana)

NOCTURNAL ANIMALS: The symbolism of Nocturnal Animals found in the dream landscape, may involve a restless and relentless psyche which searches for fulfillment in the darker hollows of the unconscious. Moreover, the tiny, camouflaged night creatures, may be indicative of the dreamer's apprehension about social discovery and subsequent admonishment. As such, in their subterfuge, these animals serve to elucidate the dreamer's preference to appear normal and otherwise complacent, in other words to become obscure, in the fully exposed landscape of waking reality.

NOISE: In the dream sense, Noise refers to the unexpected and the unknown. Consequently, we may be expressing fear and confusion concerning up-to-date developments in our waking life. For example, if we hear a series of loud crashes within a house, yet cannot find who or what causes that sound, we may be depicting anxiety about the underpinning of our psychological or spiritual beliefs. Our unconscious may be informing us that our convictions may be radically and disturbingly changing as we become older and gain more experience. Conversely, noise may represent a breakthrough in our personal struggles. Perhaps we have burst through a barrier of resistance which has held us back for a prolonged time. In this sense, noise may represent freedom and vindication. Accordingly, we need to analyze the exact sound and determine its effect upon our symbolic dream landscape representative of our entire psyche.

NOMAD: The complex symbolism of the Nomad involves incessant travel and transient goals. As such, nomadic peoples may be representative of a creative spirit which forever searches new and fertile ground. Moreover, a band of travelers may be identified with a spiritual journey. Consequently, the dream image of a nomadic tribe, may imply a quest for truth and higher meaning in our lives. On the other hand, archaic nomads practiced a slash and burn method of agriculture where grounds were cultivated until they were exhausted and entirely useless. In this sense, our unconscious may refer to our waking opportunistic behavior, which seizes everything nature and society has to offer, without offering anything in reciprocation. (see Journey) (see Vulture)

NUMB: The symbolism of the Numb body, may refer to our own indecision and/or incapacity to function in certain situations. Moreover, in the dream sense, this feeling of helplessness may be complicated by the immobile reality of our concurrent sleeping status. Consequently, our stagnation in waking life, compounded by our motionless state of sleeping, may combine to portray a dream image of paralysis. Hence, it should be understood that this paralysis is not physical, but entirely emotional. In truth, we may become numb simply because we can no longer endure the pain of a complicated reality. (*see* Antarctica)

NUMBER: Numbers are alphabetically listed in the analytical course of this text, as such, please see One through Nine. Moreover, study the Tarot Major Arcana for ancient wisdom upon numerology and its startling effect upon mankind's spiritual journey.

NUN: The image of a Nun is rather complex, involving as it does, the ritualistic denial of sex and motherhood, in favor of a spiritual union with God (a patriarchal figure). In this, we find either a miraculous affiliation of natural femininity and spiritual masculinity which ordains a saintly earthly presence, or, a person who has negated their natural maternal drive with a paternal control of instincts. Naturally, these are two vastly opposing representations of the same figure. Once again, we must ask our dream itself. Is the unconscious illustration of our nun, selfless and holy, caring for children and the family of God, or, is she an angry and misunderstood soul, who takes out her emotional frustrations on young girls and boys under her strict and quite corporal supervision. Which image reveals something about ourselves, or persons known to us in waking life? (*see* Abbess)

NURSE: The image of the nurse embodies motherly caring and a sensual form of bedside comfort. The impression given by a normal, healthy young man or woman administering to our ailing needs, is one of promise and wish-fulfillment. Accordingly, a nurse dream, may refer to hope in the face of desperation. On the other hand, our unconscious may be illustrating personal regression involving the dream nurse as mother figure.

OAK In ancient Nordic tribal tradition, the mighty Oak tree was seen as the center, or power point, of divine transfiguration. Accordingly, tribal elders performed religious ceremonies, including ritualistic sacrifice, in the husk of the tree itself. Moreover, since the old trees seemed ageless, their spirit familiars offered a promise of eternal life to mortal worshippers. Appropriately, in the dream sense, an oak tree may refer to stability, permanence and rich spirituality. Hence, we need to determine our feelings in conjunction and close proximity with the tree in the dream landscape in order to ascertain its symbolism concerning our own peculiar psyche.

OASIS: In the dream sense, an Oasis may imply a renewal of hope. Moreover, since the gift of the oasis is primarily fresh water, we may need to analyze the aspects of a revitalized emotional involvement in the context of the dreamer's life. Accordingly, we need to consider if the water is cool and refreshing, therefore welcome, or bitter and murky, representing a form of false hope. (*see* Heaven) (*see* Water) (*see* Barren) (*see* Desert)

OBELISK: The tall tower which tapers into a pyramid at its very apex, in other words, the Obelisk, symbolizes divine strength, moral direction and infinite potential. As such, its appearance in the dream landscape may imply the spiritual strength of a certain direction in life which may now stand before us, for example, the birth of a child. Conversely, the imposing tower may represent a monolithic presence which surveys and judges our wayward behavior. Along these lines, if the obelisk is destroyed in our dream landscape, our unconscious may be revealing a complete loss of personal development and the spiritual guidance which may be necessary to continue in the sound path of that maturation. (*see* Ivory Tower) (*see* Tarot Major Arcana: Lightning Struck Tower (16) arcana)

OCTOPUS: The multifarious symbolism of the Octopus involves the use of its eight legs and their objective. When all eight legs are used together we may revert to the symbolism of the numeral 8, which represents completion and organizational strength. As such, the octopus which captures and encompasses its prey, may represent the forbearance of our emotional or psychological convictions. Moreover, this particular cephalopod is known for its ink-cloud defense mechanism and solitary existence. Taken together, the octopus in our dreamscape may imply an individualistic tenet which empowers our vital experience. On the other hand, if the octopus uses its arms to perform a variety of disconnected tasks, we may be illustrating the anxiety of spreading ourselves out too thin in the daily undertaking of our numerous endeavors.

ODOR: Our olfactory senses originate in the brainstem or 'reptilian brain.' In other words, our ancient sense of smell is an integral part of our most primitive and archetypal remembrances. As such, in a dream, Odor may elicit a powerful memory. Therefore, the presence of a peculiar odor in our dream landscape may refer to the time and original event of its experience. For example, if the smell of cotton candy recalls a painful childhood memory of sickness, its appearance in a dream may imply feelings of uneasiness and disorder involving the visual symbolism underlying its presence in the dream landscape. (*see* Memory)

OGRE: In myth, an Ogre is a huge, brutish creature who happens to eat human beings. Nevertheless, the ogre is not literally evil, but simple-minded and animal-like. Consequently, he eats human beings because they are significantly smaller than himself, and thus, easy prey. As such, in the dream sense, the image of an ogre may represent our own unintentional, yet nonetheless, cruel behavior. For example, an elementary school teacher who harshly admonishes a tiny child for disobedient behavior, may dream herself as an ogress terrorizing a wayward human being who foolishly crosses her path.

ONION: The Onion represents the harsh reality of purity, which must in its faculty, eliminate persistent contaminants. As opposed to an apple, or a loaf of bread, an onion will not spoil for an unusually long period of time. Hence, we see how the onion is far stronger than most forms of bacteria. Moreover, we witness in the course of this book, how impurities have become archetypes of evil and more accurately, immoral behavior. As such, the onion is pure, healthy and virginal (untouched). It is the embodiment of dedicated virtue and rectitude. It is not fun, but darn decent, nevertheless. The onion reminds us about the difficulty required to stay the moral path. In fact, one may make the biblical analogy, that once Adam and Eve ate the apple, mankind has been forced to eat onions ever since! (*see* Garlic) (*see* Unclean) (*see* Vampire) (*see* Apple)

ORACLE: The symbolism of the oracle involves the decision-making faculty of the mind itself. As such, the oracle is shrouded in the mystery of infinite possibilities. However, some potentialities may prove to be harmful to our well-being. Hence, we find the brutality of the mythical sphinx who guards the oracle and administers its punishment. The sphinx possessing the body of a lion and the head of human being, accurately symbolizes the destructive strength of our own bad decisions. Taken together, we may need to pay serious attention to the oracle vision in our dreamscape, primarily because its riddle, or forthcoming choice, may prove to have significant ramifications in our waking life. (*see* Tarot Major Arcana: The Wheel of Fortune (10) and Judgment (20) arcanas)

ORCHID: The Orchid is a plant which grows wild and brazen in a harsh landscape. Accordingly, the orchid may be symbolic of a resolution for freedom, choice and autonomy. The color of the orchid and direction of its growth, may represent certain facets of our desire for liberation and self-sufficiency in waking life.

OUIJA BOARD: In the dream sense, a Ouija Board may represent the language of our repressed feelings which return to us by way of an apparition, otherwise known as our unconscious. Accordingly, we need to fully interpret any messages revealed on the Ouija board itself. Moreover, since the board is primarily used for divination, we may be yearning for the insight of a loved one who has passed on. Hence, the message the unconscious provides on the board, may be indicative of wisdom once gained from this highly regarded individual. (*see* Clairvoyance) (*see* Telepathy)

OUTLAW: In the archetypal sense, the Outlaw represents the potential of our immoral or anti-social behavior. Moreover, the criminal figure may represent the embodiment of all the functions which have been prohibited in our moral education and/or learning experience. As such, in the dream sense, an Outlaw may illustrate our personal frustration regarding everyday society and our normal and possibly tiresome, lifestyle. Our dream may be expressing our wish-fulfillment to seize all the goods which life has to offer.

OVERFLOW: The image of an Overflowing tub may entail an excess of emotion (water), which has a powerful effect upon our psychological outlook (house), and therefore, floods our floors, representational of our normally quiescent state of mind. In other words, our feelings in their complexity, may be interfering with our normally 'reasonable' methods of judgment. Similarly, the view of a flooding river, may allegorically demonstrate our wilder passions which can no longer be restrained in our waking experience. In a still larger symbolic sense, nature herself, accepts this overflowing river's pulsing waves as they irrigate the once arid land and bring fruitful life to the seeds of her creation. Moreover, the overflowing cup of cheer, profoundly illustrates the celebration, joy and thankfulness for the a bountiful existence fraught with miraculous wonders. (*see* Basin) (*see* Water) (*see* House)

OVERSEAS: The image of strange and far away lands, may reflect a deep longing for exotic and sensational experiences, not found in our ordinary life. In this, we witness an apparent limitation in the fulfillment of our mental capacity and overall potential. As such, our unconscious portrays the richer colors, deeper sensations and incredible variations of the collective human experience. Doing so, we may begin to see the uniqueness of our own mind and its fascinating individuality. In this sense, we understand the universality of Da Vinci's Mona Lisa, Michelangelo's David, The Taj Mahal and the Great Pyramid of Giza. Universally, They each unveil the limitless potential of mankind. Thus, the unconscious fully illustrates, that the world of experience out there, regardless of how far Overseas, remains the same world of experience found right here at home, in the soul of each and every human being, who dreams the infinite potential of self. (*see* Abroad) (*see* Path)

OWL: The archetypal symbolism of the Owl involves the keen insight of true wisdom. Furthermore, the owl flying and hunting at night, may suggest its knowledge is amassed from the dark recesses of an enigmatic unconscious. Fittingly, this sapient dream figure may represent a reflection of our own insight. In other words, the dream owl is reminding us that we instinctively possess all the necessary solutions to our own questions and personal quandaries. Accordingly, we may need to analyze the color of the owl and symbolic meaning of all characters and backgrounds which exist in conjunction with it, to fathom the presence of our obscured waking wisdom within the boundaries of the dream landscape itself.

OX: In the Chinese zodiac, the Ox personality is considered to be alert, intelligent and easy going. However, their is a tendency for quick temper tantrums and otherwise, angry mood changes. The western symbolism of the ox is quite similar. The image of a hard working animal who asks for little and returns much, is firmly rooted in the physical nature of the domestic ox. However, if the beast is mistreated or becomes agitated due to complex external situations, it may become indeed become angry and quite dangerous. Moreover, we may find an allusion to awkwardness and a general lack of the mental or physical tact involved in movement through delicate and fragile situations. Accordingly, we need to determine the temperament and behavior of the ox in the dream landscape and interpret whom the animal symbolizes in our waking experience. Furthermore, our unconscious may be revealing our own stubbornness and inability to find comprehensible compromises. (*see* Bull)

OYSTER: In the complex imagery of the Oyster, we find a plain and ordinary shelled creature, which may or may not be hiding a rare and beautiful pearl. In the symbolic sense, this mystery of the tightly shut shell may refer to an immense hidden potential. Moreover, the oyster's opening and closing shell, revealing a delicate and soft internal body, may be indicative of sexual copulation and an otherwise erotic intimacy. Taken together, the oyster dream may represent the potential of gaining love if not rare passion in ones waking life.

PAPER: In the dream sense, Paper symbolizes the physical communication of our modern world. Consequently, huge piles of paper may represent our anxiety about the 'red tape' of everyday life. The complexity of maintaining records for a huge society requires mountains of documents, which is why the 'computer' age is accompanied by the 'printer' age. Our dream therefore, may be expressing a return to a smaller, simpler and more naturalistic way of life. On the other hand, if we lack paper in a dream, we may be illustrating an insufficient vehicle, or social blessing, to fully express our creative potential.

PALM: As opposed to the hand, the Palm is primarily linked with aspects of our future potential. This kind of palm reading is associated with the concept of predetermination, which views life as a destiny preordained in the higher order of reality. Hence the term, 'things happen for a reason' or 'it was their time to go' etc. The palm lines, represent the fundamental concerns experienced in the course of a life, those being love, family, health, creativity, productivity and finally, longevity. (*see* Hand) (*see* Fingers) (*see* Tarot Major Arcana: The Wheel of Fortune (10) figure)

PARADE: A Parade may be symbolic of a communal commemoration of personal or moral convictions which are allowed to exist in a free society. Consequently, we may be expressing neighborly support for a unique system of belief. (compare March)

PARALYSIS: The symbolism of Paralysis involves an inability to function in certain situations found in our waking experience. This tendency to freeze up may involve repressed fears, firmly rooted in developmental incidents of our past. Moreover, we immediately grasp how the decision not to 'act', essentially frees us from incorrect (and therefore socially alienating) behavior. This dramatically illustrates the major social component found in the overall dream analysis. Exploring this further, we find the concept of our 'act', or performance, carries with it the very real perception of acceptance and popularity, or conversely, disapproval and rejection. As such, we appraise the social reality and decide the stakes are just too darn high and so, we symbolically stop and hope to become unnoticed in the whole reality of the situation. However, the unconscious refuses to waste its wisdom on statues and thus, illustrates the pain and vulnerability of utter stagnation and dire paralysis. As such, the dreamer is compelled to rise and move forward, slowly at first, then gradually with increased momentum and self-confident determination, into the full 'act' of a life lived, for better or worse. In short, the paralysis dream whispers faith in the effort and movement of self. (see Numb) (see Ice) (see Antarctica)

PARASITE: The rather undesirable image of a Parasitic creature may reveal the rather undesirable reality of a parasitic nature. As adult human beings, we pride our individuality above all else, because it demonstrates better than anything else, our utter uniqueness. Moreover, this distinction of our peculiar self is created and thrives in the arena of the specific choices we make throughout life. These decisions naturally, propel the free movement of our destiny. In other words, we understand how our ability to choose and make decisions, gives us independence in our living experience. When we lack this confidence in our own decision making, we may look to another person (or being) for guidance. This may in fact be normal, and expresses the full value and basic need for society and its elaborate rituals. However, when this (social) dependence erases ALL motivation to decide ones own faith, we may be witnessing a deep regression into infantile dependency, or even deeper into prehistoric lower life forms fully dependent upon outside hosts. Furthermore, when this parasitic form of blind dependency, or idolatry, sways an entire group, community or nation, the results can be devastatingly savage and entirely inhuman. Accordingly, we may need to examine and temper all parasitic behavior as it appears in our waking life. We need to realistically determine why this behavior persists and develop objectives which lead us, or others, into the gradual confidence of self. Professional counseling may be recommendable for extreme cases of dependency. (*see* Infestation) (*see* Ego)

PARK: The complex symbolism of the Park primarily involves a temporary escape from reality. The escapist trappings of the park include a tiny version of the natural environment, the make-believe world of child's play and an overall carnivalesque, essentially unreal, microcosm. Accordingly, in the dream sense, we may need to determine the intentions and motivation of all characters and situations which occur in the park landscape. For example, if we find ourselves lost in a park and nobody seems to know the way out of the park, we may be illustrating a temporary straying from society and the evident struggle in returning to that society and our old way of life. This dream may occur after a sobering transition in our life, for example, the end of a passionate affair, or readjustment after a serious addiction.

PARROT: The image of a Parrot may involve repetition, emulation, or conversely, mockery. The colorful plume of the bird combined with its permanent smile, seem to indicate jovial characteristics in all the potential representations. (*see* Bird) (*see* Color) (*see* Double) (*see* Mirror)

PARTY: In the dream sense, a Party may represent the microcosm of our social universe. Accordingly, our behavior in a party may be indicative of our relationship with our peer group or family. Moreover, the casual nature of a party may serve as a foil for the unrestrained expression of our true selves. In this sense, our unconscious may illustrate among other things, our deep connection with, or separation from, a diversity of individuals in our life based upon our unique idiosyncrasies.

PATH: The symbolism of a Path involves a way of life and the direction, or steps, taken toward that particular method of personal enlightenment. Accordingly, we need to interpret any obstacles in, or deviations from, the path itself. (*see* Tarot Major Arcana) (*see* Labyrinth)

PEARL: A Pearl may be symbolic of the perfection of beauty, affection and love. Its luster being smooth and reflective, it may also represent the spiritual wisdom of self. (*see* Oyster) (*see* Light)

PENDULUM: The back and forth swinging of a Pendulum may be symbolic of ambivalence concerning a difficult choice in our life. Moreover, the movement of a pendulum is associated with the governing function of antique clocks and other various timepieces. Hence, in the dream sense, we observe a wavering which may involve a long and seemingly endless passage of time. In other words, our indecision and hesitation may be causing distress for ourselves and moreover, for others, who may be anxiously awaiting our decision. This vacillation may serve to block the normal process of transition and any subsequent emotional or psychological healing which may be necessary in readjustment.

PENETRATE: The conceptualization of Penetration involves a complex insertion into another reality to release a part of what is known as the 'life force' in general. We seek to create a pathway from this symbolic source into our own vacuous need. Furthermore, this forced synthesis, or union, may serve as a catalyst for the newly animated 'vitality' which surges between beings, a dialectic creation all its own. (see Impale) (see Bleed) (see Imbrue)

PENIS: The overt image of male sexuality, or the Penis, may also involve complex representations of masculine characteristics. These may involve an insensitivity to elusive and fluid emotions, as well as, feminine principles of fragile earth (flesh). The depiction of the penis nevertheless, represents the potential for union between man and woman, yin and yang, sky and earth; in short, the linking of opposites. (see Genitalia) (see Vagina) (see Womb)

PERPETUAL MOTION: As opposed to the pendulum symbolism which involves decision making, objects in Perpetual Motion may imply anxiety and/or nervousness in general. The conceptualization of perpetual motion involves the constant and incessant duration of a phenomenon in time. However, real life consists of a transient series of ever-changing events. This is primarily because the human mind adjusts well to new and different stimuli. Consequently, perpetual motion, or any fixed stimulus, torments the brain whose normal function is the continual formulation of new data. In the dream sense, we may desire a change in the repetitive and/or predictable behavior found in an occupation, a relationship, or the robotic operation of modern life itself.

PHOENIX: The mythical image of the fire-bird, also known as the Phoenix, symbolizes passionate burning freedom. In the dream sense, we may witness the vision of a phoenix corresponding with the onset of personal emancipation, which wholly expands our emotional and psychological horizons. The phoenix burns down to ashes which scatter and then reorganize into the eternal rebirth of the majestic winged creature. As such, our unconscious may be illustrating the parallel and consistent reincarnation of our spiritual self which burns and flies on the divine wings of an infinite consciousness.

PIG: The symbolism of a Pig involves base actions, whether they be hygiene-related or sexually orientated, the little hog lets loose. In this sense, we must observe the sloppy, muddy appearance of the swine first and lastly examine it as a possible food source. Regarding the slop, our friend the pig may represent a fusion with earth and nature from which it came and returns daily. Contemplating the naturalistic and thus, erotic aspects of this animal's behavior, we observe a parallel with uninhibited sexual conduct in human beings. Lastly, as a food source, we interpret pork as a rich, thick and flavorful sustenance, symbolically based on the animal's free-spirited temperament. Hence, in the dream sense, we may be fully embodying our desires and earthy fervor. Alternatively, in the Chinese zodiac, the pig personality is linked with chivalry and honesty. Perhaps it is the straight forward manner of the animal, which provides us with the necessary courage to reveal truth and stand by our deepest convictions.

PINE TREE: The Pine Tree which remains green and healthy throughout the year is symbolic of eternal and transcendent spirit. The seasons which change our activity and behavior, nevertheless, cannot change the continuity of who we are. In this, we witness the unconscious revelation of the soul of life, of which the unconscious itself, is an inexorable part. Furthermore, pine needles are taught to be therapeutic by many archaic cultures and in the tradition of Wicca, or witchcraft, they are viewed as receptors of pure elemental energy. Perhaps this is why the pine tree remains forever impervious to the elements themselves. (see Evergreen)

PIRATE: As opposed to the symbolism of the outlaw, the Pirate lives out his immoral potential on the high seas upon a naturalistic vessel constructed of hardwood planks. Consequently, his iniquity garners a more emotionally disturbed and overtly sexual temperament. In the dream sense, the image of a pirate may involve a complex wish-fulfillment pertaining to dangerous and perhaps sexuality and an equal lust for freedom and adventure. In other words, our unconscious may be expressing a desire to take on more risks and chancy ventures in our waking life.

PLAY: The natural tendency of many young animals to Play, involves their inbred understanding to develop the coordination necessary for adult skills needed later in life. Therefore, in a rather complex dream sense, we may be exploring the fundamental beginnings of our own unique skills and conversely, our unfortunate limitations. In this, we may need to determine our strengths and weaknesses within the context of the games played. Moreover, we may need to analyze our social place within the group. Are we one of the gang, or a hanger on? Are we an outcast? The overall symbolism of playing involves every aspect of our memory. Accordingly, we may need to explore the restructuring of our relative abilities and real reactive potential. (see Child) (see Wall) (see Lemonade Stand)

POISON: The symbolism of Poison may be entirely dependent on who administers the toxin, and who ingests it. For example, if we ourselves are the recipient of the poison, we may be illustrating a symbolic slow death pertaining to a certain aspect of ourselves. However, if we ourselves administer the venomous substance to a known party, we may be signifying the violent release of an otherwise suppressed hostility, and perhaps retaliatory aggression, toward this individual. In both cases we may need to address the overtly violent and turbulent behavior of our conscious invention.

POLICE: In the dream sense, Police represent our own morality and conscience (Superego). In this capacity, the dream flat-foot may reinforce the internalized programming of an authority figure which guides us down the straight and narrow path of social benevolence. (see Authority Figure) (see Guard)

PORT: A Port may involve emotional, as well as, psychological opportunities for us to discover. We may need to determine whether our ship or plane is preparing to leave the dock, or has just returned. Is the dock sturdy and able to withstand a violent storm? Naturally, we need to interpret the subtle connections of earth and sea. (see Dock) (see Depot) (see Water) (see Boat)

PREACHER: The symbolism of a Preacher may involve a harsh personal lesson. Accordingly, the internal lecture may center around our feelings of guilt and subsequent self-admonishment. On the other hand, a fanatical fire and brimstone rant which seems to indicate obsessive behavior in the embodiment of the dream creature, may be an unconscious illustration of our own extremist demeanor. In the dream sense, this conduct may reveal intense over compensation and an absurdly hypocritical personal stance.

PRIEST: The image of a Priest may involve the symbolism of chastity and abstinence. In this, the dreamer may view sexuality as immoral, or in any case, removed from the tenets of spiritual life. (see Abbot) (see Preacher) (see Nun) (see Virgin) (see Church)

PRIZE: As opposed to a gift, a Prize is won for some personal achievement. Therefore, our unconscious may be revealing either one of two things. The first may entail a form of congratulations for a job well done, due to perseverance and dedication. The second may consist of a warning against material lust, which may sway us from our real goals, which should provide reward enough in their mastery and fulfillment. As such, we need to determine the nature of the prize and our reaction to its relative personal value. (see Gift) (see Greed)

PROPHESY: (see Clairvoyance) (see Telepathy) (see Foresight)

PROSTITUTE: The modern symbolism of Prostitution may involve a lack of self-esteem. However, the selling of ones body may be indicative of sexual power and an otherwise extreme separation of emotion and intellect. In this sense, we may be consciously concealing the frailty of our own emotions and replacing them with a rugged and calculating physical and psychological hide. As such, strength gained from an absence of passionate turbulence is expressed in the symbolic guise of finances. Furthermore, this wish fulfillment of open sexuality may imply a serious and perhaps fanatic repression of our natural drives and desires.

PUPPET: The Puppet is thought of as a cute, animated, highly spirited reflection of child-like and innocent life. However, with the exception of Pinnochio, who in fact became a boy; Puppets possess no soul and have no life of their own. They are controlled and manipulated by outside forces, who use their innocent and sometimes wholly inanimate charm, to convey real (live) human ideas and ideals. This is why many politicians and appointed leaders are symbolically viewed as puppets, existing at times within puppet governments. In this capacity, they are given wordy speeches written by spin doctors, which are public orations chock full of the agendas and beliefs held by a powerful organized party. Moreover, these words may not agree with the internal belief system of the speaker him or herself. Accordingly, our unconscious may be warning us against proclaiming ideals which are not even our own. Conversely, we may be wrongly seeking control of others who are to young and/or naive to resist our influence. In this sense, do we fear reciting our own message/ Are we lost without support, even it happens to be weak-minded? (*see* Ventriloquism) (*see* Parasite)

PURPLE: The symbolism of Purple involves riches, sensuality and fullness of life. As such, its presence in the dream landscape may be indicative of excess and/or erotic encounters.

PYRAMID: The image of the ancient Pyramids involves enigmatic magic and the lure of the unfathomable. Moreover, the exact architecture and compass-coordinate layout of the great structures reflect the mystery of an ancient human wisdom. Accordingly, the pyramids in a dream landscape, may represent personal power based on the faith of our metaphysical ancestry. In the vision of the pyramid we find a naturalistic union with the physical landscape, human intellect, and the expanse of the heavens. Taken together, this dream figure effectively bridges the trinity of mind, body and spirit. (*see* Tarot Major Arcana: Judgment (20) and The World (21) arcana) (*see* Mummy) (*see* Pharaoh)

PYTHON: The complex symbolism of the Python involves danger, overt sexuality and seductive, sinister evil. As such, we need to determine the location where the python slithers and what motivates its movement. Furthermore, the coiling of the python around its victims and their subsequent suffocation may be indicative of emotional pressure and anxiety associated with modern living. Conversely, the power of the snake's body may refer to an almost incredible physical or mental determination. Moreover, to be bitten by a snake in our dream may refer to a drastic change in life which may lead to a profound spiritual transfiguration. (*see* Impale) (*see* Bite) (*see* Apple) (*see* Satan)

QUARANTINE: In the dream sense, a Quarantine may refer to a personal isolation from someone or something. Our unconscious may be illustrating the difficulty and/or emotional and physiological hazard involved in interactions with certain human beings. As such, we temporarily force them or ourselves from the shared social mainstay. Consequently, the dream of the quarantined landscape involves short-term alienation which is well intentioned but is nevertheless harsh and emotionally painful.

QUARRY: As a mountain symbolizes spirituality, a Quarry dug deep into the bowels of a mountain may represent the rich depths of our earthbound soul. In this sense, we combine the embodiment of earth and sky to unearth the rare gifts of an infinite unconsciousness. Furthermore, these man-made valleys may refer to the tireless search into the self for jewels of wisdom, metals of courage and fossils of symbolic archetypal truth. As such, the dream quarry may illustrate the potential depths explored within ones own psyche.

QUARTZ: The symbolism of bright crystalline rock found in the substrata of earth may be representative of a hidden and vital potential. Moreover, this buried capacity may involve emotional or psychological clarity of which we are only barely aware. Consequently, in the dream sense, the image of Quartz may refer to a budding realization of personal enlightenment and a growing wisdom in crucial decision making.

QUAY: A Quay refers to our emotional transitions and elaborate transformations made in our waking reality. (see Dock)

QUEEN: The symbolism of the Queen pertains to mature, enlightened and otherwise supreme femininity and womanhood. As such, the queen embodies matriarchal wisdom, strength and stature. Moreover, the queen symbolizes the completion of the kingdom within the undeniable aspect of her sensitive and sympathetic sovereignty. Consequently, in a dream, a queen may represent the moral and altruistic determination of the archetypal mother figure. (see King) (see Amazon)

QUESTION, THE: When our unconscious poses a Question from its own memory banks, the implication is that we already KNOW the answer within ourselves. The dream uses the interrogation as a direct rationalizing agent of our own knowledge. Similarly, we understand how thought itself is a product of reflection and self examination. In this so called 'reasoning', we piece together the meanings of separate concepts in order to find a larger and primarily unifying, theme. As such, the dream acts as a private investigator delving into our personal behavior and belief system in order to comprehend why we may or may not enact certain responses to life's diverse predicaments. Moreover, the unconscious may become aware of our future intentions and pointedly ask us why we have made this particular choice. In this manner, passionate responses may give way to calculated reasoning, including the realization of possible backlashes. (see Oracle)

QUICKSAND: The symbolism of drowning in Quicksand may imply a stagnation in ones psychological development. In other words, we may be clinging to old ideas, or ideals, however forcibly we may be coerced into change. This resistance to a new awareness may prove to be the very catalyst which pulls us deeper into the transition itself. Accordingly, in the dream sense, quicksand represents our phobia and struggle against inevitable changes in our life.

QUIET: The dual symbolism of Quiet, or silence, in a dream may refer to inner peace or conversely, the maddening stillness of the proverbial calm before the storm. Appropriately, we must determine our relative feelings within this soundless landscape. Are we aware of life in repose or dimly cognizant of hidden life forms? If we experience anxiety in the dreamscape we may need to determine the nature of the violent storms which threaten to break in our waking life. (see Numb)

QUIZ: A Quiz may be representational of being tested by some group or individual in our waking life. Appropriately, we may need to determine who quizzes us, the nature of the questions, and our self confidence concerning our ability to meet the challenge. For example, the dream of the pop quiz which catches us off guard and in a state of panic, may be indicative of our insecurity involving a lack of preparation and/or neglectful behavior. Moreover, the regressive image of the failing grade school examination may represent adult anxiety reflecting self-worth. (see Test)

RABBIT: In Lewis Carroll's novel Alice in Wonderland, the white Rabbit represents the embodiment of curiosity which entices Alice into her surreal adventures. In the mythological sense, a rabbit is thought to be the purveyor of good luck, good news and good health. Moreover, the prolific characteristic of the rabbit combined with its benign nature may signify sound childbirth. Taken together, we realize the hare symbolizes a genesis of new and wondrous events, Accordingly, in the dream sense, the image of the rabbit may represent the ingenuous faculty necessary to step through portals of new and novel worlds. Supporting these tenets, the Chinese zodiac views the rabbit personality as extremely lucky, talented, intelligent and naturally, affectionate.

RABID DOG: The symbolism of the Rabid Dog, with foaming mouth and glaring eyes, refers to confusion, madness and dangerous uncertainty in ones waking relationship/s. The image of a canine is usually associated with loyalty, trust and friendship. Hence, this conversion of a faithful emblem into a violent, distrustful and aggressive creature, may be indicative of a reversal in fraternity and a sudden and complete loss of amity and goodwill demonstrated by a close comrade. In the dream sense, this separation of a once powerful union illustrated by our unconscious' paradoxical puppy, may entirely epitomize unwarranted and unjustified actions on the part of the dreamer against his or her social peers. Conversely, if a rabid dog threatens a friend or family member, the dreamer may be reflecting his or her own feelings of betrayal involving the deceptive and deceitful behavior of significant others.

RACCOON: In the dream sense, a Raccoon may embody a restless search through the darkness of our unconscious for goods, or objectives, which satiate our hunger. Furthermore, this inquiry into our passionate motivations may involve personal heroics and reckless behavior in general. Accordingly, the raccoon may symbolize the hazardous quest and/or painful initiation of overt physical, emotional and psychological maturation.

RACE: The symbolism of the Race may refer to a heated contest to prove oneself worthy of social praise and the attainment of life's prizes. Moreover, the nature of competition and rivalry may be inherent in this ancient archetype. For example, if a man strives for the singular affections of a particular woman, he may dream of a race wherein he is pitted against all the viable suitors of that lady. Normally, winning the race, may be an expression self-confidence, pride and conceivably, conceit. Conversely, finishing last in the race, may imply a lack of self-esteem and/or a difficulty in wholly applying oneself. Lastly, a close finish may imply the dreamer's personal and psychological struggle in the exploit of this goal. Consequently, the dreamer may need to interpret if the toil of the race in the dream landscape is worth the price of its goal and moreover, if the contest, is really necessary in the first place.

RAGS: The symbolism of Rags may refer to poverty and the otherwise insufficient wrapping of our psychological skin. In the image of tattered rags we find fragmented components of a psyche which may lack the individual cohesion of a fully realized self. Moreover, in the group sense, rags may represent a fundamental alienation from the society at large, which is primarily recognized by its communal costume. Consequently, in a dream landscape, rags may refer to feelings of hardship, self-abasement, or personal estrangement, in the interwoven fabric of our waking interrelationships.

RAIN: The archetypal symbolism of Rain pertains to psychological extinction, emotional purification and natural regeneration. As such, our unconscious illustrates the torrential skies as a tearful acceptance of death's transformation into rebirth and the eternal cycle of renewal. Hence, we are continuously cleansed in the new, yet remembered, realizations of our psyche. Accordingly, rain in the dream sense, may refer to a harsh, yet emotionally beneficial, alteration in our waking life. (*see* Boat) (*see* Baptism)

RAINBOW: Occurring after the transfigurative rains, the Rainbow represents hope and reward for prolonged sacrifice. Accordingly, the rainbow is the bridge to personal illumination. Consequently, since the rainbow contains all the primary colors, our unconscious may be illustrating the paramount gift available to humanity is the embodiment of the full spectrum of our emotions. Furthermore, since a rainbow is a direct refraction of sunlight, we may interpret the dream rainbow as pertaining to the arrangement of wisdom, guidance and perceptive clarity in our waking life.

RANCID: We often find disagreeable elements in our dream landscape. Accordingly, we need to examine the exact nature of these repellent objects. In the case of Rancid foods, we find an allusion to neglect, alienation, or a movement away from normal human concerns about health and security. As such, this rancid environment may refer to slipping into ones mental neurosis and leaving the rational (social) world behind. However, since in the dream itself, an illustration of awareness of this 'bad' food is apparent, we may be referring to an individual or situation outside of our DIRECT experience and/or involvement. Nevertheless, we may fear being drawn in by this person and/or situation and subsequently, entering his or her world of chaos. Conversely, we may seek to free this person from his or her dysfunctional, or abnormal, behavior and the intolerable price of its possible consequences.

RAT: The symbolism of the Rat pertains to shrewd faculties and their corresponding capacity for survival in horrid and utterly reprehensible conditions. Unfortunately, in human beings this instinct may sometimes involve relying on the selfish, backhanded or back stabbing temperament of oneself. In other words, a betrayal of allies in order to personally survive, may be indicative of the 'stool pigeon', or rat, (or the entire rat race) itself. In the dream sense, our unconscious may be warning us that our personal interest in survival may be suspending, or outrightly obliterating, our basic human compassion for others. In a rather interesting variation of this imagery, the Chinese zodiac finds the rat personality as charming, honest and ambitious, yet, sometimes unable to maintain long friendships and/or relationships!

RATTLESNAKE: The symbolism of the Rattlesnake involves the shrill pierce of its rattle. Hence, the snake may represent a warning of physical, psychological or emotional danger involving a recent encounter or occurrence in ones waking life. (*see* Python)

RAW: In the dream sense, Raw meat may refer to carnal knowledge and/or physical desires. Moreover, the freshness of the flesh may represent its vitality and still present potency. As such, our ritualistic devouring of this physical potential, symbolically enhances our own vigor, vivacity and endurance.

RED: The color Red is symbolic of intense passions including anger, lust and shame. Moreover, its association with blood manifests deep emotional and spiritual connotations. Consequently, any and all red figures found within the dream landscape may refer to a raise in the entire propensity and fervor of the symbols revealed.

REFLECTION: A Reflection involves the complexity of self image and self understanding. Are we who we appear to be? In the shimmering and swaying image we catch of ourselves on the surface of water, we may refer to explorations of self, as it pertains to our elusive emotional realities. Do we remain intact in these pools of self-discovery? (*see* Double) (*see* Mirror) (*see* Water)

REGURGITATE: In a dream, the image of Regurgitation refers to the expulsion of entities or individuals who are venomous and otherwise malevolent to our sensibilities. Hence, we reverse our acceptance of these people, or ideas, and symbolically send them away, in other words, back from whence they came. Conversely, the regurgitation dream may involve our inability to accept, or swallow, a difficult truth or reality. Accordingly, we need to examine the exact nature of the individual, or concept, which seems blatantly noxious in our overall discernment of reality.

REINCARNATION: Reincarnation in our dream, may represent direct associations with the tenets of this religious view. As such, reincarnation involves a continual return to worldly experience in diverse living forms. This relative formation is dependent upon ones previous incarnation. As such, a lowly, greedy person may return as a snake or algae eater. Conversely, a loyal dog or cat may return as a human being. This hierarchy of animals (including humans), links behavior with moral and spiritual uprightness. Consequently, a person who lives a moral, ethical and spiritual life will not return into the animal (or human) cycle, but will instead become pure spirit and subsequently part of heaven (the realm of eternity). In a dream image where our spirit is embodied in another form (human or animal), we may be expressing concerns about the relative 'level' of our devout behavior. (*see* Transmutation) (*see* Zoomorphism)

RELIGION: In the dream sense, Religion may refer to our moral path and resolute belief in a higher power. Accordingly, we need to comprehend the ethical message produced in the dream vision. Moreover, if the dream landscape involves a ritual, we need to examine its procedure for further unconscious illustrations. Essentially, the religious imagery pertains to our feelings of guilt concerning our straying from a moral path, our converse sensations of somber mortal humility, or passionate, nearly escapist elation, involving ethereal rewards for our devout behavior. (*see* Christ) (*see* Heaven) (*see* Hell) (*see* God)

REMEMBER: (*see* Memory)

RESTRICTION: The act of sleeping involves a relative degree of paralysis and the subsequent Restriction of certain body parts. As such, the dreaming mind often rationalizes for this physical restraint by creating scenarios involving various and elaborate forms of bodily limitation. For example, if we happen to be sleeping on our right side, with our full weight on top of our right arm, in our dream imagery, this right arm may appear lame, broken, or perhaps, in a great deal of pain. In the symbolic sense however, restriction in a dream landscape may reflect a struggling, burdensome reality which we have difficulty in escaping in our waking life. For example, if our everyday clothes suddenly do not fit us and we experience pain and anxiety about this dilemma, we may be alluding to concerns about weight gain (obesity or bulimia) or oddly enough, pregnancy. Another example of restrictive dreams invokes a room or building whose doorways and windows are too small to traverse completely through. This dream may elucidate waking relationships or situations which are arduous in exiting or entering, dependent of course, on which side of the respective doorway we happen to be positioned upon. Are we in, or are we out? In all cases, we need to examine the exact nature of the limitation (doorway, clothing) and interpret appropriate analogies in our day to day experience. (*see* Hang)

RICE: When a couple is married, Rice is thrown on them to symbolize the acquisition of a new and strong social foundation. As such, rice refers to a basis or cornerstone of human endeavors. Moreover, since rice is a basic and necessary nourishment, its presence may imply an indispensable requirement or consummate building block recently instituted in ones waking life.

RING: The archetypal symbolism of a metal circle, or finger Ring, involves the eternal shielding, or protection, of mortal human liturgies. This is why a king, magician and ordinary husband and wife all become consecrated with a ring. Moreover, the ceremonial kiss of a king's regal band, represents the acceptance of his total authority and eternal sovereignty. Accordingly, in the dream sense, a ring may depict an emotional or psychological confirmation of responsibility, status or honor in ones waking life. (*see* Circle)

RITUAL: In the dream sense, a ritual represents the physical enactment of our symbolic language. As such, a ritual, or ceremony, may refer to any number of deep, passionate transformations of self. Moreover, the determining manner of rituals are their repetitive and therefore, worshipful nature. Accordingly, in a dream, we may be expressing faith in the criterion of our beliefs to bring valid, vital and absolute meaning into our lives.

RIVER: The symbolism of the river refers to the psychological and emotional continuity of our existence. As such, violent rapids may represent difficulty in our everyday interrelationships. Furthermore, swimming against the current of a river, may be indicative of unproductive and wearisome actions, which exhaust our drive, yet lead us nowhere. (*see* Bridge)

ROAD: The overall symbolism of the Road involves freedom, movement and travel. It is the long existence into the unknown. However, unlike the highway which is impersonal and seems to go on forever, the road often carries with it aspects of familiarity in the shape of houses, street signs, people, in other words, entire neighborhood vistas. In this sense, the road may promise a new way of life which is not entirely alien to our own subtle sensibilities. Alternatively, a lone, empty road in the middle of the night, might reflect darker and perhaps frightening choices which we have made in the not too distant past. As such, do we desire this 'road less taken' , or do we find ourselves entirely lost. In another interpretation of the road dream, we examine the idea of continual movement whence we (as driver or hitchhiker) never stop to plant our roots firmly into a single way of life. This dream rather eloquently illustrates an internal restlessness which may reflect our interrelationships and social moorings. In this dream landscape, our unconscious may reveal certain images of people or places which momentarily appeal to us. We may need to explore these metaphorical offerings from our sleeping mind. (*see* Highway)

ROCKS: In the dream sense, Rocks may represent our own obstinate behavior, which must be avoided, or conversely stockpiled, to use as a form of psychological or emotional protection. Moreover, in the image of our resolute rock pile, we may find valuable gems and crystals of honor, courage and hope. Consequently, a dream of breaking rocks, may refer to a profound sacrifice necessary to reveal our hidden resplendence. Furthermore, the chiseling and shaping of hard stone may epitomize the sculpting and perfecting of our human psyche. (*see* Wall)

ROPE: The symbolism of a Rope represents help and the possibility of climbing to new summits in waking life. However, the dreamer may be referring to the tangibility of physical or emotional capture in the embodiment of a rope or lasso. (*see* Knot) (*see* Hang)

ROSE: The archetypal symbol of the red Rose refers to passionate desire and/or a deep and mature level of love and intimacy. Furthermore, the unconscious illustration of a bouquet of roses may indicate a grand gesture of hope, joy or formidable applause. Additionally, dried-up roses may refer to a flame which still burns in a love affair which has come to an unceremonious end. Appropriately, we need to analyze the condition of the roses and the initiation and motivation of the person who gives or receives the flowers.

ROUND TABLE: The Round Table of King Arthur lore, refers to spiritual equality in all men. There is no head at the table and all men figure equivalent in the decision making process. At the center of the table, we primarily find a flame, which is symbolic of God as the nucleus of creation and the universe. All men identical under the Almighty and fortified in their circuitous union of faithful humanity. (*see* Tarot Major Arcana)

RUN: As opposed to walking in a dream which refers to a search for the self, Running may symbolize an elaborate escape from ones internalized fears and anxieties. In other words, the dreamer may be expressing misgivings about stopping and 'facing the music.' Moreover, our unconscious may be indicating the physical, psychological and emotional breakdown inherent in this continual and anxious movement. As in the chase dream, therapists recommend the 'marathon' dreamer to stop and confront the source of his or her terror. More often than not, the trepidation may prove to be nothing more than a Catch-22 side-effect of the self-imposed distress.

SACRIFICE: To give of oneself completely, or to Sacrifice oneself, may involve a surrendering of ones symbolic body, in place of ones spiritual concerns. This form of martyrdom may illustrate a deep commitment to ones beliefs, or conversely, an overcompensation for a personal belief system which is not socially recognized. The question is, 'Are we saintly, or do we want to be remembered as a saint'? In the sense of a human offering, the age-old concept of the human sacrifice, not only satisfied the totalitarian gods, but also eased the blood lust of a human community, number one in the food chain for no small reason! The unifying theme in both cases is appeasement, the submission and limitation of one part of ourselves, in order to raise up high, another and yet deeper, part of our complex perceptive reality. Accordingly, we need to determine what aspect of our life is sacrificed and moreover, what is our greater reward for the ordeal and/or inconvenience, endured. (see Cannibal) (see Imbrue) (see Impale)

SADISM: In the dream sense, acts of Sadism perpetrated by the dreamer, may be indicative of repressed anger and aggression which re-emerges as a passionate and violent form of wish-fulfillment. Moreover, the infliction of pain upon captive individuals may symbolize a complex construct of psychological revenge involving forced paralysis (see numb). Conversely, sadistic behavior performed on willing participants, may be an unconscious illustration of dominant and forceful sexuality (see Leather). Accordingly, in a dream involving victimization, we may be unleashing the emotional and psychological pain carried within the depths of ourselves.

SAINT: The conceptualization of a holy man or Saint may be paradoxical in nature, yet the terminology conveys a bridge from ordinary human frailty to profound inner strength. This leap of human potential is accomplished by a total conviction and dedication to faith in a supreme being. In the dream sense, we may be utilizing the image of the saint to metaphorically relate moral fortitude and/or deep faith in something (not necessarily religious) in which we profoundly believe. It should be stressed that a saint, unlike an angel, began his spiritual journey as an ordinary man or woman. This undeniable aspect of sainthood appeals to our very own mortal humanity. In the religious sense, we attribute certain saints to their particular worldly deeds. Therefore, if the saint is known in the dream landscape, we may be able to gain some insight into our own particular nocturnal vision. (*see* Icon)

SALT: In the dream sense, Salt may represent added flavor and a new found flare in the experience of life. Moreover, in the biblical sense, salt is symbolic of the greatest stature of life itself. Hence, the salt of the earth, represents the very pinnacle of creation. Accordingly, in a dream, salt may refer to increased zest and vigor in ones life and an elevated sense of individual worthiness. The dream may also refer to our truth, dedication and creativity in every day life.

SAND: The complex symbolism of Sand refers to the transient impermanence of being. Moreover, sand may be indicative of the dualism of the microcosm and the macrocosm, representing simultaneously, a single grain of sand and a mighty desert. Additionally, the diverse illustration of comfort offered by a beach and the sudden violence of a sandstorm, both pertain to this enigmatic dream imagery. Accordingly, we need to interpret our interaction with, and manipulation of, the dream sand, in order to understand how its multifarious and elusive nature may figure into our current waking circumstance and/or predicament.

SATAN: The devil Satan is often depicted as ingenious, deceitful, smooth and entirely full of evil. In this extremity of behavior, we witness how influential this personage can be upon our mortal being. In the spiritual and intellectual sense, this dark demon is able to prey upon us via the large array of our weaknesses. It is interesting to note, while a saint or angel motivates our personal inner strength, the devil asks us nothing but the indulgence of our worldly desires. He is happy to speed down life's low road, laughing crazily behind the wheel. The interpretation of this dream image is split, dependent on our reaction and interaction with this powerful allegorical being. Are we drawn within its charms and ease, or are we repulsed by its lack of any and all restraint. In the psychological sense of the former example, we in fact be overcompensating for the mundane reality of our day to day existence. (*see* Demon) (*see* Tarot Major Arcana: Devil (15))

SAVAGE: The wild individual who practices little or no restraint whatsoever, may be indicative of our own need to figuratively 'bust loose.' Moreover, the Savage illustrates darker proponents of our psyche which may be repressed in our waking experience. Furthermore, in a not entirely separate interpretation, the wild man may illustrate a spiritual visionary or shaman which guides us with the eccentricities of his naturalistic movements, gestures and elaborate dance. With this in mind, we may need to determine the symbolism of the savage's mask, clothing and other adornments. (*see* Aboriginal)

SCAR: The symbolism of a Scar, may represent old wounds, or bad feelings, which never entirely heal and linger in our memory. Primarily, these psychological and emotional injuries occur in our youth and remain repressed and buried in our unconscious. However, when personal regression develops, a dreamer may call upon these memories to support his or her irrational behavior. Accordingly, in the dream sense, a scar may be representative of a deeply seated insecurity which may be holding us back from accomplishing our adult endeavors and fulfilling our well-deserved goals. Conversely, a scar may epitomize the struggle we have gone through to become self-realized individuals. In other words, do we display the scar as our personal badge, or does the scar display us, as its hapless and defeated victim?

SCHOOL: In the dream sense, a School may represent the foundation and beginning stages of our earliest social skills. As such, we need to honestly confront the memories of our shy, awkward and painful, or conversely fun, lively and animated scholastic interrelationships. The appropriate memory depicted in a dream landscape, may be entirely reflective of these identical emotions rekindled in a dreamers waking life. (*see* Academy) (*see* Quiz) (*see* Scar)

SEA: The complex symbolism of the Sea represents the embodiment of our entire emotional matrix. Moreover, an endless body of water which reflects the sun and sustains a multiplicity of wonder below its depths may be indicative of our unconscious. As such, all movements directed into the sea may imply an immersion into our unconscious. Conversely, physical movement rising out of the deep waters may refer to memories recalled from our own personal depths. Accordingly, in the dream sense, a sea may refer to the symbolic transition from our unconscious to our conscious and vice versa. In so doing, the sea may represent the plateau between our waking mind and our dreaming mind. (see Drown) (see Baptism) (see Unconscious, the) (see Water)

SEASONS, THE FOUR: The Four Seasons may be symbolic of the entire cycle of life. As such, spring refers to birth, youth and potential, while summer alludes to the zenith of life in full bloom and blistering enterprise. The fall, or autumn, represents a gentle dismissal from the climax of young adulthood, into the wise, reason of weathered maturity and steady industry. In the end, gentle winter numbs our bodies into a lingering detachment of worldly concerns and prepares us for the profound transfiguration of our own death. In turn, this passing allows for the completion and new beginning inherent in the eternal cycle of divine renewal.

SEED: The image of a Seed involves potential for life generation and growth in general. As such, everything in the realm of hope and possibilities may find a symbolic allusion to the living seed. In the judgment that a seed once planted, needs water and sunlight, we witness a representation of the wise acceptance of emotions in order to grow to ones fullest potential. Furthermore, the memory of seed gives primary strength to the mighty tree. In other words, transformation is not separation, but rather, transcendence, which is the goal of existence and unequivocal completion of being. (see Acorn) (see Garden) (see Growth) (see Overflow) (see Water) (see Sun) (see Light) (see Earth) (see Womb)

SEVEN: The archetypal symbolism of the number seven refers to chance, luck and the divine animating power of God. If these representations seem too diverse and radically opposed, the reader may want to consult modern theories of quantum physics. In quantum theory, the only provable certainty is uncertainty, or randomness. Another branch of modern physics called Chaos Theory wholeheartedly agrees with this random, or arbitrary, approach to the workings of our material existence. In other words, theorists exclaim, 'God plays with dice.' (see also

Tarot Major Acana: Charioteer (7))

SHADE: The dream imagery of Shade illustrates a temporary relief from the heat and exposure of direct sunlight. However, since sunlight is symbolic of reason, clarity and revelation, shade may refer to mild deception, harmless subterfuge and sensual foolishness. Moreover, shade may represent an elusive union of light and dark which may reveal a peculiar conglomeration of good and bad intentions. Accordingly, we may need to analyze the individual and combined natures of these consorted feelings and decide if they are well-balanced in our psyche, or thoroughly muddled and consequently, alienating.

SHADOW, THE: Carl G. Jung referred to a person's dark, and perhaps repressed, inner self, as The Shadow. In the figure of the shadow we find the intense passions of self which are too powerful and too individualistic to reveal in normal society. In Robert Louis Stevenson's short story entitled: Dr. Jekyll and Mr. Hyde, the author reveals the physical embodiment of ones repressed self through chemistry; a sort of anti-reason elixir is created by the good doctor, which involves opening portals into the dark regions of the human psyche. The tragedy of the story is not found in the form of the evil Mr. Hyde, but rather in the unbalanced natures of both Jekyll and Hyde. The same lesson holds true in the dream sense, which reveals the shadow as a figure who is overtly repressed and must emerge, at least partially, to complete the balanced psyche of the dreamer.

SHAMAN: In ancient times, Shaman, or the spiritual messengers of tribes, looked to dreams to guide them in their social instruction and inspiration. The visual quest of the shaman became the singular embodiment of the spiritual needs of the entire clan. Accordingly, in the dream sense, the vision of a journeying shaman, may represent the incarnate motivation of our own spiritual search. As such, any and all gestures and rituals performed by the shaman, should be interpreted for their appropriate symbolic meaning in our own life.

SHARK: The symbolism of the Shark refers to swimming in dangerous emotional waters. The several million year old shark species is known for its fierce aggression and razor sharp teeth, but not for its colorful body or physical nature. In fact, the cold predatory eye of the shark displays no emotion whatsoever. Accordingly, this large-jawed creature may represent a lack of sensitivity concerning our own sentiments and the inherent danger involved in this behavior. In the dream sense, the unconscious may be displaying our own cold and ruthless insensitivity, or conversely, warning us against the actions of a known individual whose intentions may be less than noble.

SHEEP: In the Chinese zodiac, the Sheep personality is thought of as being elegant, artistic and religious, yet shy and sometimes baffled by life's complexity. In the west, the symbolism is not entirely different. The sheep is thought of as innocent and vulnerable in a harsh and complex world. Unfortunately, this longing for belief and understanding may lead sheep into slaughter, their own, or someone else's. As such, the concept of blind trust, or faith, while admirable in a certain sense of humility, may also spell disaster. As human beings, we are not sheep, and have the ability to think for ourselves. We have the ability to reason and estimate the repercussions of our behavior. When we blindly follow, we negate our foresight into the forward future, instead relying on trust and the ensuing of rear ends before us, in the herd at large. The dream drastically illustrates the nature of our own behavior, or conversely, the nature of others who follow our lead. Sheep or shepherd, we still rely on some form of hidden truth. (*see* parasite)

SHELL: Because of its bright color, feminine shape and proximity to water (ocean beaches etc.), a Shell is intricately associated with emotional relationships which transcend the normal tenets of lust and desire. The nature of the shell involves pure love, spiritual ascendance and a mystical union with nature. In the ancient Kabbalah, the tree of life is generated and enlightened via the transfigurative associations of archangels, otherwise known as 'shells.' From still another point of view, the sea shell tells the story of an entire life, its once cephalopod inhabitant. Taken together, we understand the poignancy of the shell dream. As such, we need to determine all the factors surrounding the discovery and employment of the shell in the dream landscape. For example, the image of walking upon broken shells may symbolize the caution we exhibit in relationships, fearful of the heartbreaks or disillusionments endured in our past. (*see* Oyster)

SHELTER: The image of a hiding spot which momentarily saves us from the harsher elements, may be directly symbolic of real hope amidst violent chaos. However, what makes this imagery unique, as opposed to a house or apartment sanctuary, a Shelter is not permanent and will eventually deny stability. In this sense, we must interpret the short-lived extension of hope offered by its dwelling. The unconscious may be alluding to much needed assistance offered in waking life via a person, family or organization; however, a conscious realization asserting a re-emergence of self-determination may equally be implied in this dream communication. accordingly, we need to analyze the condition of this shelter, either man-made or natural, and examine the steps we take to prepare for our emergence back into the real world. (see Den) (see Cabin)

SIX: In the Tarot deck, the number Six major-arcana, refers to naturalistic and divine love which is not based upon simple carnal desire. Moreover, the Star of David in the Hebrew tradition, illustrates a balance of strength, counterbalancing as it does, the powerful triad forms. Accordingly, in the dream sense, the number six may represent the fortitude and solid prosperity of family and otherwise, consecrated union. (see Tarot Major Arcana: The Lovers (6) figure)

SKY: The archetypal symbolism of the Sky refers to infinite vision and/or wisdom. Moreover, the masculine aspect of spirit resides in the sky above and compliments mother earth below. Furthermore, the light blue reflection which veils the atmosphere is indicative of boundless potential and eternal grace. Consequently, all entities which move through the vast horizon, illustrate freedom and the zenith of existence. (see Fly) (see Light) (see Blue)

SLAVE: In the dream sense, a Slave may be indicative of our servitude to individuals who forget, or ignore, our basic humanity. Moreover, the representation of slavery may involve our unconscious illustration of a sudden personal loss of individuality and inherent liberty, for no justifiable reason. Consequently, we may need to analyze our lack of autonomy in our working relationships, including our own family life.

SLEEP CYCLES: (see Alpha & Delta waves)

SLOW MOTION: As opposed to dream paralysis, which involves an entire loss of movement, including escape or retaliation, Slow Motion dreams seem to focus our mind on the temporal unfolding of symbolic events. In this sense, our unconscious may be revealing minute peculiarities and subtleties in our behavior. This may be an indication of slight personal changes occurring in our waking life which may be causing us anxiety. Moreover, slow motion imagery seems to add a poignancy to our dream situations. Accordingly, we may need to determine if certain waking events are exaggerated in our consciousness and justifiably, need to be placed in their proper psychological or emotional context.

SMOKE: The complex symbolism of Smoke is innately involved with flame and therefore carries all the tenets of danger, passion, deception and creation which one associates with fire. In the realm of sensuality, smoking continues to induce feelings of calm, cool control and an almost emotional toughness. This lure of smoke is so powerful and humanly transcendent, it causes teenagers to begin smoking even though they are deluged with information about cancer and the string of other respiratory illnesses linked with the use of tobacco. Far from being a defense for smoking, one finds a far superior alternative in the Native American practice of smoking the peace pipe to mark social unity and tribal bonding in sacred ceremonies. In a single instant, these people (especially the Dakota Sioux) combined ritual, creation and communal sharing to incorporate a powerful, reasonable center of human wisdom. So, we must ask our dreaming mind; is our smoking a healthy religious experience, or just a 'cool' deceptive fog? (see Fog)

SNAKE: In the Chinese zodiac, the Snake personality is considered deep, wise and romantic. These individuals are also thought of as being strong-willed and very determined, despising nothing more, than their own failure. The western image of the snake is not entirely different. The natural allusion to stealth and sexuality infer quiet wisdom and an almost hypnotic romanticism. The strength of the entwining serpent, illustrates a kind of gradual and building determination, which finds little room for real compromises. Taking all this into account, our dream may imply something about our internal force of will, which may move beyond our ability to stop its sometimes damaging effects. (see Python)

SNOW: The complex symbolism of Snow involves purity, childhood and rudimentary pleasure. Moreover, the image of a silent and tranquil snowfall, may be indicative of spiritual peace and/or somber wisdom. As such, we need to determine our exact feelings in and around the snow.

SPIDER: The image of a Spider may represent a loner, or lone being, whom it may be wise to keep away from, even though he or she may be extremely alluring. In another sense, a spider's danger is aimed primarily at unwanted pests. Therefore, the stranger referred to in the form of the dream spider, may in fact illustrate a positive force eradicating the prevailing infestation of negativity. In the connotation of a female, Black Widow etc., we may be revealing fear or uncertainty concerning relationships and their intricate ensnarements. (*see* Vampire) (*see* Bleed)

SPOTLIGHT: In the dream sense, a Spotlight may refer to the strict focus and intense concentration upon our actions. As such, we may be expressing a desire to be noticed by a particular individual, including a parent, or romantic interest. Moreover, this spotlight may be an indication that we have perfected some behavior which may have been previously ordinary or nondescript in our waking character. Along these lines, our unconscious may be illustrating overcompensation regarding the nature of our own insecurity.

SQUARE: The Square shape implies strength, stability, honesty and a conservative outlook on the future. Furthermore, we see the sound foundation for building upon ones own physical, psychological, emotional and spiritual development. (*see* Form) (*see* Eight) (*see* Four)

STAGE: As opposed to the symbolism of the spotlight, which focuses individual attention, the Stage refers to the social choreography of our interrelationships and the subsequent reaction from our audience of peers. In this sense, the stage is representative of our communal behavior. Accordingly, we need to analyze our relative success, or failure, upon the dream stage. Furthermore, if we find ourself on the side stage, our unconscious may be elucidating the reality of our introverted behavior. Consequently, we may need to storm the stage of our interpersonal existence with style, poise and confidence.

STAIN: As opposed to the symbolism of a scar, which refers to a deeply seated and difficult memory, the mark of a Stain may allude to the remembrance of a superficial and therefore, wholly reversible mistake in our life. Accordingly, we may need to analyze the substance and color which stains our clothes or body, and the clothing or body parts, themselves. (*see* Imbrue)

STARS: The symbolism of Stars, or celestial bodies, refers to the hopes, dreams and aspirations of man immersed within the boundless reaches of creation. Moreover, since light represents wisdom and clarity, flickering stars reflect enigmatic, unfathomable and incomprehensible cognizance. As such, star gazers, star readers and especially, star travelers (aliens), are consulted for knowledge and guidance. Accordingly, in the dream sense, a starry night may typify future knowledge and the potential to use that wisdom in a peaceful, benevolent and steadfast manner.

STOMACH: The food we eat and the desire with which we consume it, illustrates a great deal about ourselves and our respective needs. In the conceptualization of the stomach, we examine foods (or information) ingested, and our digestive (acceptance) of them accordingly. Hence, the feeling of our stomach reveals the temperance of our belief system or relative way of life. When certain situations appear before us which are entirely unacceptable and lack the basic humanity we are accustomed to in life, we find ourselves nauseated and wanting to purge the entire matter. We are therefore, in a very real sense, ruled by what we are able to stomach. Consequently, in our dreams, we need to analyze all effective stimuli concerning our stomach, otherwise known as our 'gut' instinct. (see Abdomen)

STORM: Used extensively in art. literature and film, Storms eloquently symbolize internal turmoil and seething anguish. The combination of dark skies, harsh winds and flooding, drowning torrents of rain, illustrate the instability of emotion and the relentless punishment and ruthless unanticipated effect they unleash upon our psyche. As an archetype in human consciousness, the eruption of elemental forces signals caution and danger. This is the time to hide and find shelter. In the wisdom of the animal world, the calm BEFORE the storm, is the time to work and make preparations for the impending havoc. Therefore, our unconscious may be implying, we are too late for carefree preservation and now we must 'weather' the symbolic storm before us. Once again, similar to the animal world, the survival against the elements builds our character and strengthens our life force. (see Boat) (see Rain)

STRANGULATION: The restriction of breathing essential to the process of life, signals an innermost danger which we feel may harm, not only ourselves, but our loved ones as well. As such, our own Strangulation may involve a sickness in our family or

a threat to our livelihood in general. In this sense, any stress related to ones survival, including and especially the aforementioned, economic failure or accomplishment, implicitly reflect
this nightmarish dream imagery. Alternatively, a strangulation
may imply a suffocation of ideas, passions, and otherwise suppressed instinctual drives. Events which produce shortness of
breath, including eroticism, may be illustrated in a suggestive
sense. (*see* Hang)

SUCCUBUS: (*see* Incubus)

SUGAR: In the dream sense, Sugar may be representative of instant, yet short-lived, gratification. As such, the sweetness of
sugary pleasures may be symbolic of a compensation for the true
happiness found in love, charity and devotion. Moreover, the
sweetness of sugar may be indicative of personal, and therefore
selfish, enjoyment and/or debauchery. In any case, sugar can be
used as an exceptional ingredient in healthy and nutritious
cooking. Accordingly, the symbolic sweet crystal can be used in
good measure toward sound and meaningful relationships. In
the dream landscape, we may need to determine the amount of
sugar used and the nature, and motivation, of the individuals
who produce and serve the confectionery substance.

SUN: The symbolism of the Sun dates back to earliest stages of human development and involves the hope of a new day, the al-
leviation of our fear of night (more appropriately the unknown)
and a basking in the warmth and sensory brilliance of creation.
Primitive cultures world-wide, including the Aztecs, Celts and
ancient Greeks, held elaborate ceremonial rites of worship to
their SUN deities who reserved great force and aided mankind
in an almost day to day, interpersonal fashion. Today, as in the
countless millennium past, the sun dream indicates immense
radiance and outright wonder, the eternal exploding energy of
the ceaseless fire bearing star which sustains life and illuminates
being. Naturally, the negative or flip side of illumination is exposure. In this sense, a blazing desert heat might evoke a fear of
being seen, discovered, revealed and thusly ravaged by elements
out of our human and/or immediate control. (*see* Light) (*see*
Tarot Major Arcana: The Sun (19) figure)

SURGERY: In the dream sense, Surgery implies a radical intrusion
into the foundation of self. Appropriately, we need to interpret
whether this encroachment is for our own emotional or physiological benefit, or conversely, an attack upon our stolid psy-

chological meddle.

SUSPENDED ANIMATION: The surreal image of floating in Suspended Animation, may involve various levels of alienation and isolation. However, in this circumstance, the detachment and seclusion experienced, may not be entirely unpleasant. When the external muscles of the body relax, we may become aware of our internal processes. Gradually, all biological operation is accounted for, and otherwise overlooked. When this separation from our physical self occurs, we begin to be able to move directly into our neural imagination and the full repertoire of its deepest memory. In this externally motivated journey into the unconscious, we may or may not find what we expected. Herein, lies the paradox of suspended animation. We may feel a desire to surrender ourselves to the vast internal world of perception, however, we may not be stable enough and secure enough, to relinquish ALL external physical control. In fact, we may panic at the thought of a situation without means of physical escape. In this sense, we become suspended, immobilized and entirely vulnerable to all forms of perceived danger, which of course increases with the steady rise of our irrational panic. The panic may become so violent and taxing to our central nervous system, that we awake from this nightmare physically exhausted and utterly entangled with anxiety. Conversely, the biological release which leads us into the unconscious, and otherwise spiritual awareness of self, may bring memorable elation and inner peace which lasts a life time. Taking all this into account, we need to understand our relative ability to animate ourselves without the control of our usual faculties. Moreover, is our fear too overwhelming, to allow for the full disengagement of body, absolutely necessary to explore the uncharted worlds found in this so-called, suspended animation? (see Float) (see Numb)

SWAMP: The symbolism of a Swamp may refer to an unstable foundation in ones waking endeavors. Moreover, a swamp may represent murky and obscure emotional involvements, which may in fact, be confusing and desperate in scope. Taken together, we see how the swamp landscape in our dream, may be indicative of an unconscious warning concerning the shaky groundwork of a recent emotional undertaking. (see Drown)

TABLE: The image of a Table may represent the potential for a meeting or gathering. In this sense, our unconscious may be signifying a need for talks, to perhaps bring together social unity, or in any case, purposeful unification of some kind. Moreover, the contents upon a table may symbolize a person, or an entire group's psychological makeup. For example, a lone plate, full glass and burnt-out candle may symbolize loneliness, or the lack of human socialization, while on the other hand, a map, pointer and ashtray full of cigarette butts, may certainly indicate an organized plan involving a considerably large group of people. (*see* Dinner)

TABOO: In the dream sense, any personal behavior which is strictly Taboo, may be referring to actions repressed in our unconscious. Along these lines, a tribe, or cluster, may be indicative of our moral and social code. Accordingly, we need to determine the tribe's grounds for the suppression of this behavior. Does the dream clan's taboo match our own social prohibitions? If the group's restriction is radically different from those of waking society, we may need to interpret all of their public and community differences. Hence, when we build a psychological awareness of the group and its motivations, we will have begun obtaining an accurate description of our own psyche.

TAIL: In the dream sense, an animal's Tail may refer to our feelings of happiness, fear and/or sexual arousal. The latter example may allude to the symbolism of the male phallic. In yet another sense, our tail may refer to our point of vulnerability. As such, we may be taking risks, for which we are not prepared to pay the full consequences if caught. In this case, we may place our tail between our legs, symbolizing fear and outright embarrassment. The tail as hind quarters, may refer to a form of sexuality which is hidden and unable to face up to its true reality. Furthermore, when we view objects of desire from behind, we may be illustrating voyeuristic tendencies and perhaps a coy form of repression.

TANGO: The passionate dance known as the Tango, may have little to do with rhythm and music and everything to do with the
hypnotic nature of sensuality. In its torrent, wave-like repetition, we find the building of carnal heat and an almost burning
sexuality. Nevertheless, the tango adheres to rules of society and
gathers its strength from mutual sexual tolerance. Therefore,
should one partner lose the passion found in the ritual, the
tango becomes no longer relevant. In a dream tango, we may be
reflecting the building passion of a particular situation, especially involving opposing forces who are attracted by the measure of their mutual emotion. The dreamer needs to analyze the
direction of this passion and its metaphoric connection with
waking realities.

TAPESTRY: The combination of disparate materials and diverse
color woven into a Tapestry may be symbolic of community
unity and the lengths we as human beings are willing to go, to
achieve these ends. Accordingly, we need to analyze the condition of the tapestry, as well as the colors and material chosen.
We also need to determine if the tapestry is completed. Understanding these precepts, we may begin to understand the organization of parts (people, situations) in our life toward a greater
and grander whole.

TARGET: The Target dream may involve dualism depending on
whether we view ourselves as the symbolic victim of life's arrows, or conversely, the active and brave archer reaching the
bull's eye in admirable achievement of self. To ascertain this distinction, we need to uncover all the representational tenets and
images in both the arrow as well as the launcher. Moreover, do
our emotions signal fear and anxiety in this dream landscape, or
thrill and exhilaration. (*see* Arrow)

The
TAROT
Arcana

TAROT: The complex symbolism of the Tarot, refers to a language of divination and a multi-dimensional mirror into our own unconscious. As such, we see a random selection of cards, each pertaining to a facet of our human psyche, laid out before us to illustrate the past, present and future. Appropriately, we analyze the meaning of the cards, which in theory, reflect the arbitrary reality present in our concurrent awareness. This essentially means, a Tarot card reading performed two days hence, may be radically different than one performed today (in the present), simply due to the new arrangement of thoughts and worldly attitudes which are ever changing in our perceptive awareness. Consequently, in the dream sense, a Tarot layout may involve a description of a dreamer's current, yet entirely changeable, feelings concerning reality, or some specific point effecting his or her waking life. The four respective suits of the Tarot: Wands, Swords, Cups and Pentacles are synonymous with the four elements: Fire, Air, Water and Earth. In this sense, the fire element of the Wand represents inspiration and the spiritual, psychological and physical reality of action and initiative. The air element of Swords refers to the determination and strength of an individual who conquers fear and inner paralysis with complete faith in oneself and ones purpose. The water element of Cups refers to ones emotional capacity and furthermore, the purity of ones soul and spiritual outlook in general. Is the cup of love shared with others in the hope of interactive communal hope? Conversely, is the cup spilling, or empty and void of the fullness of life? Finally, we come to the earth element of Pentacles where we find a concern about worldly experience including and especially money and social influence. However, the Pentacles may also refer to our ties with the natural world around us, in other words, man and mother nature. Is the connection mutually fulfilling or one-sided and thereby destructive overall? We will explore each of the twenty-two major arcana in the course of this publication beginning with the Fool and culminating with the World. (see Seven) (see Collective Unconscious)

THE TAROT DECK (Major Arcana): The Tarot deck is fundamentally used as a system of divination, however, many historians and theologians worldwide have agreed that within the boundaries of the Tarot deck, ancient belief systems and otherwise secret doctrines, are encoded for all times in picturesque

.... **TAROT**

symbols, in an effort to implement the understanding of a mankind which is willing to take the time and care necessary to unravel its labyrinth-like system of personal and spiritual wisdom. Occultists sight the beginnings of Tarot law in Egypt's Book of Thoth, whose followers followed the Royal Path of Initiation toward the spiritual understanding of divine reason. Tarot, Rota, and the Hebrew Torah, all reflect connections with this conceptualization of the cycle of life which reveals truth and wisdom to each and every one of us in repeating spiraling steps of ascending and descending events of experience and our accompanying appropriate (or not so appropriate) personal decision making process. (compare Jacob's Ladder) Notwithstanding, the controversy of the Tarot deck's absolute beginnings, it is well known that esoteric and deeply philosophical structures of faith including the Kabbalists, Pythagoreans, Astrological and Alchemical traditions, Enochians, Rosicrucians and the Hermetics, as well as eastern incarnations, such as Buddhism, Hindu and first stage Shinto, all contain, and in a very real sense, figure in the creation of, tarot symbolism as it exists today.

In examining the 22 major arcana, from the (0) Fool card, to the (21) World card, we will explore the central idioms and ideologies, as well as generic social dynamics, which the cards represent and (to this day) continue to tutor within the scope of our universal culture, therefore figuring preeminently within our overall psyche and dream understanding of the outside and inside worlds of consciousness.

Sequentially, in an initial viewing of the deck, we find the four respective suits of the tarot: Wands, Swords, Cups and Pentacles, which are synonymous with the four elements: Fire, Air, Water and Earth. In the first link, we discover that the Fire element of the Wand depicts inspiration and the spiritual, psychological and physical reality of action and initiative, the slash or spark of being. Secondly, the Air element of Swords refers to the determination and mental strength of an individual who conquers fear and inner paralysis with complete faith in oneself and ones purpose. The Water element of Cups beckons to ones emotional capacity and furthermore, the purity of ones soul and spiritual outlook in particular. In this sense, is the cup of love shared with others in the hope of interactive communal integrity, or conversely, is the cup spilling, or empty and otherwise drained of the fullness of human potential? Finally, we come to the Earth element of Pentacles where we find a concern about

KEYS TO YOUR DREAMS
193

worldly experience including and especially material gain and social influence. However, before we color this suit with an entirely negative sensibility, we learn that Pentacles and Earth also refers to the natural, living, and highly visible world around us. Is the connection of man and nature mutually fulfilling, or one-sided and thereby destructive overall?

Concluding, in the examination of each of the twenty-two major arcana in the tarot deck we will reveal color, shape, numerical and all other coded symbolic meanings inherent in the face of the card itself. In this way, we may attempt to find our dream connection with the fool's journey into the world of realities wisdom on the Royal Path of every human beings course of self discovery.

THE FOOL (0) (Tarot Major Arcana): The Fool figure does not begin with the number 0 to symbolize nothingness in the sense of loss. In fact, quite the opposite is true. The emptiness of the fool represents his potential to obtain all the wisdom the world has to offer. He will accomplish this feat only by operating on instinct and furthermore, and quite naturally, is fearless in his faith in the necessity of the experiences which await him. Similarly, when we play the fool, we follow our most base, raw emotions rather than our reason. The fool has not learned how to reason as of yet. he is instead inspired by the fervor of his emotions. As such, he is lured by his curiosity into the unknown.

On the card itself the fool figure is about to step off a cliff with all the assurance of a man stepping into his own garden. He is at one with creation in this absolute faith in the soundness of the reality which supports him and drives him forward. In this fashion, the fool is latent energy awaiting a connection and spark of active, operational and indeed, essential, life. The fool is associated with the element Air because of this spirited and highly transient movement throughout existence.

In another point of view we find the fool's flexibility concentrating all his concern upon the future. The past is behind him and because his eyes, like man and other predators are fixed forward, this is the point where he needs to stay, the point of potential. Reflection will be saved for another day.

In the Jungian sense, this point of the fool's potential is roughly comparative to the limits (which are actually limitless) of the unconscious He is the collective unconscious before it collects data and focuses on viable solutions. He is the unseen law behind a physical system which produces actual and viable results. In this, he represents the onset of the initiate into the folds of spiritual reason and the wonder of creation. Moreover, this exuberance of the fool is reflective of his absolute purity. Life has not yet punished him and in fact cannot punish him, because he has lured (and is the initial push of) life, into the realm of all inclusive reason. At that subsequent stage of discovery and self knowledge (tree of knowledge) and the punishment which goes with it, the fool can no longer be present. He has moved into new realms of experience.

In this fearless/impenetrable riddle we find an association with man, mind and god. Accordingly, the gods associated with the fool are Jupiter and Zeus. The animal linked with the fool card is the eagle who sees all and yet cannot be reached. In the truest sense, the fool is ever matched up with the individual who uses the deck, whether for divination or serious philosophical or religious study. The initiate needs to remain the fool in order to move through the wisdom of the tarot, which may seem frightening through the eyes of ordinary reason, but become ever clearer to the newly enlightened. The card itself depicts this constant approach to enlightenment with the shiny yellow sun which seems to fill the fool with warmth and encouragement while lighting his way into the great beyond.

In some decks, a dog is pictured yapping at the fool as he begins his perilous journey. This simple representation symbolizes leaving home and the familiarity of friends and family, who sometimes bind us with their own emotional ties, wishing us a well structured safety net and overall sanctity. In spite of this, the initiate understands that he or she must experience the realm of existence in its fullest and purest sense; in all its splendor, harshness and outright severity. Only by overcoming these hardships again and again in a spiral cycle of stages can the individual gain the true meaning of the Royal Path of existence, the ROTA, the Tarot...

THE MAGICIAN (1) (Tarot Major Arcana): The Magician represents the spark of the fool's potential. In this, the white robed figure brings all of life's possibilities into full physical existence. Accordingly, he possesses control of the four suits which lay horizontally on a table before him, they are: Wands, Swords, Cups and Pentacles. As stated earlier, these four suits are symbolic and synonymous with the four elements which are: Fire, Air, Earth and Water. It is the magicians singular position to reveal the world and the promise of its abundant application, in other words, its miraculous completion. This is why he stands below the figure-eight infinity symbol which demonstrates an infinite reality surrounding mankind.

As he simultaneously points to heaven above with his right hand and earth below with his left hand, he becomes the incarnate symbol of man who exists between heaven and earth, a yin/yang axis between spirit and body. The magician acutely understands that all these levels of perception embody the oneness of self. Naturally, he is the beginning of self awareness and social awareness. This is why, on most decks, the figure is depicted on stage performing to an outside world. However, unlike the fool, the magicians confidence upon the stage is reflected from the fullness of the knowledge of his enterprise, not upon blind faith.

The magician in some decks is portrayed as young and virile. There is a double-fold application for this rendering. Firstly, his youth represents the initial 'spark' of life, previously mentioned, and secondly, an articulate symbolism is revealed of an individual wisdom gained through knowledge and reason rather than experience. This calculated 'reasoning' shows us an objective perception of the world rather than a personal, self-orientated subjective perception of reality. This immediately connects the magician figure with the severity of pure mind and hard logic. As such, he sees and comprehends the path which the fools has undertaken and allows entry into each of its portals of learning. In this sense, the Hebrew letter Beth is attributed with the magician. Beth means house, and as we have come to learn in the course of our study, house is primarily symbolic of the world. Hence, the magician is master of the household and moves through its rooms swiftly and effortlessly.

In yet another connection with this reasoning we find the figure associated with the gods Mercury, Hermes and Thoth who are known for their speed of thought and infinite vision. In fact, the Hermetic order, followers of Hermes Trismegistes, or thrice great Hermes, believed that the forty-two books of their master revealed the secret knowledge of both the ancient Greeks as well as the ancient Egyptians. It was said that Hermes Trismegistus was the divine incarnation of both the gods Thoth and Hermes, who were similarly associated with universal wisdom, a mastery of magic, the swiftness of thought itself and the healing power of the caduceus. Historically, the T-shaped bar with entwined snakes called the caduceus, is said to date back as early as Mesopotamia, 2700 BC and has always been associated with the powers of healing the sick. In a similar correlation, the Hindus believed the caduceus to be symbolic of the kundalini force which travels up the spine over and betwixt the six major chakras in every human being on the course of becoming whole. Involved with this life flow, we find the magician associated with the element Air, which is once again synonymous with mind, but also spiritual freedom to explore the visionary world of his understanding. In this, we find the position of his experimentation and its subsequent learning. In other words, his power of healing is not incarnate, but a product of his swift and curious mind. Moreover, he is not afraid to fail in his attempt to discover implicit truths about his elemental reality. This viewing of the life potential in all its harshness is fundamentally what separates the Magician and the Fool, and yet, at the same time, bonds them together as one in the same. However, enduring at two separate levels of existence, one always following the other, creation ensued by an entirely inevitable, manifestation.

In as much, we see the absolute, albeit austere, purity of life in its beginning stages, eloquently represented here in the Magician card. Exactly how this relates to our unconscious awareness of our whole world, replete with four elements and infinite possibilities, we must assess for ourselves. Nevertheless, the confidence and assurance of the card cannot be ignored and may serve as a starting point in our conceptualizations of our own capabilities in handling the countless realities of an ever emerging unknown, with a well balanced mind (insight) and body (grounded), infused with a spirit which is indeed 'thrice great.'

THE HIGH PRIESTESS (2) (Tarot major Arcana): Following creation and manifestation, it is only natural to find separation and its subsequent developments. The High Priestess represents the first division of the whole world necessary to bring a return or reunification of that world. This restoration to wholeness produces the birth of an ever evolving cyclical creation.

Seated between the negative and positive pillars of Solomon's temple, respectively Boaz and Joachin, the High Priestess creates the manifest duality of the magician's replete and infinite universe. In the depth of her calm introspection, she seems to pull the world into its absolute opposition of physical realities, especially man and woman, generating a chasm of infinite potential. In this dynamic wielding of the life force, she brings about the inspiring and flooding torrent of inconceivable attraction and miraculous union. In her beauty, youth and perfection she forms the deepest well of first love, romantic love and begins the voyage into spiritual love, all born from opposition and attraction; an ocean created from drops of rain, swelling emotion energized upon the human psyche.

Naturally we see how the High Priestess figure is associated with the element of water and its multiplicity of forms and expressions. In this vain, the Hebrew letter connected with this card is Gimel, which means camel. The camel brings life into the desert because of its ability to store water and reserve its force and vitality. Moreover, the shape of its hump also implies a potent sexual ability and survival cunning. The High Priestess too has demonstrated her cunning, by separating the world in order to continuously rejuvenate its essential being. In her wisdom she fashions both a cup and water from life's completion, to provide thirst and celestial quenching.

The figure is often associated with inspiration and the divination of DREAMS, in particular. She accomplishes this by existing in harmony with the deepest pool of the unconscious, with which she is synonymous. In this way, her resplendent, yet deep tranquillity, teaches the tenets of wisdom honed carefully by reflection and abstract musing. Still further, in many ways, she is the combination of the Fool's faithful instinct and the Magician's keen intelligence. As such, she is awareness taken to its deepest, yet not entirely unattainable, level.

The color associated with the High Priestess is sky blue because of its infinite scope and welcoming clarity. As such, the figure seems to stretch her arms under the light of wisdom and new found love and fashions the very sky in the doing. Yet, at the same time, night brings darkness and moonlight (emotion) and this too is symbolic of the High Priestess, for she is the beginning of the Yin/Yang struggle of all cyclical opposition. However it must be remembered, unlike the Empress, she is in no way a balance of these apparent opposites, she is instead a FUSION of opposites, a brand new birth of living self. In short, she is the regenerative principle masterfully and forevermore embodied.

As such, the High Priestess is connected with Adam, Eve and the serpent, Pandora and her box, and lastly the gods Rhea, Isis and of course, Venus (Aphrodite). The universal and common denominator of these female archetypes represents an involvement or struggle with evil (or evil forces) in order to begin the order of the world such as it factually exists. These figures become a rationale or disclaimer for the tragedy of life. however, in the process, they equally assume credit for the peaks of human existence, crowned by the emotion of love and the bearing of life itself.

In this, we understand why the figure is seated between the pillars of Solomon's temple and likewise possesses the sacred Torah which she solemnly holds in her lap. It is because only She whom we name the High Priestess, who has created the chasm in reality, who may hold and manifest the very rules necessary in order to return to spiritual wholeness.

This is our final clue concerning her symbolism in the unconscious of the dreamer. It involves the patience necessary to disassemble an object in order to learn its proper function as a reconstructed unit, intact and perhaps, interacting. Accordingly, the High Priestess may be the architect and engineer of our deepest psychic understanding of the world. She has single-handedly, in her symbolic appearance in the Tarot, set infinity into motion...

THE EMPRESS (3) (Tarot Major Arcana): The Empress in her feminine principle, seeks to join all states of being (divided by the High Priestess) in the stolid faith she holds in mature, natural and otherwise spiritual, love. In this sense, she champions Acceptance of reality, regardless of its multiple contradictions, and as such, hopes to bridge the separate facets of the world together in fluid harmony. She is a sovereign in this singular desire for social order and outright cohesion in the cycle of life.   Her Hebrew name is Daleth, which means door. A door joins isolated rooms of meaning and provides an interchange of ideas. In the deepest philosophical sense of this wisdom, all that is necessary is the absolute existence of both rooms. Herein, we also find her connection with mother nature and the living chain. It is her contention that when we account for the balance of complex elements of existence, these disparate levels of reality will find a way to coexist without complication. Hence the symbolic door is a passageway into separate worlds and an invitation from each respective side to the other.

We find in this card a desire to control the impassioned love of the High Priestess and then generate it into a common good. This moral and common denominator is understood as maternal love. The Empress cares for the miraculous child she has been allowed to carry, nourish and labor into physical birth. The mother, child and their mutual bond (for example, safety, warmth, affection etc.) represent the completion of her three-fold nature.

Exploring this trinity of worldly acceptance, we find associations with the three fates of ancient Greece: Clotho, Lachesis and Atropos, as well as the Hindu trinity: Brahma, Vishnu, Shiva, not forgetting ancient Egypt: Osiris, Isis, Horus, and of course, the Christian trinity of The Father, Son and Holy Spirit. In the physical, scientific sense, we may compare the three-fold completion with our worldly perception of past, present and future. In other words, the Empress creates and allows a space for an enigmatic reality within our capable abstract reasoning. For this act of genius, she is forever connected with the planet Saturn, as well as its cohorts: time and music, which connect reality and perception in the nonphysical realm of conscious logic.

In fact, since the Empress exists in perfect harmony with all the planetary spheres, she is linked with the twelve signs of the zodiac, which not surprisingly, appear as solar rays emanating from her matriarchal crown. Along these same lines, the figure vibrates to the color emerald green, which is representative of infinite (and therefore cyclical) life. Moreover, she is linked with the swan and the scorpion, both creatures noted for their acceptance of the variables of death. In this, she finds herself in continuous transcendence and transformation of life which is her sanctity and her reason for being. She will complete the chasm created in the master plan of the High Priestess, with her simple and straight forward worldly love. Naturally, her element is the combination of earth (the physical world of reality) and water (the emotional world of spirit), creating soil which nourishes the seed of life which she deems to flourish and strengthen absolutely.

Her three-fold strength, visualized in the triangle (pyramids, geodesic domes etc.) underpin her glorious balance of universal mind, body and spirit. Like Atlas, she supports the natural world of being in all its harsh complexity. She is a door and passage into perceptive awareness, providing a level, fertile ground for sober and entirely subtle, reasoning. She has embraced the world in its astounding and limitless measure, culminating the infinite love of the High Priestess herself, whom she cherishes and humbly follows in the eternal dance of the spiritual path.

In a dream, the Empress figure may imply an acceptance of a very difficult situation including pregnancy, or conversely, the passing of a loved one. The capability of collecting facts and reasoning a valid position is also suggested in the maternal and naturalistic world of the Empress who sits calmly in the seat of life in her long flowing robe of patience, tolerance and above all, the forbearance of absolute mercy.

THE EMPEROR (4) (Tarot Major Arcana): A suitable mate for the material grounding of the spiritual world embodied in the Empress is the Emperor, who provides order, stability and purpose in life. Here we find the beginning of law and self-discipline. The Emperor exists in the logic of mind, laying down its foundation upon the randomness of physical reality. As the Empress grounds the spiritual world, so the Emperor grounds the physical world. He accomplishes this by utilizing his old, wise and virtuous mind. In other words, he is the first physical completion of the Fool's quest for experience. Consequently, his knowledge is not necessarily instinctual, but rather learned over a lifetime, and as such guided in part by the spiritual acceptance of harsh existence, parallel to his mate, the Empress.

The Hebrew letter for this figure is Tzaddi, which means to lie in wait. The wisdom of age comes slowly, yet methodically. The jubilations and tragedies which define a life are indicated in this card when, and only when, their lessons are imprinted in our memory. In other words, when we have truly learned from their consequence, lessons about good, as well as, evil.

The mental rulership over the spiritual and material world can only be described as judgmental. Since only God may judge, the Emperor merely interprets the will of his God through the vehicle of his experiential knowledge. In this, we witness the beginning of social structuring. The Emperor must choose the limits

of choice in the free range of reality to provide the most beneficial good possible for all of his subjects. These limitations or
'cultural norms' become law and should be obeyed by all. In as
much, to disobey the law of the Emperor, is to defy both God
and man by refusing to accept the responsibilities of human interactive living. This is why the mineral associated with the
Emperor is found to be the crystal. Intact, the crystal is rare, precious and reflects equal light in all directions. However, when
the crystal is broken, shards of glass fragment reality and deceive
perception. We are left in an unbalanced kingdom with little direction and even less value. In order to retain our sense of
worth, we need to firmly establish our personal belief system
and stand by it as much as we possibly can. This increases the
sense of self and self-awareness through choices.

The color bonded with the Emperor is violet which symbolizes
royal splendor. The animal linked with this same imperial format is the peacock. To this end, we understand why the element
associated with this figure is Air. All encompassing, life-giving
air, demonstrates the free range and valor of the card proper.
The Emperor gazes his noble face and steadfast principles into
the multiple angles of the four cornered world. Akin to the
square, and number 4, the figure is fair and just and acknowl-
edges the rightful place of the four elements and four cardinal
points of the world. He has set the macrocosm into order and
within it, justified all human productivity and subsequent interaction. In short, he is recreating the catalyst of the Magician
on the physical plain of organized reality.

In the dream scenario, the Emperor figure describes the need for
brave decision and perhaps new directions in life. He symbolizes the world of logic and pure mind, as if to say, our emotions
have led us where we are, now we need an organized plan of action to lead us where we actually need to be. Furthermore, the
necessity of self-discipline in life, is squarely laid out before us in
the assurance of the emperor. We exist in a world of free
choices, exercise this right and crystallize who you are and
where you want to be in the natural scheme of things. The Emperor welcomes all into his splendor of logic, fairness and compassion.

THE HIEROPHANT (5) (Tarot Major Arcana): In many ways, the
Hierophant is the extension and in fact the completion, of the
Emperor. This is because the creation of physical laws which

pertain to faith and the spiritual life in general, fulfill the entire purpose of the Hierophant. In this, the figure logically and with personal and social authority, returns us into the purity of the Fool's world of absolute faith. We have completed the four corners of the physical world around us. Now we are able to return to a fifth point within the center of the square. This point is our soul or spiritual center. In this, we understand the representation of the pentagram and the number five in particular, as Mankind. Man is a product of the physical world, infused in spirit, 4+1=5.

The journey into high initiation, or the path of God, is indeed difficult and at times, self denying. We must surrender the material world in order to claim the spirit within that world. In this sense, the Hebrew letter for the Hierophant is Vau, which means 'nail.' We must nail or stop our forward progress on the physical plain in order to see, feel and know God, who is omnipresent and without direction. The purity of martyrdom is implied as well in the 'nail' translation, as many prophets, and more exclusively, the Christian God, Jesus Christ, were crucified with nails upon an upright and extremely symbolic, cross. In as much, we all have a cross to bare, a higher power to answer to, much higher than either the Emperor or the Hierophant, and that is the purity within ourself, our God understanding.

The sign which vibrates with this figure is Taurus and appropriately, the animal linked with the card is the bull. We find in this connection, a stubbornness of faith and will, a vision of charging ivory horns of purity which defy the obstacles of a physical world and penetrate instead the very mind and heart of animated human reasoning. In this, we have punctured the deep well of emotion and filtered its life-giving waters in preparation of a flowing baptism into God's unseen kingdom of universal love and innate perfection, the source of everything in existence, past, present and future.

The element associated with the Hierophant is Earth. This is logical in that it portrays a physical realm which should be transcended by the logical approach to spiritual and moreover, moral realizations. This wisdom reached by an awareness of absolute love and mercy dictates the tenets of the naturalistic world toward its ascending enlightenment. In fact, the number five is often depicted in occult texts of the ancient world as the foundation of light, and metaphorically, the light of knowledge.

Furthermore, the color orange/red of the hierophant is synonymous with the radiance and illumination of the heart. In this we find the passage, 'See with the heart and not thine eyes.'

In music, the fifth tone of the octave produces the initial stage of the next cycle and musicians worldwide learn early in their instruction to play and recognize the infamous circle of fifths. Continuing with the conceptualization of 5 as spiritual form, we examine the human hand whose five digits including an opposable thumb, virtually separate him from all other life forms.

However, man has been known to grasp the power given to him by spirit and utilize it for material gain. In this sense, we must challenge the veracity of organized religion, which may in some cases fall prey to the surrounding physical world which has brought it into being and utterly nourishes it. Observing this statement in its truest sense, we look to the Hierophant as spiritual guide and not vainglorious ruler of the pulpit. The temptation on this level of the royal path of the Tarot is perilous indeed. The message may indeed warn against the lust of power and greed.

In the dream sense therefore, we come in contact with a figure who takes the whole of man and the physical world and attempts to lead it forward (a rather dangerous task) into the enlightenment of God and spiritual faith. Hence we must ask ourselves, are we strong enough in our heart and in our mind (decisions) to follow this filtered path of love, charity and at times relentless self sacrifice? Conversely, are we using this martyrdom to gain support and a kind of perverse and reverse domination? Moreover, are we able to transcend the apparent contradiction of organized society and personal faith? In short, are we soulful within ourselves even in the sphere of a social and sometimes depersonalized world of sensations? The unwavering Hierophant re-establishes the deep faith of the Fool, whom in truth cannot fail, but in spite of himself, can lie (or be caught up in the deceptions of the Moon), and in so doing, return to mortality in an infinity of repetitions and eternal oversights.

THE LOVERS (6) (Tarot Major Arcana): In the journey of the Tarot, the initiate must come to terms with his or her own sexuality and the responsibility of intimate union with a partner who may represent a mate and the eventual source of family. Inherent in this understanding we witness the initial innocence and shame experienced in first attraction and the choices which inevitably develop around it. Furthermore, as the relationship grows, we find the struggle and jubilation of the mature loving commitment, replete with physical desire and spiritual adoration. In the extent that these principles are balanced we find a merging of two individuals into one higher realm which may provide the impetus for birth and the subsequent continuity of life. However, when any one figure of mind, body or spirit is not present, and or mutual, in the confederation of two people, hardships, deviations and misunderstandings may replace the true sanctity which is the ageless and timeless domain of Lovers.

The Hebrew letter for this figure is Zayin, which means sword. The prominent symbolism of this association refers to the double-edged nature of the sword itself. The Lovers, akin to a medieval saber, become one unit with two separate and unique sides which cut in two different directions. In this, we find a reference to the painful aspects of unrequited devotion or desire. Likewise, the sharp blade may heal and motivate.

In a very real sense, the figure itself depicts both physical and spiritual opposition. The division of male and female is most prominent in this plain of experience. In childhood and old age, the carnal feminine and masculine aspects of our being is less harsh and plays a smaller role in our direct interrelationships. The Lovers however, are attracted by their split and seek to explore the elaborate connection of their intense differences. On the spiritual side of this investigation, male aspects including logic and determination come into contact with feminine principles such as deep emotion and heightened sensitivity. Placing these aspects into a complex labyrinth of social union has been a focal point of human understanding since organized society began.

In this we see the struggle or double-edged sword inherent in the Lovers. Love may become a shameful battle ground when power and misdirected passion directly interferes with the natural alliance of the couple's masculine and feminine ideals. In this circumstance, we may find a constant wrestling of personal ideology which often may turn into bitter animosity and outright hatred if not properly diffused and given ample opportunity to heal and return to sanctity. In another very serious sense, we may find within the context of an unbalanced union, situations where lust or material gain utterly dominate altruistic caring and emotional commitment. In the complexity of these relationship out of kilter, we find painful pitfalls which are able to run the gamut from psychological abuse to infidelity, battering, even murder.

The other side of the double-edged sword demonstrates the love which most people prefer to think about. The affiliation of man and woman represents the chosen joining of spirit and consequent initiation of family. As such, the cycle of life, death and rebirth vibrate in complete harmony in the earthly sphere of this stage of human enlightenment. We witness the mental, spiritual and physical fulfillment of two separate and entirely unique individuals who celebrate in their wedding of Yin and Yang, the merging of humanity on the royal path of the Tarot.

The astrological influence of The Lovers is Gemini, the twins. The secret of the twins lies in their strength together. Apart and losing their cyclical cohesion, little is left but an utter imbalance demonstrated in evils such as distrust and deceit. This is why The Devil card (15) (1+5=6) displays a smaller version of the lovers chained below him, prisoners of his lustful and chaotic revelry. Due to the nature of the double-edged sword which allows an equal opportunity to elevate to spiritual oneness or drop into the pit of physical and psychological loathing, the element we find associated wit The Lovers is Air. We envision the sword as it slices through air on its way toward self sacrifice and purification or doubling back, cutting through human sanctity and destroying even the strongest hearts among us. In the modern jargon, we may utilize in the place of air, the conceptualization of time and space respectively to clarify this connection. Time is the abstract notion of mind, order and reason, in other words, male. Space on the other hand is physical, infinite and ever changing, in other words, female. However, one cannot be understood without the other and upon reflection it becomes clear that space and time are one in the same, via the perception of measurement and our relation to that measurement, the space/time continuum. In this we clearly see the riddle of The Lovers, opposites who are in fact inseparable, and hence complete the cycle of life in an incredible display of living potential.

In the dream sense, all of these tenets may need to be explored to unravel the complexity which is love and relationships. The dreamer needs to thoroughly reflect on the card itself and determine which aspects of the figure stand out foremost. On a superficial level, the cards appearance in the dream may reveal a need, want or desire to find a significant other to share in the revelation of ones individual contentment of being; perhaps to unravel it, beginning the next cycle of life and learning.

THE CHARIOT (7) (Tarot Major Arcana): The joining, and more importantly in this Arcana, control, of spirit and matter, brings great jubilation and potency to the initiate on the royal path of the Tarot. Accordingly, the individual on this path finds a goal and immediately and confidently moves forward in the conquest of the sometimes elaborate undertaking. In this, we visualize how The Chariot figure represents perseverance, determination and direction in particular, once we have completed the growth of our personal and social self. In other words, we now utilize the power we have been given, striving to bring this ability into action, mortal composites of The Magician who brings the spark into the potential world of The Fool.

However, we must avoid the temptation to lose ourself in the capacity of our labor. The loss of our spiritual center is at risk in the building edifice of our material ego. We witness this in the Arcana displayed in The Tower of Destruction (16) (1+6=7). The tower is hit by lightning signifying that man has built himself, and more significantly the belief in himself, too high and now must suffer the consequences of a displeased God or source spirit. We witness a crowned king and ordinary man both falling from the destroyed tower. This demonstrates the potential corruption of all men regardless of social standing and relative authority. The lesson to be learned therefore in The Chariot figure is a proper use of power. The charioteer harnesses a white and black sphinx and wears a vestige insignia of a triangle within a square. Both images represent the ideal goal of force, initially with the sphinx/steeds who are held together and work in unison rather than veering apart into chaos and secondly, the triangle, synonymous with spirit and maternal acceptance, firmly centered within the square, synonymous with an ordered and well planned physical universe. In short, the heart beating inside the sound body.

The Hebrew letter associated with The Chariot is Cheth which means fence. On first analysis, we may believe the fertile con-

ceptualization of 'bridge' may have been a wiser choice of symbolism in this arcana due to the presupposition of the charioteer
as bridging opposite states of being. However, this is not entirely, if in fact at all, the case. The charioteer harnesses his
steeds so that they cannot veer away from one another AS
WELL AS not crashing into each other. As such, he does not
merge, or 'bridge' opposing states of being, but rather allocates
their separation and dictates the unity of their meeting, in other
words, he builds a fence between plains of reality. In placing this
sound fence between spirit and matter, he is able to move
swiftly, efficiently and accurately atop its sturdy, well measured
posts. In as much, his direction and worthiness is insured by the
balance of reality itself.

The astrological sign associated with The Chariot is Cancer, the
crab. In this symbolism we witness the durable (masculine) shell
which is also turned within itself and brilliant in color, suggestive of femininity. Moreover, we find an amphibious creature
who is equally at home in the water, or dug deep within the
earth. In both cases a fluent and well controlled (not to mention
purposeful) balance of elemental reality is not only exhibited but
utilized. Moreover, the patience of the crab whispers another secret of this figure. The initiate on this path must be patient in
order to build his fence and properly plan his forward direction
and the worthiness of its relative goal.

The element linked with this arcana is Water. This is primarily
because water as a substance is able to exist in all three states of
matter being respectively, solid (ice), liquid (water) and gas
(steam). Moreover, water is able to easily pass from one state to
another via heat (fire) which connects it to the four elements
themselves: Fire, Air, Earth and of course, Water. Furthermore,
while water may easily transfer through each of these states of
matter, it remains separate and unique in each relative state. In
this, we find another reference to Cheth, the fence, which is the
prime character of The Chariot Arcana.

Placing all these tenets together, we see in the context of the
dream, the card assertively represents a desired goal and conquest which may be imminent in our experience. The card also
tells us to hold strong in our determination and jurisprudence
of the aspired purpose. Above all, the card is indicating that we
should not lose our sense of self and maintain an equal balance
of physical soundness and spiritual reverence in attaining the

truest worthiness of the goal itself. Lastly, the card straight out tells us our success is impending and guaranteed in our stead-fast and just integrity. In as much, we are the charioteer and our intent is fruitful to our overall experience. The time is here and now!

Strength (8) (Tarot Major Arcana) The Strength Arcana brings the initiate yet further down the path of self. It is at this point that the individual learns inner calm and quiet, the control of control per se, the transfiguration of force into inmost stillness. The tranquil female figure which serenely tames the lion on the Arcana depicts this celestial wisdom gathering our replete human drive into its folds. In as much, this path is the first lesson of the release of self, in that it demonstrates a deep faith and assurance in the perfection of being which prevails over our heated personal ambitions and passionate crusades.

The figure eight which sits halo-like atop the peaceful young girl in The Strength card depicts the infinity of creation and reality itself. It is to this end that finite human endeavors and goals in the physical world are in fact noble (seen as they are represented as the courageous and powerful lion), but ultimately limited, and NOT AT ALL, all-encompassing in the plain of absolute existence. They are instead reflections, or manifestations, of the omnipotence of God and the spiritual truth thereof; the unseen yet undeniable undercurrent of everything perceived in the real world. This is primarily why silence is associated with wisdom, permitting as it does, in an almost abstract and entirely ethereal, inner stillness, the sensing of the world within and the world without. Silence brings the perception of the world and the innate knowledge of the higher realm closer to hand. This wisdom is not developed in a series of hard calculations, but rather, felt and understood, in an otherworldly comprehension void of any and all earthly language.

The Hebrew letter for The Strength Arcana is Teth which means snake. The biblical association of the snake in the tree of knowledge is a rather elaborate labyrinth of symbolism involving as it does, the fall of man implicit in gaining material knowledge. However, the fascinating two-fold meaning of this archetypal image involves the return path, the return to grace. As it is necessary for the tree and the snake to be close to God, for they exist as prime archetypes in the garden of Eden, relatively speaking, we find their presence inevitable in the return to His celestial plain. Herein, we find the symbolism of Teth. The tree, which is silent and therefore wise (wisdom, as well as knowledge), carries the serpent which depicts force and sexual awareness. In the royal path of the Tarot, the initiate learns to traverse both paths of sexuality and force in the forms of The Lovers and The Chariot, respectively. In other words, overcoming the downfall of the serpent's desire for lust and blind ambition in man, replaced by love and honest perseverance in the path of The Lovers (6) and The Chariot (7). Moreover, in the sense of numerology, 6+7=13, which in turn vibrates with The Death (13) card has extreme significance. This arcana maintains a presence which we fully realize is necessary in our natural development. We must feel confident in the transfiguration of death, the ability to transcend our physical and material conquests in favor of a mortal redemption into simple, yet absolute faith. In this well ordained passage, we are allowed to finally approach the Tree of knowledge once more. We have returned to the Garden of Eden. However, in this cycle we are equipped with the certain realization which involves the unconditional surrender of our knowledge to the higher, celestial realm of wisdom found in the calm stillness of spiritual faith, accordingly, we are able to return to God and the source of reality, intact once more. We have withstood the test of our own empowerment upon the earthly plain of reality and its elaborate temptations. Conclusively, we are allowed to focus and master the purpose of our existence once more and justify the validity of our being.

In the dream sense, we approach a dramatic cessation of our physical force in this figure. Accordingly, the unconscious reminds us to reflect on the higher purpose behind our passionate and otherwise ambitious drives. Calm meditation upon the overall social and communal merit of our personal achievement may transcend an initial vainglorious gratification of individual megalomania. Stated another way, if we believe our physical accomplishments separate us from ordinary men and women and deem us god-like; we certainly will be in for a rude awakening when we inevitably fail in the natural imperfection of our quite mortal human nature.

On the contrary, if we gain wisdom from our serenity, we will comprehend humility and the frailness of our being. Doing so, we will find the real strength in silent stillness and work in earnest toward the purity and craftsmanship of the spiritual (or God's) plan, also known in terms of Plato as the Ideal Form of all being.

In this, we realize the master design, blueprint and purpose provides for all life forms with a balance of equality and innate perfection which can never flourish in the isolated vacuum of an individual's material separateness and fearful selfishness.

THE HERMIT (9) (Tarot major Arcana) The Hermit arcana continues and completes the journey into pure spirit which is begun in the path of the Strength arcana. The deepest form of meditation depicted in this card reflects the complete removal of our physical self in place of humble spiritual awareness and the selfless prostrations involved in the ego-defying endeavor. In as much, The Hermit, as man, is bent before his God and relies only upon his staff for support and antique lantern for real and purposeful guidance. The upright staff is symbolic of righteous faith and the will necessary to link the straight and narrow line between heaven and earth. The staff remains continuous and direct, even when the mortal body bends and falters. Further in the representation of this figure, we find the lantern which displays the spiritual light of truth which shines a brilliant path blazing through the darkness of ignorance. Unfortunately, the lantern also throws shadows upon our remaining worldly and physical reality. These delusions must be ignored by The Hermit in his unswerving and forward destiny into the purity of truth.

Accordingly, the Hebrew letter for The Hermit is Yod, which loosely translates to foundation and 'firm' truth. In this, we find the completing aspect of this figure in the royal path of the initiate in the Tarot labyrinth. In fact, the last numeral, number nine, fundamentally linked to this arcana and path, represents the stability and finality of the three triangles and the subsequent realization of the necessity of death in order to return into the soul of God and being. In other examples of this numerals significance, we find the Eleusinian Mysteries which involved nine spheres, through which the consciousness of the initiate needed to pass, prior to becoming born again. Similarly, we pass through nine months (moons) of gestation in the womb of our mother before we are born and otherwise allegorically delivered into the physical world. Moreover, in the strict mathematical sense, we see how the numeral 9, when multiplied by any number becomes 9 once again. Some examples: 9x3=27 in turn 2+7=9, 9x6=54 in turn 5+4=9, 9x38=342 in turn 3+4+2=9 etc. Furthermore, any number when added with the numeral 9, becomes itself once again. Some examples: 9+4=13 in turn 1+3=4, 9+138=147 in turn 1+3+8=12 and 1+4+7=12, 9+6=15 in turn 1+5=6 etc. In this mathematical exposure, we find the fixed and conclusive reality which is the number 9.

Accordingly, the spiritual transfiguration of The Hermit brings with it the conceptual power over our fear of death and death itself, in the intrinsic sense. This empowerment over mortal trepidation prepares the initiate for the necessity of isolation from the outside world. As such, the journey in the Tarot at this point becomes one of total solitude, the symbiotic return to the purity of new born innocence. In this pristine state of native consciousness, unclouded by personal and social preconceptions, we are able to fully meditate on the oneness, completeness and truth of being, and, our inexorable role within its divine drama. Furthermore, we see in this figure the predisposition toward a personal relationship with God, faith and salvation for the initiate, rather than the form of enlightenment found in organized religions chock full of rituals and agreed upon ethical standards. The ancient theological argument examining the whereabouts of the true house of God, whether in the human heart, or human place of worship (church, temple etc.), is approached in this high spiritual arcana. The Hermit recognizes God as absolute within and without and finds his deity not merely within himself, but beyond himself. As such, the residence of God has no physical location, instead, the source of God becomes the invisible, underlying principle which animates the whole of the physical world. In the platonic point of view, this unseen life source is known as the Ideal Form. Curious, yet logically sound, this idea of God as perfection dates back to the earliest and most primitive cultures known to civilization. Perfection exists in a very real sense on a perceptual plane, but cannot be achieved in the material and imperfect world.

Naturally, the astrological sign which vibrates with The Hermit is Virgo, the virgin. Hence, only in our purest state of acceptance can we comprehend the absolute resolution of death. Only in the innocence of our birth, can we enter deaths finality and transcend its plain into the Ideal Form of the eternal.

The element associated with this figure is Earth. In this, we find a very crucial point about this path in the Tarot journey, which certainly was not lost on the ancients. Only on the earthly plain of existence can the initiate begin his consummate and unequivocal transformation into the spirit world. This rite of passage is common in the primitive world and reflected in young warriors who are sent out into the natural world to brave the elements to learn their potential and ultimate faith in themselves and creation and the elaborate connection thereof. In these ornate and at times bloody, survivalist functions known as Vision Quests, the young warrior witnesses the heaven and hell of existence which dynamically changes their characters forevermore, eventually to become the communal wisdom which permeates the mind of a people through successive generations. Hence, in traversing the entire cycle of matter to spirit to matter once more, can transfiguration be ultimately achieved. In this we find a precursor to the next full cycle of the Tarot path, beginning appropriately with The Wheel of Fortune which signals the need for acceptance of both heaven, as well as, hell.

Taking all this into account, what we experience in the dream appearance of The Hermit may concern our ability to sink into the deepest part of ourselves through meditation, and in so doing, leave the material world behind. As such, we may be reminding ourselves about the things which are most important in life, things like love and absolute faith in the self and spirituality. Furthermore, we may be signaling that we are too involved with the every day trappings of the physical world and losing sight of who we really are as an individual. Hence, the arcana demonstrates how we need to stand back and become isolated and self-sufficient once more; secluded enough in fact, to lose our artificial sense of personal grandeur and return into the wholeness of being; becoming once more finite matter animated by infinite spirit. In this, we illustrate the socialization of the individual and the individuation of society; one person, one people, one spirit. One reality expressed in an infinity of multifarious faces.

THE WHEEL OF FORTUNE (10) (Tarot major Arcana) The next cycle of the major arcana begins with The Wheel of Fortune and a return to earth, replete with the wisdom of its divine and inherent completion. We visualize in this arcana, a wheel of physical, mental and emotional ups and downs centered by a spiritual axis which is entirely neutral concerning the position of the wheel itself. In other words, the Wheel of Fortune demonstrates how today's hardships will be replaced by tomorrow's triumphs (and vice-versa) and there is no control over this random selection whatsoever. The lesson is we must and in fact, can only, endure the present and remain as spiritually centered and faithful of life's innate order (axis), as we possibly can.

Let us delve into the symbolism of the axis. This concept of the axis and upon further meditation, the unifying principle of matter, holds true in living biology, planets and entire universes. We observe in material reality both a cohesive adherence to a structured organization and a helical rotation which creates a circuit from negative to positive and back to negative once more. This binary loop allows for elaborate patterns of information which interweave in their complexity and relative codependence. Nevertheless, this enigmatic double-polar source remains unseen in its overall organization. We are left only with the operating physical manifestations of this pulse-creating blueprint. From brains to blood to radios to satellites to star clusters to movable joints to tires, arch-ceiling, audio equipment and every day, ordinary alarm clocks, we depend on the end result of the unifying principle, or universal scheme. In as much, we witness in the enactment of our physical reality the behind-the-scenes foundation of an infinite God. To this end, we experience the underlying divinity behind all things, high, low, good and bad. This is what is meant by the antique phrase 'God works in mysterious ways.' Likewise, the strength of faith is tested in the harshest of times, not in joyous days when worship and thankfulness come easy. The biblical story of Job relates this lesson and is paraphrased in reverse by Jesus Christ in the new testament in the quote, 'What gaineth a man who inherits the world, but loseth his soul?' Conversely, Job in the old testament loses his entire world of family and possessions, but maintains his faith in God in direct resistance to Satan, or the dark side of the wheel.

The pointed symbolism in these narratives elucidate the necessity of both good and bad fortune. The path of the initiate in the Tarot maze is fortified explicitly with obstacles which need to be overcome before transfigurations allow the ultimate return to pure spirit. Hence, the movement of the wheel is synonymous with life and the continuous nature of an enigmatic future. Accordingly, to transgress and transcend each successive stopping point and resting place of The Wheel of Fortune as it occurs, brings the initiate that much closer to the cyclical uniformity of the consolidated center, the axis mundi of all creation.

This rather abstract conceptualization of the physical world spinning indeterminately around an unchanging and central spirit, may be difficult to assimilate in every day life. However, the key to this elaborate figure's symbolism absolutely relies on the initiates understanding of the wheel's relation to himself and the people who surround him in the material world. Hence, where the initiate finds anger, jealousy, hatred in his own heart and the hearts of others, he must remain strong in the faith that God continues manifest beyond the immediate reality of all physical weakness. Likewise, where the initiate finds joy, pleasure and contentment, God is here too, as always, the unmistakable spring. As such, the student gains the wisdom that all actions, all behavior and all movement, each step and each breath, animate the spiritual center within us all. In as much, each gesture we make and every word and deed we express, becomes a prayer to the infinite source of creation. In addition, we perceive this thinly disguised divinity in the people who share the earthly plain with us and accordingly, we gain the realization that we are blessed in their presence, regardless of their mortal standing and behavior. In our humanity, we may feel offended, antagonized, hurt and conversely, jubilate, flattered and otherwise intoxicated, by the actions of these our fellow men and women. However, The Wheel of Fortune reminds us to weather ALL social storms, good or bad and look far within the ornate shell of our mankind and find the heart beat of life there, which quite effortlessly ignores the emotional gradations of color which displays the material world in its brightest and darkest hues. In other words, when we allow for God's (Ain Soph Aur) ongoing creation in the acceptance of our own heart, we begin to move closer to that God who exists simultaneously in past, present and future. In this understanding, we begin to feel the presence of our own eternal soul, as we walk, talk, eat and sleep with the infinite reality of the divinity each moment of every single day of our entire life span and in faith, beyond.

The Hebrew letter for this figure is Kaph, which means palm of the hand. Palmistry, once called Chiromancy, is the oldest form of divination and long predates written history. In ancient Persia, the palm was believed to hold an individuals relation to the stars, planets and other mystical spheres. The future was preordained in the intricate lines, curves and shape of the hand itself. In Asia, Zen masters practice the shaping and proper aligning of the contours of the hand of the initiate as he or she gains inner wisdom. In yet another example, the ancient Chinese healing art of acupuncture recognizes the palms relation to internal organs. In this, we witness the ancient and ongoing belief of an individual's outlined self and fate, laid bare in the palm of their hand.

How we use these hands to fulfill our respective destiny reflects our awareness of self. Accordingly, we see how our physical manipulations, the Latin 'mano' meaning hand, shape our continuous opportunity to return to spirit and enlightenment. Furthermore, in our steady grasp, we stay the course of our existence and internalize its progressive lessons. To deviate from our preordained (innate) wisdom and ability and otherwise lose our 'hold' upon the world around us, may well spell disaster for our individual destiny. The phrases, 'He is not himself', or 'She isn't her usual self." are based upon this duplicity of being. Free will allows for this dislocated journey away from ones natural path of existence. In this wayward semblance of reality, the initiate loses the balance of his or her acquired experiences and becomes drawn toward an excessive behavior. This unbalanced scenario may involve sickness, drug abuse, mental neurosis and a host of other mutilations of self. Painfully, the firm grip of a steady, well-adapted individual, becomes the shaky, numb and ravaged hand of a person in dire need of help. Nevertheless, in many cases, this hand may be clasped by an outside influence or force and returned to its former passage. That is, if the initiate, utilizing free will, regains inner realization and is able to rationalize him or herself once more. As such, the student allows him or herself another chance to vibrate in perfect balance and harmony with his or her own natural destiny. He or she has returned to the world.

We observe in this symbolic formulation, The Wheel of Fortune operating in its full complexity within the reasonable compass and hold of each human being. Additionally, we are rewarded for this insight of our unique destiny and its dynamic fit within the universal scheme of things. We are blessed with a perception of the world and a place within its confines. The Wheel of Fortune elaborates upon this primary knowledge, necessary before the initiate can transcend into final spiritual wisdom.

Additionally within this figure, we find the Sphinx depicted, a figure who represents the ambiguous riddle of universal existence. The Wheel of Fortune reveals the paradoxical nature of this ultimate question which can have no direct and concrete answer, other than the cyclical and lasting path of experience and insight. In other words, the Wheel and the Sphinx are one in the same, the experience of life. This is why the Sphinx promises death to the seeker who answers its final and paramount riddle incorrectly. Put simply, to live unaware of Earth and God, is to have no connection with creation at all, and that is a tragedy, beyond compare. In as much, the Sphinx is merely a metaphor for human realization, in and of itself.

In this sense, the element which vibrates with The Wheel of Fortune can only be Air. The character of air is light, omnipresent and clear as mind and reason itself. As we have seen, the capacity to understand the world and its complex foundation is at the heart of this all-encompassing arcana. This point of the Tarot path is like the wheel itself, the beginning and end of The Fool's world labyrinth discovered and then transcended, only to disappear once more.

There is no coincidence that this Wheel of Fortune appears where it does in the path of the major arcana. The ancient Greeks and Hebrews both believed in the absolute divinity of the numeral 10, which explicitly vibrates in this representational figure. The Tree of Life in the Cabalistic faith, reveal the ten emanations of the Ain Soph Aur (God). In addition, the beginning of man's journey into God Consciousness is found in the infinite, cyclical conformity of the metric constant which is the numeral 10. Finally, the ancient Greek philosopher Pythagoras, who believed in the mystical divinity of numbers, instructed his pupils about the significance of the first four numbers, which when added together in succession, could only form the perfection of being; that is, the number 10. $1+2+3+4=10$. The first four numbers represent the four elements and the four corners of ordered reality. In this, the numeral 10 becomes the underlying principle of the physical world, the axis and eternal foundation of being.

All in all, The Wheel of Fortune has illustrated from antiquity, reality, both inside and out, seen and unseen, beyond any form of language and all five senses. In this path the initiate rings in tune with The Magician and his or her own inner magic, aware of the flash and spark of life becoming. It is at this point that the wholly ordered Magician (1) and the chaotic Fool (0) join forces and become one, the alpha and the omega. This is the enlightenment of darkness and wisdom of the unknowable. Upon the wheel itself is the word Taro, or Rota, which is the revelation of Heaven, Earth and Man; the unchanging foundation within the ever-changing eternal creation.

When this card appears in our dream, we must be prepared to look beyond the physical reality which we directly perceive before us in our lives. We may need to gain an awareness that behind our good and bad experiences is a constant source of divinity and personal destiny which wholly transcends our present emotions and immediate reactions. Furthermore, we are reminded that this spiritual truth is reflected and manifest not only in our deepest, isolated meditations, but also in the outside, every day world in every situation at hand, and justifiably, we must act in accordance to that full realization of an entirely consequential existence.

JUSTICE (11) (Tarot Major Arcana) As stated in The Wheel of Fortune delineation, life out of kilter, without balance and purpose, is detrimental to the initiate on the path of spiritual truth. In the Justice figure of the Tarot, we learn to balance the scales of our paradoxical physical spectrum. In as much, we must determine a suitable equilibrium for our diverse human natures. These include: individuality and socialization, concern with the spiritual world as well as the secular world, anger and forgiveness, love and lust, greed and martyrdom and finally, perseverance and obsession. Naturally, we find an implicit connection within these opposite states of being in that they are attached by the same experience of existence. Formally, they exist as two sides of the same coin, separated only by the decision making process of free will. In other words, the initiate is given the opportunity to make of, and take from, the experience, whatever he or she chooses. However, there is a definitive and unavoidable balance in nature, explored in The Wheel of Fortune, which must be recognized. Hence, if the initiate chooses obsessive, unbalanced pursuits, he or she must be prepared to pay the price of the harsh and extreme return to natural equilibrium. This is why the wise king pictured on the Justice card holds a sharp and threatening sword aloft, to remind The Fool, or initiate, of the inherent danger found in the foolish enactment of unbalanced deeds.

However, in the simultaneous awareness of diversely opposed

behavioral attitudes, otherwise known as well-rounded wisdom, we find a dynamic canceling out (at least on the conceptual level) of extreme and single sided prejudices. Therefore, even when we find ourselves in a predicament, where we may have become momentarily lost in the excesses of an emotional outpouring, we still maintain the perceptive ability to find the other side, or alternative, involved in the full scope of the particular situation and reasonably, justify a return into healthy emotional equilibrium, given time and patience. For example, if a man decides to work two jobs in order to provide a healthy income for his family to fulfill all their economic needs (and desires), first he must consider the effect of his consequent absence in the day to day dynamic of the family's social unity. In order to accomplish this, he must examine in great detail the pros and cons of his real time spent within the family. In this, he may eventually come to realize that what is lost in the togetherness of family, cannot possibly be compensated financially. This is merely an example and may not hold true in many real circumstances. The point is, however, found in the wisdom of examining fully the opposite alternative of our contemplated decision. In this observation of both realities, an internal compromise may be reached which satisfies both fronts. In the prior example, the man may decide to work several hours more each week or each day to provide extra income, yet still remain in the presence and union of a loving family.

The scales therefore, are a mental construct and operate prior to the visible choices made in life. In this sense, we understand why the element which vibrates in this particular path is Air. Air is synonymous with mind and reason. Justice is the concrete materialization of reason in its highest human sense. In fact, in the legal terminology, being of 'sound mind', refers to ones ability to justify ones actions and behave in a just and reasonable manner in society. In other words, the mind is itself, balance. In this logic, we fully understand the advice to stop and think, before acting. We are infusing reason into our emotional instincts, and consequently widening the viewpoint of our overall situation. Accordingly, we begin to see the entire projection of the potential of our behavior and can deliberate upon the consequence of our reactions.

Herein, we discern the connection of age, wisdom and justice. The data base of experience gained in ones life assists in the process of visualizing possible outcomes. Therefore, an older individual enjoys a greater understanding of reality's multiple faces. The elders mental framework is a veritable storehouse of memories taken directly from the context of life. In this, he or she is less likely to repeat mistakes, and conversely, more likely to engage in reasonable endeavors.

The royal path of the Tarot is well aware of this connection of age, wisdom and justice. Appropriately, the Justice (11) arcana is a combination of The Emperor (4) and The Chariot (7), which represent respectively, order and forward movement. In short, we witness what amounts to a keen insight into potential and the ensuing confidence to proceed in an irrefutable direction, undaunted. Conclusively, we learn to fully utilize the gift of an experienced mind in our elaborate choice of movements throughout life's labyrinth. Moreover, in this wisdom, we seek to obtain the fairness and equilibrium natural to creation and hence, select and support the options we honestly deem necessary, for a healthy and relatively complete existence.

The Hebrew letter for the Justice arcana is Lamed, which means ox goad. In this symbolism, we re-establish the sound and productive groundwork for life, found in carrying a steady mortal load (rational and material choices). If the goad is unbalanced, the ox will lose its ability to perform work (achievement) and in all likelihood, may injure itself. As we have seen, this depiction holds true for the initiate as well. (*see* Wheel of Fortune)

We have noted a variety of associations in this figure with the natural world. Nature in inseparable from the concepts of balance and parity in the world environment proper. The relative food chain is supportive of each group of predator species which subsists upon an equal and available supply of prey species. These prey species, conversely, depend upon the availability of insects, flora and vegetation respectively. These distinct living creatures, in turn, rely on microbes and favorable weather conditions. In each case, a delicate equilibrium of need and subsistence must be maintained. If any of these consistent variables change, the effected breed of living creature must adapt to the occurrence and find a new method, or balance, of survival. History has demonstrated how nature was, and still is, unjust for certain species who were unable to cope with sudden changes in their environment and subsequently, became extinct. Dinosaurs and Wooly mammoths are two examples of once dominant creatures which were entirely unable to alter their lifestyles enough to withstand the sweeping environmental changes which caused their ultimate demise. In this, we see how Justice is relative and sometimes extremely harsh. Likewise, the real life decisions we may be forced to make in life, can be inhumanely rigid. For example, murder is by and large (with the exception of fanatical groups) unacceptable to all cultures, however, the concept of 'kill or be killed', when we are attacked by some unreasonable and violent force, is called self-defense and found to be entirely acceptable behavior in the justice system of the United States and many other countries. Wisdom helps us discern necessary actions in life, such as the previous example, sometimes known as fight or flight.

Notwithstanding the United States legal system and universal philosophies on ethical standards, the Tarot demonstrates that final judgment is reserved for a higher power than ourselves and our social mechanisms. This is why Justice, as a concept and faith, is understood as the principle of learning. It is the method we utilize PRIOR to making decisions and ultimately, taking real action.

The appearance of the Justice card in a dream may simply be a warning to be cautious in the approach of an upcoming decision. Yet, on another level, our unconscious may be reminding us about our next stage of maturity and the necessary development of a sound, well-rounded and open-eyed wisdom. This may occur at a certain point in our life, when our judgment and decision making may have a new and powerful effect upon our overall social structure. For example, when we leave school and enter the work force, or when we bring a child into the world, or perhaps, when we become a political leader or conversely, a head CEO in an international conglomerate. Regardless, when wisdom is needed, Justice is paramount in our perceptive organization. We must learn to trust ourselves in judgment, without looking back. Prudence is built upon our ongoing and broadening experiences, for better or worse, richer or poorer, till' death do us part. Albeit, before we can get to this Death (13), we need to examine the next arcana on the path, and that is, The Hanged Man (12).

THE HANGED MAN (12) (Tarot Major Arcana) There are times when ones wisdom and worldly experience offer no solution for difficult questions and predicaments encountered in life. Nevertheless, decisions need to be made in the continuation of life and forward progression. It is to this end that the initiate encounters the path of The Hanged Man who dangles from a crucifix-like tree, suspended by one leg. This is the passage into the surrender of faith. Hanging perilously from the material world, the initiate places all his trust in the higher power of God (Ain Soph Aur) and the spiritual plain. His fear of falling is overcome by the physical sacrifice he offers to the wisdom of creation, reiterated in the symbolism of the tree of knowledge/wisdom/life, from which he hangs. As such, The Hanged Man is precariously fastened between two worlds to find guidance in the trying mortal decision he now faces. In many ways, this path echoes The Fool's prayerful step into the great unknown, pictured in the (0) major arcana. It represents the plummeting descent into absolute faith in the universal blueprint, falling into the hands of God, per se.

However, The Hanged Man is not as pure as The Fool and must rely on his steadfast trust and belief in creation, in the humble wish that God may return wisdom into his operating world of experience. As such, The Fool seeks all experience and conversely, The Hanged Man aspires for momentary and specific guidance. God helps those who help themselves, (see Justice) however, we find in this path an inability to help ourselves any longer, through reason alone, and instead we must surrender to the eternal wisdom of the primal creator.

The image put forth in this arcana, of faithfully dangling over the unknown, is highly representative of immersing oneself into the unconscious. In this sense, we conceptualize falling into a deep sleep and sinking into the surreal abyss of our symbolic and otherworldly dream consciousness. Moreover, as we have witnessed repeatedly, ancient cultures around the world have associated this procedure of dreaming with their particular deity and His or Her respective message to a waiting humanity. In this, we evoke Carl Gustav Jung's idea of The Collective Unconscious which links all life forms, transcends linear time, in an eternal past, present and future and nonchalantly accommodates within its framework, all worldly knowledge. At this point, we ask ourselves, where does the collective unconscious end, and God (Ain Soph Aur) consciousness, begin? Are they one in the same? The Hanged Man figure, though silent, seems to answer in the affirmative. As such, he is unremittingly associated with dreams, his own and those of the Tarot initiate. Accordingly, The Hanged Man must leave his waking body behind in the corpse-like state of sleeping and approach the higher wisdom of his eternal self, which is also his absolute trust in creation. Like Native American Shaman, he embarks on a journey, otherwise known as a Vision Quest, where his body remains earthbound, while his mind, heart and soul enter the immortal realm of spirit. In this spiritual world, everything heard, felt and seen is understood in terms of eternal, archetypal symbolism. Hence, a spirit familiar, or guide, may appear as a hawk, donkey, waterfall or spider, depending on the enlightenment sought after and received by the Shaman. In as much, the physical reality of the guide in the waking world of consciousness is meaningless, only the characteristics and behavior of that representational form can be analyzed. As such, a bald eagle is more than just a majestic bird, it is the far-seeing vision of wisdom and the very image of tranquil spiritual peace. Its white head signals purity and purpose as it circles, high above the world of mankind's follies. Moreover, it flies alone, in the replete confidence of self in a trance-like and utterly timeless, devotion to its creator. In parallel fashion, this visionary symbolism pertains to our own unconscious and its dynamic language of dreams. The Hanged Man seeks answers in his spiritual dream world, a world, or plain, which is perfectly removed and apart from himself and all his respective manipulations.

This linguistic point needs to be examined in closer detail. It discloses the fundamental difference between what is known as 'The Subconscious' as opposed to the concept which we have been discussing in the course of this book, which is called 'The Unconscious' The term 'subconscious' refers to our deepest seated actual memories, remembered experiences which may have been repressed, or perhaps remain suppressed, yet nevertheless, continue to exist as a part of our physical selves. They are alive in the banks of our memory and in theory and in practice, we are able to recapture, or 'recall', these bits of information, by way of hypnotism or psychoanalysis proper. Once these buried memories are retrieved, a process known to psychologists as 'breakthroughs', the individual is given a chance to face the reality once more and having done so successfully, may begin to overcome the effects of those traumatic experiences. In a very real sense, the memories no longer seethe at the edge of consciousness, but rather are thrown into the full light of reason and mature individuation, which more often than not, quells their once profound effect. This is what is called the subconscious. However, The Unconscious, and moreover, The Collective Unconscious, as we shall see, is quite another matter. The root word 'sub', as in 'subconscious', means 'under.' In other words, the subconscious is 'under', or below, our ordinary consciousness. Conversely, the root word 'un', as in 'unconscious', means 'not.' Which is why when somebody is knocked out cold, we say they are unconscious, or 'not' conscious. The psychological terminology for 'The Unconscious' operates on this same linguistic tenet, only in far more complex manner of perception. The Unconscious is an allegorical plain which exists beyond our own unique and personal plain of experience. It is a concept beyond our trace memories and ongoing consciousness. In this sense, we cannot capture our dream world, we can merely learn from its highly stylized revelations. This unconscious exists apart from us, in a timeless plain of being. In our dreams and deepest meditations, we are allowed to momentarily cross the threshold into this visionary land as a perceptual observer, but never as an inhabitant. In every way, we must return to consciousness, of which this reality is 'not' a part. The cosmic scheme of life grants us the temporary and fleeting permission to move beyond our visible world and tap into this eternal realm of wisdom. God-like as it may sound, this is what we consider the unconscious and more precisely, The Collective Unconscious.

In dream symbolism, the predominant representation of the unconscious revolves around images of mighty oceans, because of their immeasurable depth, ongoing, enigmatic mystery and overwhelming force. Moreover, an ocean can carry us in its wake and current and is in its very presence, the outline of our emotional revelry. Additionally, we may sink into its depths in order to re-engage our primordial past. In this, we return to the primal pools of our ancestral strains of DNA/RNA protein complexes, when we were a part of the massive living swirl (or what they call, soup) of the new and miraculous molecular structuring of a living world biology; the scientist's Garden of Eden. The journey from sperm cell to ovum, which merge into blastula, zygote and eventually, fetus, does so in a liquid environment, not altogether unlike, those protein and vitamin rich pools of earliest creation. In fact, the fetus, in its nine month gestation, moves through various bodily stages of aquatic capability, otherwise known as evolutionary memory, including the appearance of a tail, gills and fins. Naturally, these appendages morph into arms and legs etc., but the ancestral process is not lost. Consequently, only when the baby is delivered, fully formed, into our oxygen breathing present adaptation, can it surrender its sack of amniotic fluid in which it survived and gained nourishment. In the Soviet Union, infants are delivered from the womb into an environment of warm water to lessen the trauma of this birth into a world of direct light and air. However, regardless of technique, the new born child must eventually emerge into his entirely novel world. In so many ways, this baby's first breath, is the harsh, revelatory entry into real and complete waking consciousness. Little wonder the poor little thing screams for dear life!

In another symbolic link, we examine the ritual of Baptism, where a child is submerged into holy water by a priest or minister in order to purify his mortal soul. In essence, the individual has returned to the innocence of his maker and creation itself. Once baptized, this child can live in peace, anointed into the immaculate spirit of God. In fact, he or she is now considered to be a true child of God. In other words, one of His own.

In all cases, this symbolism was not lost on the ancients and accordingly, the Hebrew letter for the path of The Hanged Man is Mem, which naturally means water. In as much, the figure searches for spiritual rebirth in the baptismal waters of the eternal creation. He needs to purify himself by removing his awareness from the physical world. He does this through self sacrifice and the deepest faith he can fathom, leaving behind in the process, the society of man and their inevitable public opinion. Once he has left behind this consciousness, he may or may not be allowed a glimpse into the Unconscious. If he is allowed entry in this symbolic world of visions, whose wisdom is eternal and archetypal, he must remember it as best as he can and transcend its message into his own conscious world of experience. God has given back to him his own birth and innate knowledge. Accomplishing this great, sacrificial, and humbling task, notwithstanding his position, upside down and hanging from a tree, he has in spite of himself, begun anew. This is why the figure is pictured with a halo shining brightly around his head and facade. The Hanged Man has found enlightenment.

In order to fully contemplate the dream interpretation of this figure, we must first turn to its connection with The Empress (3) Arcana. The Hanged Man (1+2)= The Empress (3). The feminine aspects of acceptance and maternal sacrifice, natural to this path of the Tarot, demonstrate the humility necessary to surrender ones built-in human egoism. In other words, there are times when we need to submit to powers greater than ourselves. To this end, we need to admit our own ignorance and intolerance and ask for guidance in certain predicaments which appear in our life. This is not to say, that we should surrender our individual wisdom to societal pressures and opinions placed upon us. In fact, The Hanged Man demonstrates quite the opposite. His arcane presence reveals the imperfect consciousness found in the whole world of man. He in turn, surrenders this limited wisdom of man, to the eternal promise of God and the Unconscious. He invites us into a vision quest of our deepest reality, which is far beyond the zenith of our human awareness and comprehension, in order to find wisdom far removed and otherwise unattainable by the self. In so doing, he challenges us with a smile to keep a faithful bridge between our own wisdom and the erudition of the entire folds of an immeasurable creation.

DEATH (13) (Tarot Major Arcana) There is no thing in the physical world which begins from nothing. New life can only spring forth from the death and gradual dissolution of some other entity. In physics we learn that matter can neither be created nor destroyed; it can however, be changed into another state of being. In all these examples, we witness the inseparable reality of life and death. Without the definitive and concrete end of singular experiences and physical structuring in total, otherwise known as extinction, we could not possibly progress forward into new life and fresh creation. In other words, death stands for the full readiness of change into new existence. As such, we rather dramatically learn in this arcana, to surrender fear of loss and ultimately termination. Consequently, as we witness ideologies and physical realities dissolving before us, we must accept their disappearance and boldly prepare ourselves for new and unique beginnings. Therefore, the Death (13) card should not be faced with trepidation, but rather welcomed into our field of experience with open-eyed respect and tolerance. We are given the opportunity to change and therefore, conclusively grow as individuals and human beings.

In the spiritual sense of the Tarot wisdom, we comprehend this path as an invitation into the divine scheme of existence. It demonstrates the necessity of our eventual passing from life on earth. In examples of this austere truth, taken from the real world of human tradition, we look to the recorded accounts of

Near-Death Experiences. These descriptive accounts have been told all through chronicled history by individuals whose biological functions and heartbeat had ceased and whom were subsequently pronounced dead by medical professionals. In these detailed narratives of post-dying experiences, we find a similarity in retained perceptive images including glowing white, angelic figures, many of whom are deceased loved ones, who welcome the newly departed into the next plain of existence. These depictions of the afterlife encompass feelings of warmth and overall well-being. In most cases, initial fear is transformed into ecstatic emotional revelry and a feeling of humble thankfulness. There are audible references to drumming and clapping, sometimes ethereal singing and chanting which quicken the departure of the soul from the enclosure of the physical body, reminiscent of aboriginal shaman who create trance-like beats to enter spiritual vision quests in search of communal wisdom and transcendent enlightenment. Moreover, these Near-Death Experiences perpetually relate a transfigurative image of an otherworldly sensitive and serenely agreeable light which lulls the individual into a peaceful, yet unknowable porthole into a new plain of reality. The entire scene is roughly comparable to birth from the womb. However, the process and conditions are reversed. Instead of traumatically bursting into the harsh, oxygen-filled world of earthly consciousness, this birth is closer to a return to the comfort and security of the womb, placid and forgiving, all nourishing and in touch with our creator. In this way, it is a trip into the Unconscious, dream-like in every detail, infinite and timeless in all imaginal scope. We have returned to our innate beginnings, the ancestral plateau where birth and death are one in the same and the once all-important sense of our own individuality has undergone celestial transfiguration into our singularity with the oneness of being.

In this discussion of Near-Death Experiences, we observe the creativity of death itself. In essence, we are recapitulating the wisdom of the ancient Tibetan Book of the Dead and other spiritual reflections from around the aboriginal and civilized world upon the ultimate passage into the afterlife. In a preponderance of these cultures we find a method of preparation for a peoples inevitable finality. In some of these cultures, death is absolutely and proudly welcomed. For example, a good part of the Asian world celebrate funerals as sanctified passages into the celestial realm. The deceased are given letters, gifts and well wishes to guide them in their beginning journey into the netherworld. Furthermore, descendants of departed loved ones, continue to respect and honor the dead and often call (pray) to them for advice and worldly guidance. In Tibet, children are encouraged to play with the mortal remains, including bones and skulls, of their ancestral dead. This deeply embeds the idea of death as normal and grateful in the sublime world order of things. The process erases fear of death in an intrinsic spiritual world, which is nonetheless harsh and sometimes devastatingly cruel. Moreover, the lesson of gaining an awareness of being which is beyond the perceptive five senses, lends spiritual transfiguration to an entire culture, rather than merely a chosen devout person (Magic Man, Shaman), and his or her respective familial line. In short, every Tibetan understands that their Great Great Grandmothers continue to share love with the family and her tribe, even though she is not there to break bread with them. Instead, she has played with the children and enjoyed their company, as they have enjoyed hers. It has continued the ever-weaving fabric and cohesive nature of life, on every level of understanding and human comprehension. This is death embraced in unconditional love and a replete metaphysical insight which brings man into the very heart of an infinite creation. Another example of death wisdom is practiced by the Dakota Native Americans, or Plain Indians, who fully welcome their ultimate parting without fear or regret. To fear death is to challenge the great plan and may cause the deceased agony and peril in his or her entrance into the netherworld. Various books of the dead describe this monstrous association with the afterlife, replete with mutant-beings, fierce obstacles and eternal suffering. Medieval Christian teaching decided to utilize this approach to the hereafter, as a dogmatic system of reward and punishment bestowed on humanity. In other words, if you're good, you'll end up in a good eternal place, namely heaven, but if you're bad, hell and Satan's infamous demons is all that will await you in their eternal hot house far below both heaven and earth. In any case, the native Americans had no such distinction. Instead, they followed the simple tenet of achieving a proud, direct acceptance of death. This tranquil recognition is believed to ease the ultimate dissolution into the unconscious realm of spirit. There is one condition which the living can place upon the messenger of death, available to elder warriors and shaman who have proved themselves in all matters on the worldly plain. Death must wait and listen patiently, while the wise old man or woman relive and relate the great tales and honors gathered in his or her life. Only after life's glories have been retold, can the elders soul depart into the welcomed beyond. In a myriad of ways, this conceptualization of encountering and overcoming fear is central to the lesson given in this path of the Tarot. Conversely, clinging on to a familiar past, due to concern and worry over an unknown future, induces and provokes this figurative image of a difficult, awkward and painful entrance into an inevitable new realm of experience. The horrific, inhuman conceptions associated with the harsher aspects of the Persian and Celtic afterlife and the medieval Christian elaboration of hell, equally demonstrate the effect a persistent resistance to death and change in general. The early Christian movement and later Islamic principalities, used this representational fear to insure moral behavior within the context of culture. The societies law, or rules of conduct, once established, were to be followed without question and certainly and absolutely, without deviation. To disobey these cultural ethics became equivalent to a personal acceptance of divine retribution and in fact, an invitational request for this terrible punishment. At some point, in a harsh history of western Europe, cultural leaders decided this sublime penance could happen a bit sooner and consequently, clergy and religious participants could perform various tortures upon accused sinners right here on the earthly plain. In these cases, the misunderstood fear of death became an active consternation about worldly existence and more specifically, independence of thought. It is well documented in the annals of human history, where creative thinking led many to castigation, excommunication and even public execution. Ironic, how the ancient wisdom found in the Egyptian and Tibetan Books of the Dead, which instructed methods for a release of fear and a personal acceptance of death, could be turned upside down into an increase of cultural terror, on both the metaphysical and material plain of existence. One must remark upon the various interpretations of the written word and moreover, oral accounts and their respective effect upon the human psyche. Notwithstanding, and within the context of our naturalistic evaluations, certain ancient truths remain persistent age in and age out.

With this, we return to the next phase of our discussion. This concerns the wisdom to surrender our past without fear and subsequently, progress an allowance of free movement and thoughtful reflections into new and creative modes of existence.

This point was not lost on the mystic tradition of the Kabbalah. Accordingly, the Hebrew letter for the Death arcana is Nun, which means Creation. Appropriately, we find the symbolic associations with imagination in general and the creative principal, specifically. Only with a fearless break from old ideology, can we progress into a new and innovative birth of ingenuity. The afterlife and an entrance into an enigmatic netherworld, reveal a rather dramatic symbolism of creation in its sum total. In this formulation, we unearth the means and courage of invention. Furthermore, this figure reminds us to keep faith in our innate ability to continue exploring new and better approaches to life and its ever expanding spectrum of probabilities.

Binding all these symbolic elements into a cohesive interpretation, involves one last look at the Death (13) card itself. In the Waite-Rider deck, an apparition dressed in the regalia of the Black Knight, rides a noble white steed and carries a black flag emblazoned with a flower-like emblematic bloom. The upright stature of the figure seems to reflect its righteous place in the physical world. Simultaneously, a sympathetic allusion to mankind is offered in the visible suit of armor, worn only by men who risked and at times, sacrificed their lives to support the cause of their belief system. Moreover, this metal suit demonstrates man's inborn will to live and the need to protect the sanctity of his own originality. In short, the card tells us to live our lives to the fullest and harness the mastery of our own unique skills. Herein, lies the unifying source of this arcana. Becoming in tune with ourselves, our strengths and our limitations, we are able to comprehend when a real change in our mortal course is undeniably necessary. Once realized, we seek ingenious ways to create outstanding metaphorical bridges to God, Self and Society. In this wisdom, we lay down the armor of our present ego structure and fearlessly step into new perceptions of the tangible world. We are no longer afraid of change and we embody our innate creative future with pride and our deepest reverence to the life/death cycle of sublime existence and beyond.

TEMPERANCE (14) (Tarot Major Arcana) The striking journey into the Death (13) arcana, teaches the inevitable requirement of absolute change in our lives and our ability to cope with these dramatic transitions. To this end, we need to maintain flexibility in the waking choices we fashion in our being. The wisdom of the Temperance (14) arcana is centered around finding harmony and balance in the scope of our experience. Conversely, extreme, one-sided, behavior can be devastating in the face of unyielding change which forces transition away from the fulfillment of that singular obsession. In finding some measure of emotional moderation and a modicum of self-restraint, an individual may remain pliant and therefore compliant, to the reality of change.

However, we should never confuse this sensitive equilibrium with mediocrity and a general lack of passion. In fact, a major component of emotional maturity is built upon tempering the childish behavior of operating exclusively upon our instinctual impulses. The ability to stop and think, to measure our feelings and motivations and to ascertain the real consequences of our actions, deepens the capacity of our emotional commitment to any and all given situations. We may choose to withdraw from a particular experience, or spend the rest of our lives enriching its most articulate details. In any case, our decision will be steady and fervent, rather than superficial and reminiscent of the immediate gratification sought after by a child, who in reality, doesn't no any better. In stark contrast, the initiate on the illuminating path of the Tarot has already moved past Death and now enters the realm of deepest self knowledge. He comprehends in this arcana, the overall need to sight his parameters and realistic limitations. He has come full circle from The Fool (0), who leaps without thought into the great beyond. The initiate has since learned the significance of this leap of faith and its concern with the spiritual world and ones relationship to God and creation. However, on the earthly, physical plain, Temperance guides the wisdom of man, allowing leeway, for the ever changing nature of the sometimes severe, universal realm.

In the Temperance (14) card itself, we observe an angel-like being who pours liquid from one cup to another. The winged angel maintains a calm demeanor and an almost surreal stillness, which defies fallacy and mortal stumbling. He/She is in a state of timeless, static bliss, a kind of relevant Satori on the worldly plain. Behind the winged being, a path leads to an illuminated mountain which glows in the promise of high and uplifted spiritual transcendence. To further emphasize this point, the angel wears the emblem of a triangle inside a square, centered upon his/her chest. This symbolizes the nature of spirit residing inside or within matter, which is itself external and conversely, comes into contact with the data receiving five senses. This realization of spirit-infused matter, or what the alchemists term the Operatum Modus, holds the philosophical key to enlighten-ment. In this sense, the blissful angel may have originated from the mountain itself (spirit from matter) and followed the de-scending path to where he/she now stands, or, may have mate-rialized from the netherworld, otherwise known as the Uncon-scious, solely to guide the initiate, The Fool (0), to his highest earthly plateau. In either case, his/her effect of perpetual motion allows for free movement from the spiritual to the physical plain.

On the card itself, this visible and perpetual interplay of liquid from cup to cup parallels the ebb and flow of life. Moreover, the necessity of emptying one cup to fill another, displays the ever changing focus of material existence. In other words, we right-fully juggle the strength of our being, (in whatever form that strength may take), into the position where it is foremost re-quired. Consequently, we find ourselves with a list of changing priorities, which must be addressed in the zenith of their rela-tive importance. Naturally, this variable focus of priority may become a maddening, unending cycle of behavioral drudgery without an operational set of fundamental parameters. To this end, we must know when to push and when to pull, likewise, we need to be aware of our energy expenditure, and when to re-lease pressure altogether. In short, we must gain the wisdom to perpetuate a fluid and flexible sense of self, capable of adapting to life's multidimensional complications. In direct response to this conceptual belief, the Waite-Rider deck displays the fluid flowing from cup to cup in the Temperance card, suspended be-tween the cups themselves. In this sense, our ability to compre-hend a wide picture of the world around us and immediately accommodate and adjust to each situation as it occurs, becomes preeminent and retains our strength in a graceful, rhythmic state of readiness. This is understandably superior to a chaotic state of unmapped and unprepared late responses, coupled with an overcompensative and potentially harming, amount of ar-dor.

In another symbolic formulation, the suspended flow of fluid found in the arcana, is roughly comparable to ones possessions and worldly gifts. This endless cycle of continual filling and emptying, prevents our metaphorical cup from being overfilled and consequently, wasted in its excess. Instead, we return our good graces into the world from whence they came and retain a dire appreciation and hunger for life and its generous miracle.

Moreover, we cannot possibly horde what we choose to continually reinstate into our surroundings. This idea is echoed in the doctrine of the Karmic wheel, which is an allegorical device signifying the ten-fold return of good deeds released from oneself into the external material world. Naturally, this truth is also reserved for bad deeds sent out into the world and returning cataclysmal in their ten-fold vengeance. In any and all cases, we find a direct cause and effect mechanism operating in the world of the Tarot, as it does in the recognized world of science, where the delicate ecosystem maintains equilibrium via a dramatic succession of checks and balances within nature's tolerance. Darwin's theory concerning Survival of the Fittest demonstrates this abstract link in the picture of the weakest animal in a herd, say a bison, becoming injured, falling and ending up as prey. On the other end of the chain, we find the strongest predators, lions, for example, killing and eating the prey's carcass. Descending down the line, we may find a pack of hyenas, who will devour all the scraps and most of the bone structure. Next in line, scavengers such as vultures, will gnaw at the fetid corpse and suck the pulp of the marrow from the softening bones. The process is still not complete, as insects invade the oils and bacterium of the remaining strands. Eventually, only the single-celled bacterium will linger to feed on the animal. The last stage is the once living animal's complete absorption into the soil itself, as fertilizing nutrients for plant life which will in turn be ingested for nourishment, perhaps by members of the very same herd. All in all, nothing is lost, or wasted and virtually every part is utilized for the common good. The Temperance card is the full representation of this simple truth in its depiction of the perpetual movement of the fluid, held aloft betwixt the two cups held fast by the serene angel (spirit).

This idea of the 'common good' previously mentioned, refers to the communal reality of any given conceptualization. In terms of this discussion, we look to a few of the real social implications of Temperance, as a working human behavior. The initial treatment of the subject should perhaps begin on the rather broad examination of interrelationships themselves, in other words, the 'group dynamic.' In this thoughtful procedure we regard the connection of self-control and personal flexibility with external attachments within society. With this goal in mind, we note that outgoing persons, who display easy and immediate accessibility and adaptability to others, seem to universally possess at least three common traits. The first and foremost of these characteristics is an almost innate ability to listen attentively to others. The second trait involves gathering up a real concern for the speaking individual's quandary or crisis, however removed from the listener's own experience it may be. Lastly, the listener is able to portray his or her own individuality and wisdom by making the speaker aware that this conversation, consideration and concern is by choice and not by chance. In this subtle comprehension, the speaker realizes that any particular wisdom he or she may receive in this meeting, is not offered to just anybody, without any discrimination whatsoever. This is for the listener alone and no one else in the universe. Naturally, this gained feeling of special individual attention, serves at least two basic and fundamental purposes. The first is the accumulation of trust, which is paramount in the union of fragile and cautious human beings. A willingness to set ones own concerns and needs aside to champion and assist the trepidations of others, signals a real civility and altruistic human kindness, which inspires the profoundest confidence in all relations. The second purpose may seem contradictory to the first, but in truth, the first cannot function without the second. The second purpose of special attention, directly involves revealing the listener's own individual identity and sense of self worth. Without a solid foundation of self identity, all selfless behavior runs the risk of appearing spineless, weak and ultimately, displaying a kind of hidden and larger ulterior motive. In other words in the sense of dialogue, 'I'll help you, because then you may like be better.' as opposed to, 'I'll help you, because I want and choose to help you.' The difference in these two statements is as large as the human ego itself. We witness the balance of Temperance within the individual, becoming the very support mechanism in social relationships. The flexibility and balance of self, assures the imbalance and fear of others.

As in the entire Tarot Arcanum, this wisdom was not lost on the ancient Kabbalah mystics. The Hebrew letter for this path is Samech, which loosely means tree which supports. As we have seen repeatedly, the symbolism of tree refers to well rounded knowledge and wisdom. To support others with our prudence and ground their roots firmly so that they may help others is paramount in the full understanding of the Temperance (14) arcana. The animal associated with this path is the Horse. In this allusion we embody the strength of individuality which when trained and focused, may acquire the skill to run faster than ever thought possible and fly through the living experience of this deft magic, in unique and complete appreciation of self-awareness and self-control. Moreover, with the acquisition of personal flexibility, (innate in most breeds of horses), otherwise known as adaptability, we see in the implicit social sense, why man and horse have been set together in mythical union, two beings functioning as one, with pride, love and archetypal poise.

Taking all this into account, we see how the presence of the Temperance card in a dream may refer to gaining self-control and balance of self in a particular waking situation, which may be pulling the dreamer into self-absorbed, obsessive, or, one-dimensional behavior. Understanding the parameters of self and maintaining personal balance figures prominently in the social context of our existence. If we are able to learn from our mistakes and study the spectrum of possibilities in a presented situation beforehand, we may not become cornered and paralyzed by the difficulties of that situation. This strength of wisdom is in turn infused into our social environment and can provide support for others about to embark on similar journeys as we the initiate have successfully passed.

THE DEVIL (15) (Tarot Major Arcana) Contrary to the myriad of media-related images presenting the prediction of certain and unchangeable evil in the appearance of The Devil (15) arcana, the card itself is entirely instructive to the initiate in his last stages on the path of the Tarot. The card reminds the initiate of his human frailty, even at this latter echelon of the royal path. In this sense, the card is not in and of itself wicked, but rather demonstrative of our deepest internal fears and mortal, earthly weakness. In the darkness of this arcana and this figure, we logically surmise a link to our repressed unconscious desires and emotional passions, unclouded by reason and subsequent temperance. This is the arcana of instinctual drives, which quite literally, damn all consequences. Moreover, this dramatic primal memory is etched upon the background of our psyche, a naturalistic reminder of all worldly possibilities, which are carried within our physical human forms. To ignore this reality surpasses all ignorance and denounces creation itself. However, to become possessed by this earthly plain of experience is, or at least can be, equally devastating to the ever-learning initiate. In total, we see how the demonic figure in this path illuminates the extreme nature of worldly indulgence, yet only offers us a slight hint as to the real consequences of this overall earthly influence over our being in the journey through the Tarot.

Curious enough, this ambivalence is part of the archetype of the Devil figure itself, as it appears throughout human history, forever the sweet tempter and irrepressible trickster. From antiquity to modern times, we see good, heroic archetypes paired off with evil, treacherous villains whose power and seductive influence is equal, if not greater, than the hero him/herself. Naturally, this is entirely logical in the theological sense, since there can be no understanding of good whatsoever, without an equal and opposite evil, to weigh it against. In fact, good deeds can only be internalized and appreciated after the reverse consequences of bad deeds have taken their cruel and fully comprehended toll upon our memory. This is why a cat taken home from the freezing cold of a shelterless existence, will in general terms, be more grateful of his new abode, than a similar feline, born on the living room sofa. In other words, good, or God, needs evil, or the devil, to create brutal hardships which human beings must overcome to realize the intense joy of good, or God's holy enlightenment. But there is far more to the conceptual reality of the trickster than adversity and burdensome tasks given to man to prize and relish the superior world of spiritual existence. The real strength of this demon lies in his replete knowledge of man's full range of physical desires. Subsequently, the devil understands the craving of each mortal man and woman and it is his mission to lull humanity into this entirely personalized and rather extreme world of physical pleasure and material seduction. In this scenario, man must use his own reason, wisdom and faith to overcome his passionate impulsive drives when they become too obsessive and out of all reasonable control, to return intact to the sublime balance of nature's overall equilibrium. In other words, man must surmount his indulgent gratification as well as his grievous suffering, to return to the center of God. Undeniably, we see how the trickster is playing with a full deck and exists on all sides and parameters of reality. He is the positive/negative influence which keeps the soul suspended over the incomprehensible vortex of God. This is why the Devil's appearance is so dramatic and captivating, in both its diametric faces of seduction and repulsion. The Devil (15) arcanum in the full representative sense, is God's complete vision of the world. The initiate must pierce directly though this fervent image, in order to reach ever deeper into himself and move ultimately, beyond that self.

Little wonder, the Hebrew letter for this path is Ayin, which can mean both eye and foundation. To see the infrastructure of the establishment of the world is to possess that world in the elaboration of thought and memory. Furthermore, to carry the image of the earth and cosmos in ones mind, opens up the possibility of manipulating that conception and hence becoming part of the ongoing creation itself. Herein lies man's glory as well as his downfall. The mastery of God's creation placed in the hands of human beings demonstrates the Supreme Being's faith in man and full use of his prior creation, the devil. Here we see God giving mankind the chance to create and fulfill the wide breadth of his existence without question and with complete creative solitude. Of course, as in all endeavors of the divine consciousness, there is a catch which enables man to prove his ultimate worthiness as a manifest prodigy in the grand stratagem of his creator. The trick of fate lies in the reality of potential, the chaotic elaboration of possible existences to create. This chaotic revelry of prospective reality keeps man spinning in the delirious swirl of his own unending multitudinous vision. His need to experience further and deeper corporealities, can and often does, prevent him from completing any final creation and more importantly, thwarts him from thankfully and humbly returning that creation unto God. The test which man must pass involves once again moving beyond his mortal self and his own gifts, in order to maintain God within the miracle of his existence and celebrate ALL creation in union with the creative source (God) itself .

Hence, The Devil (15) arcanum and the archetypal Devil itself, must provide sight and knowledge while remaining darkness and eternal chaos. This is why the card is pictured black and utterly ominous. In the center of this stark reference to the dark realm, we find direct polar opposition to God's light and holy transfiguration, in short, spiritual enlightenment. This symbolic representation of celestial brilliance is not however, to be confused with our normal conception of earth's illuminating solar light. The radiance, or light, of God, refers to the clarity and purity of truth, wisdom and faith. As such, it will never be witnessed by the naked eye, yet burns eternally, inside our very own spiritual center, or soul. This leaves the physical conception of light, or perceptive awareness of the world, by (our) humanity's five senses, in the hands and direct manipulation of the devil himself. This is why the self-same evil one is called Lucifer, which means bearer of the light. However, this does not mean that the natural and physical world is evil. or immoral, nothing could be further from the truth. It simply implies that

beyond the physical awareness of the world, their lies an underlying mechanism which maintains its very order and direction, a random quantum pulse, or code, which generates the
formal structure of the entire visible miracle. Furthermore, the
human perception of the world operates on these same unseen
principles of biological logic and wholly organized cellular
memory. The Life we live is an enactment of principles evolved
over millennia and perfected by the needs of creation and the
survival thereof. Therefore, when we speak of a cat, volcano,
your mother-in-law, the law of gravity, or your boyfriends eye-
lashes, we do not refer to Satan's Physical Universe and otherwise, fun loving ideology. In fact, this is not our submitted argument, whatsoever. Specifically, it is only when we become
OBSESSED with the materiality of these realities, in and of
themselves (ex: 'My cat is the greatest feline in the world and
she loves me more than anyone else possibly could!') this is
when we begin to lose sight of their true meaning and underlying arrangement, both symbolically, scientifically and especially,
spiritually. In such a state of obvious and gross materialization,
The Devil has us viewing his face, the superficial and highly influential contours of the world. In this way, we behold a world
without spirit and blindly surrender to the domination of its
emotional sway. This mastery of evil is hastened by a steady
flow of earthly gifts and horrors which reserves the attention of
our external senses, rather than our well rounded and balanced
wisdom. In this persistent light, the devil is the chaotic whirl of
undisclosed potential. He is the eye wide opening, the clarity of
all things seen simultaneously, the horrific revelation of all being, present and future. He is the flash of insight before death,
the entire lifetime captured in frozen comprehension of all
human memory. All things considered, he is time and space incarnate. In this physical kingdom of emotional comprehension,
we internalize the extreme parameters of love as well as, hate,
extraordinary measures of love and hate. Eventually in this
tempestuous conceptualization, anguish and fear underlies our
daily existence as the cruel pendulum swing of reality moves us
with very little warning from absolute elation to dire suffering.
Accordingly, it is our purpose as spiritual and spirited human
beings, to move beyond this blinding, mesmerizing vision and
regain the order of supernal spirit, which faithfully delineates
and balances the world of our external five senses. To this end,
we can overcome the pain of heartless injustice and heart-
breaking, grievous loss and its antithesis, the transcendence of

pleasure, in our sole earthly existence. Moreover, we have surrendered understanding reality only in as much as it effects our
own individual being, rather, we have brought a life and spark
back into the world into which we humbly and thankfully unite
ourselves, through our own spiritual insight. In so doing, we
are given the opportunity to become, as the mystics say, at ONE
with the universal truth. Only at this point, can we begin a discussion of specifics.

It is relatively safe to say, the human union known as Love is
the deepest emotional and passionate drive in the spectrum of
our human comprehension. It is built upon the necessity of procreation and the continuation of life as we know it. Without it,
humanity disappears forever. Therefore, it is only natural for
society to have written extensively and figuratively about its
eloquence and the zenith of its absolute culmination, which is
of course, marriage and family. In this sense, The Devil (15) path
is linked with The Lovers (6) card, (note:1+5=6) in as much as
the devil represents the downfall of the lovers and hence, mankind in general. The tragedy of the lovers is depicted in their
blind lust, which supersedes their highest purpose, which is of
course, Love. The Devil (15) card portrays the lovers chained to
Satan and more importantly, to each other. This symbolism refers to our past discussion about the devil and his worldly influence. The lovers in lust, desire the physical carnal reality of each
other and lose their true spiritual union in the process. Their
connection involves self-gratification which is fed simultaneously, one from the other. Conversely, Love is selfless and altruistic and hence, concerns itself predominantly with the needs of
the other, in sum total, beyond physical desire. Moreover, this
desire remains, in a natural sense, a means towards an end
(birth). The love of another (mate), leads to love of still others
(children) and eventually, all others (society). In theory, this is
all well and good, however, modern society has demonstrated a
formidable need to reconsider our attitudes about relationships
in general. We have gone through the sexual revolution and
gained a basic understanding of man and woman as sexual beings, who do not necessarily wish to mindlessly populate the
world with children, just to experience a modicum of intimacy.
We must ask ourselves if this is an insurmountable contradiction to the ancient laws of union. The question has long been
answered by humanity itself, which has demonstrated and still
demonstrates a myriad of loving relationships which produce
no children and most certainly do not lead to marriage. In fact,

society condones this behavior and calls it 'dating.' We experience honest, open alliances, where the needs and apprehensions of our significant other is addressed and with any luck, merge with our own in agreeable consolidation. Nevertheless, If we cannot find this spiritual, mental and physical link, we are given the societal permission to gracefully discontinue the union and try again elsewhere. We are not castigated by our community and sent off alone into the wild woods, or worse, damned to the perception of a metaphysical hell. We have progressed to a new stage of behavior and all these charted mechanisms of modern behavior, because of their concern with the requirements of others, reflect real spiritual Love in the course of human interrelationships. Desire, or lust, is merely a part of the overall connection, perhaps only the catalyst in many long term relationships. Hence, The Devil (15) arcana is still something the lovers need to worry about, because it is the limitation of their real union. In spirit, even in today's world, The Lovers can find true love.

In the dream therefore, the appearance of The Devil path refers to our obsession with the physical side of reality. Hence, we may need to review current situations in our life and try to decide if we have removed our own soul in our relative behavior within the context of these experiences. The realization of a greater meaning and eternal purpose beyond our physical selves and the world we perceive with our five senses, may aid us in our treatment of that reality and our self awareness within its absolute and utilitarian framework.

THE TOWER (16) (Tarot Major Arcana) The Tower (16) arcana is a direct expansion of The Chariot (7) card, (1+6=7), in its symbolism of our need to harness control and drive forward toward ever-increasing goals. However, this path reminds the initiate about the danger of climbing too high in his ambitions. The lightning which strikes The Tower is reminiscent of an all-powerful divinity who can dismantle our lofty worldly plans whenever He chooses. As such, man is ultimately and always subservient to God, regardless of his personal status in the kingdom, or society, of mankind. In fact, the card depicts two figures which are blown out from the heights of the once mighty tower itself. One is a crowned king and the other, an ordinary citizen. This split image naturally carries a dualistic meaning. The first embodiment demonstrates the equality of man under the Supreme Being. In other words, whether a man be a king or a pauper, as far apart on any relative scale, from all other individuals in the entire social structure, he still remains a man and hence, far below the creator, who is the absolute author of the world. In his appropriate humility under the Almighty, man remains equal in his wisdom upon the earthly plain. Secondly, the card examines the folly of personal ego. In this sense, both a king, or an ordinary man may become wholly enamored with his own accomplishments, status or self-image. Moreover, in this empowerment, a man may believe himself equal to a divinity. While this may seem illogical, history has demonstrated whole societies who worshipped specific men as Gods, for example, the pharaohs in Egypt, the high emperors in Rome and countless megalomaniacs such as Alexander the Great, Genghis Khan, Napoleon, Hitler and Jim Jones in the modern world, among others. These men all faced The Tower of their self-grandiosity blown to smithereens in an instant of grim and all too mortal realization, whether on their death beds, or hiding under-ground in meticulously preplanned concrete bunkers, which doubled rather congenially as tombs.

The logical continuation of this discussion involves the blind-ing lust for power, regardless of the human mechanism used to achieve this end. This includes politics, business and not too surprisingly, religion. The written record of organized religion and its terror campaigns against humanity in the name of God, Allah and Christ, fills volumes of text and continues into the present day all around the circumference of this otherwise con-temporary world. Put simply, any murder in the name of a Su-preme Being, past or present, places the acting individual in the judgmental role of the creator Himself. Needless to say, The Tower (16) arcana has a special message for such an individual and the so-called holy organization, who supports his or her ac-tions. Paraphrased, its sounds something like this, 'Judgment will be His and His alone, those who would take into their own hands, judgment, will themselves be judged in turn.' In other words, don't do a divinity's job, worry about your own mission here on earth instead. However, if you believe yourself to be more capable than the Almighty himself, then God will demon-strate His very own unique capacity, in his own way and his own time, upon you yourself.

There is another side of this figure which conversely parallels our fall from grace and the utter deflation of our human ego. This involves the presence of a benevolent God whose lightning bolt is representational in a two-fold manner. Accordingly, within the context of this symbolism, the flash of lightning refers to divine insight which serves as a brilliant illumination of self-realization. We suddenly find the answer to our perplexing questions and riddles in a virtual instant, a nano-second. Furthermore, in our astonishment, we acknowledge this flash of genius comes from outside ourselves, as if from nowhere. In this approach, we find an allegorical reward from a Supreme Being or Entity, who follows our perseverance and worthy aspirations. In both cases, the creator has demonstrated His absolute dominion over physical man. However, when man follows his spirit and sound judgment, divine intervention is always welcome and fully appreciated.

Perhaps this is what the ancient mystics had in mind when they associated the letter Peh, with the devastating path of The Tower. The letter Peh, translates to assessing an agreement. As such, when the mortal initiate aspires to selflessly achieve his or her goal for the greater good of mankind and in full humility and thankfulness to a Supreme Being, he or she may be aided, rather than thrown asunder. In this case, man has thought out his goal, his prerogative and his catalyst, hence, a natural concordance has been determined and all is well in the overall scheme of existence.   In another sense, the purifying fire of the lightning blast, renews our course in life and returns our previous and primal balance of perceptual awareness. We have rediscovered divinity's place in our heart and in our daily lives. This is why prophets from diverse religions and globally crisscrossing historic faiths reveal a common theme in their rhetoric involving an individual's need to Repent and actively change his or her ways, in order to be redeemed under the all-encompassing sight of God, be that prime mover: Allah, Jesus, Yahweh, Shinto, Buddha, Shiva, Krishna, Horus or the four compass points of Waken-Tanka. We have to fall headlong before the Almighty, prior to completing the return upward cycle of spiritual awakening and final enlightenment. The Tower (16) arcana represents this fall into the primal waters, which is the eternal spaceless, timeless vortex of the many named and yet nameless, unknowable God.

In the dream appearance of the lightning struck tower, our unconscious may be warning us about our lofty status in the society which surrounds our daily existence. We may feel untouchable and impenetrable. As such, we may have built and fashioned walls around ourselves which are seemingly insurmountable and can withstand all efforts to break through to our rather fragile inner sanctum. The Tower arcana reminds us that this self-imposed safety net is not at all fool proof. When we least expect it, we may find disaster and a drastic alteration of our lifestyle and social position. However, this lightning bolt is double-sided and consequently, its flash of divinity may embody a needed psychological break-through into the very framework of our rather elaborate belief systems and waking consciousness on the whole.

THE STAR (17) (Tarot Major Arcana) Having traveled this far down the royal path of the Tarot, the initiate has nearly reached the goal of finding his own unique place in the order of the world. He has struggled with his own ideology, fought to maintain physical, mental and spiritual balance, transcended death and the temptations of the kaleidoscopic devil, finally and barely reaching the absolute apex, his zenith of personal potential. Unfortunately, only to be struck down to nothingness once more. However, in the process, he has been given a clear glimpse of divine enlightenment and the full culmination of his goal. In his fall from grace from The Tower (16) arcana, the initiate has regained his innocence and purity. He has been granted the insight into the real meaning of his faithful beginning as The Fool (0). Without purity, curiosity and belief in fate, the Fool would never have been granted this remarkable journey into the royal path of the major arcana.

The ancient Kabbalah mystics, being well aware of this final positive cycle in the transfigurative path of illumination, identified this arcanum with the Hebrew letter He, which means window. The appearance of a gateway which reveals a world outside our own realm of experience, gives us strength and determination on this, the last leg of our voyage into completion. In this sense, we see the connection of The Star (17) with the Strength (8) arcana, (1+7=8). However, the force we accumulate in this path slightly differs from that of the Strength path. The Star figure represents more than Strength's spirit overcoming matter, it symbolizes instead, the internal faithful wisdom of God consciousness, which transcends both matter AND spirit, revealing knowledge far beyond our ordinary sense of self. We watch in slow motion as the stars illuminate the night sky pulling our perception out past existence and into the infinite reaches of the everlasting heavens. As we gaze through this 'window' at the limit of our own grasped reality, we feel in the core of our being, the undeniable assurance of celestial order and the incomprehensible scheme of far-reaching, yet wholly consonant, divinity. Herein, lies the true strength of this path, the clockwork turning and tuning of our dreams and aspirations into hope and eventually absolute faith. In a warm, welcoming swell of increasing inner light, the initiate assimilates and embodies in this cycle, the highest wisdom of self. This is the Self as an intricate and intrinsic component of creation, past, present, future and in fact, beyond all conceptions of measurable time.

The Star (17) arcana portrays a nude and divinely pure, female figure. We recall the symbolism of the feminine aspect comprises two definite and nearly opposing principles, The High Priestess (2) and The Empress (3), respectively. The High Priestess represents the split of reality and the beginning of conceptual awareness. As such, she creates the nature of opposition and the energizing axiom of negative and positive polarity. Creating this gap in the center of existence, the High Priestess allows her counterpart, The Empress, to begin the process of healing and maternal union, the bearing of unconditional love. In short, the successive arcana demonstrate how the feminine aspect creates and completes itself by dividing nature and then returning that austere division into finite and cyclical order. Accordingly, the female figure in The Star (17) arcana utilizes both principles of her nature to bridge the internal world of our unconscious with the external world of our conscious awareness, the union of utmost polar opposition. This singular metaphoric enactment is depicted by the nude figure placing one foot in the water and one on dry land. Simultaneously, she pours from her two earthen and womb-like vessels, soil into the water and conversely, water onto the dry land. In placing each element into the heart of its opposite, the feminine aspect has gained the strength of divine acceptance and universal redemption.

This oneness is still further emphasized in the connection of The Star (17) with the combination of the Magician (1) and The Charioteer (7) arcanas. The path of the Magician initiates the spark of creation and embodies its underlying uniformity. The alchemist-like figure represents the balance of the four elements, or four corners of the universe, crowning him with the halo-like figure-eight symbol, representing infinity and divine wisdom. The Charioteer, we remember, depicted conviction, controlled perseverance and ultimately, forward progress. Together, these respective arcana bring the erudition of an eternal persistence in the sublime order of all things to the initiate, on this his final cycle upon the royal path. The ongoing creation illuminates the darkness of our potential human ignorance and blesses us with the sanctity of our own soul.

The appearance of The Star (17) card in our dream, may well refer to feelings of sanctity and security surrounding a wide variety of circumstances and our responsive behavior in their immediate context. The acceptance of our necessary place in the world, fills us with glowing compassion and a functional ability to provide confederation with our fellow man in the cerebral society which he has a tendency to create.

THE MOON (18) (Tarot major Arcana) The last obstacle in the initiates journey through the major arcana and toward enlightenment is the unforgettable influence and elusive deception of The Moon (18) path. The world of shadows, illusions, magic and enigmatic emotions, fills the realm of this rather complex level of the Tarot. We are faced with a warm inviting light in the night sky, which pulls at our impassioned embrace of reality. The light is merely a reflection of the sun, yet nevertheless and without fail, the initiate is craving to confuse it with the guiding light of spirit. The alluring pull of shadows and emotions, especially romantic ones, keep the initiate bouncing from light to dark, in search of the dynamic cycle which will announce his definitive revelation. In this mad rush, the initiate mistakes The Fool for The Magician, The Devil for The Hermit and most importantly, The Moon for The Sun. Operating from this complete deception, the initiate tangles himself tighter into the web and deeper into the perilous labyrinth of his intricate path of learning. Lunacy becomes so prevalent in this arcana, that the Tarot deck itself, becomes confused with worldly powers and unalterable future prophesy. The initiate believes his spiritual learning up to this point, has given him strength in and over his outside world. In this, he muddles matter and spirit and loses all sense of balancing their real diversity . He wildly dances with little real faith in himself. Instead, he relies on the divine knowledge of his past journey and respective collected experiences. Unfortunately, his voyage is wholly incomplete and in this extremely self-evident void, the initiate leaves himself entirely vulnerable to the worldly pull of Self Aggrandizement. Needless to say, the initiate has returned to the most foolish behavior of The Fool (0), and worse, he has no awareness of his own folly. He has entered with exuberance, the rather visceral psychosis of personal delusion which could potentially cause him immense harm and relentless distress. On the other hand, if he remains rational enough to believe the reality of his own hype and establishes a foundation upon its frantic groundwork, he will conversely return, to the reality-check of The Tower (16) of destruction, given ample time. Unfortunately, this miscalculation may cost him a majority of his life time here upon the good earth. Accordingly, it may have been The Moon (18) path itself, which inspired the phrase, 'So close and yet, so very, very far!' In any case, the Tarot works in strange ways and the Moon card is the litmus test for this timely realization of our own artifice.

The ancient mystics learned from experience and wisely associated this arcana with the letter Qoph, a frightening written term, in and of itself, which means Rear, or Back of the Head. The symbolism prevalent here is extremely remarkable, in that it examines a rather well known figure of speech, concerning Ideas lodged in the back of ones head. We somehow have been behaviorally programmed to scratch the back of our heads when thoughts are muddled, or at least not readily available. Its as though, we plan to shake the concepts loose from the rafters of our own cranium. On the other hand, our perception and memory is linked with our eyes, ears, nose and mouth, which are located in front of our head and facing an oncoming reality. In this paradox, we witness the metaphor of The Moon: knowledge which is ours, yet not quite, ours. The back of the head holds wisdom, but we have yet to scratch it loose. Herein, we begin to discern the key to The Moon (18) arcana.   In the study of witchcraft, the student is warned about influential elementals or wandering spirits which possess a great deal of strength. The fledgling is instructed in exact procedure when casting spells and performing rituals. To misread a chant opens the initiate up to immediate and very real danger. There is a simple reason for this technical mastery. The wise old crone is quite aware of the hazards of shadows and misunderstood spirituality. It is her business to open the eyes of her students to the oneness of being, rather than the limited force of material manipulation. God, or the creation, is not a parlor trick and certainly should not be taken lightly. These harmful and undesirable elementals represent the initiates folly into behavior modulation, their own and others in their sphere of existence. This weakness of worldly control obscures the real journey through the nature spirits into the singularity of creation, known as the Ain Soph Aur. Likewise, when a Zen master asks, 'What is the sound of one hand clapping?', he expects no reply other than some formulation of, 'It is the center of being which allows me to speak of its singular glory.' In other words, to answer literally, would reveal the limitation of language and human awareness. Instead, the student must demonstrate his ignorance and humility under the eternal and many named creator. All in all, we find an aversion to trickery and self-deception in all forms of authentic spirituality. In wisdom, when the answer is not known, no answer should be offered. However, before we condemn The Moon (18) entirely, we must understand that the force of language and the elementals of the spiritual and natural world need not be ignored at all and are in fact, needed in the path of enlightenment. Simply put, we need to understand the force of the underside, or reflection, of being, without being dragged into the alluring circus mirror maze of hallucinatory and nonsensical reality. This necessary reflection of being, gives the natural world the gift of depth and complex dimensionality. It reveals the subtle energy flow of creation and its healing and furtive principles. To follow our naturalistic drives, while mastering the balance of our internal energy swirl, offers us a significant glimpse into the overall miracle of creation, without being the absolute end all, be all. After all, we must not mistake the forest, for its lovely and exquisite leaves. This is the elusive lock which the key of The Moon (18) arcana, cranks wide open.

The Moon (18) waxes and wanes and follows cycles which effect the rhythm of the seas, the skies and all life forms. Female Wicca tribes, dance under the moonlight in singular appreciation of this fertile and dynamic principle of swelling emotional power. Nature worshippers and nature herself, all species of life to the letter, react to the spinning, revolving moon orb and are drawn toward its intense pull. Mammals bark, yelp and howl at its pale facade in the night sky. When the moon is full the police force readies itself for an increase in crime and mayhem as lunacy grips the populace of mankind. The astrological wheel and the subtle principles of psychic awareness all steady their focus upon the melodious pirouette of the moon beam upon our relative plain of existence. All in all, we observe the real influence of the moon in our life. It is a force which drives us, yet one which should not be followed blindly. Rather, its reality should be integrated into our daily awareness. When we consider the all absorbing madness of desire for example, we examine the sharpness of its double-edged sword. In one manner, the 'romantic' individual expresses his or her love under the moonlight and finds eternal bliss in the eyes of his or her soulmate. If the mate reciprocates this emotion, they may well live happily ever after, or at least for a little while. However, if the madness is not mutual, a broken heart may be the least of our very real concerns, which could easily run the gamut from abuse to rape to outright murder. Courts of law recognize the outstanding number of these crimes of passion and this brutal account is as far from our Valentines Day association of romance, as we care to think about. We see in grim detail, how the subtle force of the moon must be recognized, internalized and then absolutely held in boundary to run its proper course, balanced by the confidence of our clearest wisdom. It is plain to all, just how elusive this proposal can be in the genuine intricacy of life. Little wonder this is the last and greatest obstacle for the initiate, before he or she can cross over into enlightenment. In so many ways, the mystics had found the correct symbolism in placing this force at the 'back of the head', where it properly belongs.

As The Moon (18) arcana enters our dreaming mind, we must examine the complexity of its imagery in order to understand its statement in our waking experience. We witness the melancholy moon overhead two towers, in between the towers, yet far off in the distance, we witness a mountain range with a river emanating from its central apex. This river flows directly toward our point of perception traveling a supposed great distance. At long last, it becomes a tiny stream which empties into a still pool directly before our frame of reference. Out of this pool, a crayfish crawls up toward the moon. Near the pool and ignoring the crayfish altogether, two large dogs are also captivated by the face of the moon and bark at its morose expression. In this expansive symbolism we find a deceptive destination incurred by the potency of the moon itself. We are drawn toward the spiri-

tual mountain beyond the towers of our own psychological development. In fact, our natural instincts seem to push us forward toward this immense pilgrimage of sorts, represented in
the embodiment of the crayfish and dogs. The subterfuge becomes fully apparent when we realize the river from the mountain flows toward us. The journey has been taken, and we have
already arrived at the pool of creation. To move toward its
source would be the equivalent of walking backwards, or following the force at the 'back of ones head.' In as much, the unconscious bids us caution in following false prophets and spiritual duplicities. Furthermore, the arcana may be reminding us
to 'keep our heads' in romantic situations which could lead us
astray from our own better judgment and higher wisdom. Last
but not least, the card tells us that we have approached sanctity
in our own lives, we need not be drawn away from that illumination, by an illogical necessity to possess its power to
overcome the world of hardships. We must learn not to conquer the world, but move with the rhythm of its dynamic spirit.

THE SUN (19) (Tarot Major Arcana) In the full, life-giving radiance
of The Sun (19) arcana, the initiate has attained the final stage in
his search for enlightenment. In his calm and inner stillness, he
accepts the presence of God within the totality of his being. He
no longer needs to find, or chase, the truth of reality, as it symbolically shines above him and within him. This is the spiritual
sun of God, or the midnight sun, as the practitioners of witchcraft, appropriately call it. This is the sun which never sets and
hold us steady within its omnipotent luminescence. If we are
centered within ourselves and our reality, we will surely be in
tune and in line with its brilliance. The Fool (0) had walked
away from the sun to find himself, nonetheless, he was completely empowered by the faith of that same radiant orb, which
gave him hope beyond hope, that he would discover a true
place and meaning in the world. After his entire journey
through the arcana, he finds himself under the same Sun (19)
from whence he began, however, he is now deeper in knowledge, experience and everlasting faith. After all, he knew full
well, the surety of his innocence and belief in the wisdom of
creation, would lead him back 'home.' Likewise, in The Sun (19)
arcanum, we find a nude child with arms outstretched, joyfully
riding a white horse. In this symbolism, we witness the glee of
childhood innocence and its natural connection with purity.
Taking this to heart, the initiate on this path has surrendered all
his worldly motives and motivations. He has returned to the

purity of his utmost faith in life. He can now bask in the direct sunlight of his creator. The path of the Tarot is not complete, yet a center has been found which will remain the absolute beginning and ending of all return journeys into self discovery. Furthermore, only in the wisdom of this singularity and purpose of existence, can the initiate complete the final two stages of the Tarot major arcana, Judgment (20) and The World (21), respectively.

The mystics of the Kabbalah, associated The Sun (19) path with the letter Resh, which means Face. This symbolism refers to the face of man and the face of God, facing one another in union, as one being in the totality of creation. This is what is meant by the biblical passage, paraphrased thus, 'God created man, unto His own image.' The wisdom is not literal, but metaphoric, as the ancients understood the 'face' or 'image' as it refers to human awareness of the divine. The face of creation upon us and within us, guides our way in the world, which is gained through our comprehension of the one spirit, our soul of being. Moreover, we face this reality with faith in our purpose and overall meaning in existence. When Descartes said, 'I think, therefore I am.', his words echoed the concept of our awareness as the paramount and prime mover in reality. Naturally then, complete awareness of experiential life and its innate and flawless foundation, replenish the objective of our appearance in the universe.

The sun provides ongoing nourishment to all life forms on earth and holds the planet itself in a constant sustaining orbit even when it is not visible to a good measure of humanity and the earth's multitudinous other inhabitants. Before science, only faith guaranteed the return of this imperative sun each and every morning. Likewise, The Sun (19) card may be viewed as the supporting sustenance of our worldly behavior. It is the center which bolsters our spiritual awareness through all calamity and distress. It is The Hermit's lamp, which guides him through the darkness of worldly fear and the physical unknown. It is through this spiritual light that our own mortality is transcended. In this, death itself is accepted in its due time, without fear and with replete assurance of the oneness of creation, unto which we return. In so many ways, The Sun (19) has been the spiritual light at the end of the tunnel, which revealed its omnipresent radiance in each stage of our otherwise blinding journey. In fact, the most perilous stage of the major arcana was the elusive Moon (18) path, simply because it falsely depicted The Sun (19) and sent the initiate reeling backwards, instead of forward. However, even in this stage, when the initiate finally realized the reflective powers of the moon, he could reverse his heading, turning one-hundred and eighty degrees, directly toward enlightenment, fully empowered by the forceful, effectual moon 'behind his head.' In all cases, the reality of a source of faith is acknowledged prior to our passage into its complete erudition. As such, The Sun (19) is the final wisdom and knowledge of faith itself. The concept of knowing faith, is not a contradiction in the land of the Midnight Sun, where the Unconscious guides the conscious and The Fool (0) holds all the world's wisdom in a tiny satchel cloth, suspended on a fragile branch, resting upon his narrowest of shoulders.

If The Sun (19) card should happen to appear in a dream, we may well be embracing the wisdom of our decision making. In such a scenario, we demonstrate a complete confidence in our inner faith. We have behaved consistent with our integral and vital spiritual conviction. Nevertheless, chances are pretty high, we will continue to make foolish mistakes, but as long as the source of our wisdom remains within us, we will maintain a fairly reasonable balance and relatively clear outlook on things. However, there is a negative side to this dream imagery. If the card should be turned upside down, we may need to question the absolute clarity of our insight. We may be offering our innocence to a worldly or deceptive force which seeks to turn us away from ourselves. We may need to reexamine powerful influences in our life and their actual motivating factors.

JUDGEMENT (20) (Tarot Major Arcana) The previous arcana referred to man's unique place and purpose in the world. Conversely, the Judgment (20) figure points to God's singular intention for mankind and the future of reality itself. Is the diversity of human events, including war, famine, murder, injustice, clairvoyance, lust, hunger, greed, passion, transcendence, control, elation, devastation and mayhem all created for man's own amusement? The Tarot doesn't think so. Instead, these daily realities represent the replete learning process of humanity and one by one, test his ability to remain centered in spite of their overwhelming effect on his body, mind and soul. In short, the source of creation engages man to be at one with universal transfiguration. The Judgment (20) figure calls man, woman and child, all pictured on the card itself, to join in the union of creation. The archangel Michael/Gabriel blows his horn in triumphant announcement of the oneness of being. The human personifications emerge from coffins and their own figurative death. Those who cannot hear the horn, remain dead to the truth and suffer the consequences of an entirely disjointed and meaningless existence. This fundamental loss of truth and the eternal spirit is presented as an archetype throughout human history in a variety of metaphorical images of the afterlife and its counterpart, the end of time.

At this point, the conceptualization of Judgment (20) becomes a rather complex issue which involves several cross-cultural theological viewpoints with diverse discernment, pointing nevertheless, toward some common central denominators. In all cases, the central denominator, or theme, of these arguments demonstrate the discipline and otherwise punitive aspects of The Almighty, in connection with the human soul.

First off, great traditions such as the ancient Egyptians and Celtic Druids, linked the human soul with the mouth, or breath of life. In Egypt, mummies were given the sacred rite of 'The Opening of the Mouth' to insure the powers of speech, hearing, sight, smell and awareness in general in the afterlife. In other words, the soul was prepared for its journey into the underworld, or netherworld of Osiris and the dead. In similar fashion, The Celts believed in the concept of an immortal soul which necessitated three human aspects to assure its transition into paradise. They are crabhadh, creideamh and iris, which can be loosely translated as soul, heart and mind, respectively. If the individual lacks an equal measure of any one of these three components in his existence, his or her soul may eternally wander away from the body into other spheres of worldly existence, including animals, plants, even inanimate matter. The connection is made when we witness how this wandering soul may pass from the mouth of its original owner, into the mouth of another person through ingestion of any one of its worldly manifestations. Hence, the mouth becomes the portal of the soul. In this sense, we understand the interpretation of the Hebrew letter Shin which is associated with this Judgment path. Shin is translated as Fang or Tooth. Accordingly, as was presented in the previous arcana, Face represents God, then intuition would follow the sharp Tooth upon that Face, rather graphically represents the ferocious bite of a singular Supreme Being. Concerning that exact bite, we analyze the controversy around the specific nature, or punishment, implemented upon each individual human being who refuses his or her souls' entry into the spiritual light.

We begin this discussion with a few words about choice and its compass-like targeting of either the humble light of spirit, or conversely, the proud darkness of the physical world and self-will. The decisions made in the course of a life-time sway from one extreme to the other, depending on a wide complexity of factors. The path of the Tarot examines this ongoing trial of errors and assesses the initiates wisdom and faith to 'stay the course' toward enlightenment. The royal path has been a maze of distinctly human possibilities, which involved several stages of reason and wisdom, justly needed in order to maintain forward progress toward the knowledge of self. However, before this goal, or treasure, of the labyrinth can finally be attained, the seeker must ultimately face himself. This fatal confrontation is represented by the minotaur, symbolic of every individual's final test of inner strength. Man must overcome all his fears and passions to complete the journey into spiritual fulfillment, which ironically, was with him and in him, all along. To this end, the royal path has reached the culmination of its second cycle and the final aspect of its teaching. In another allusion to this conclusive investigation of self-worth, necessary before the human soul can voyage into eternity, is found in the embodiment of the Egyptian Sphinx. The mysterious half man/half lion giant, which guards the entrance to the holy city of the great Pyramids of Giza, is regarded as the 'guardian of the soul.' The ancient Egyptians believed in eternal life for individuals who preserved their bodies and directly aligned and sustained their respective spiritual essences, Ba and Ka, or mind and heart. Having done so, the Pharaohs and kings designed houses of eternity, fashioned in the exact measurements of the miraculous pyramids. These structures made up the eternal city of the royal families. The Sphinx, which has faced the same sunrise for thousands of years, represents the lion strength of the Pharaoh's perfectly sustained spirit, or soul, which has thereby remained eternally intact and has moved into the realm of the gods Ra, Horus, Osiris and Nuit. Having reached the afterlife, the Pharaoh began a whole new existence fraught with dangers which would be successively overcome, simply by the possession of the just spiritual union of Ba and Ka. The proof of a deceased individual's worthy spirit in the afterlife was determined in a place called the Judgment Hall, where that individual demonstrated his or her 'declaration of innocence' in the past physical existence in the world of man, to a collection, or jury, of forty-two gods. The last stage of this judgment involved the weighing of this persons Ba/Ab, or heart, against a feather, which represented divine truth. In this, we find yet another allusion to the final self-examination, necessary before entry is permitted into eternity, exemplified in the images of the minotaur and the Sphinx. Accordingly, humanity is reminded in this same awesome sight of this Sphinx, which guards the entrance to the timeless city, that only strength of spirit and deepest faith may lead one into everlasting immortality. As such, both the minotaur and the Sphinx represent the Supreme being's horns, or teeth, challenging man to prove his worthiness in the picture of ongoing creation, most importantly, to himself.

The Judgment (20) arcana, in this same age-old tradition and wisdom, indicates the inevitable point in time when the initiate must ultimately face him or herself and choose between the internal light of truth, or the external world of selfishness and social deception. If the wrong choice is made, the light of eternity is denied in favor of a finite material existence, replete with physical, as well as, spiritual death.

Before we further explain this point, we should first address the cross-comparison between the Christian Bible's Book of Revelations, remarkably similar to the Quran's view of judgment day entitled: The Great Event, and the Tarot's Judgment (20) arcana. We observe in both traditions a call to redemption and a rather practical 'end-time.' In Revelations, we witness the end of the known world, with the second coming of Christ the redeemer. As opposed to his first appearance on the worldly plain, Jesus is no longer tolerant of man's sins. The time for judgment is at hand. Jesus brings with him, the seven angels of plague and wages an all out war against Satan upon the physical world of man. Inevitably, the human race is divided into two armies, the faithful who stand alongside Jesus and the wicked, who wear the mark of 'the beast', or Satan's antichrist. In a violent upheaval of reality, including the great seas changing into fiery cauldrons of peril, good systematically conquers evil and those who sided with the devil perish into the torturous darkness of nonbeing with the antichrist and Satan himself, who will not emerge again into the world of man for one thousand years. Conversely, the one hundred and forty four thousand 'without sins in their mouth' (another allusion to soul) follow Jesus and join Him in a new Heaven upon the earth. Additionally, those who have died throughout history with faith in God, raise out of their coffins and resume their previous forms, now unified with the Supreme Being. Those who have not died in Christ, remain in the death and darkness of Satan and await Judgment and individual punishment from God. The symbolism of the Tarot, on the other hand, begins with this same vivid imagery, but varies quite a bit in its metaphoric translation, bringing it closer to the understanding of ancient Egyptians, Celts, Oglala Sioux Native Americans (who practiced a ceremony called: The Keeping of The Soul) and modern Christian theologians. The end of time as it is portrayed in the Judgment (20) arcana, pertains to an individual and his or her reflection upon society, rather than the drastic end of society itself. Emerging from death, as pictured on the card, the initiate removes him or herself from the darkness of nonbeing. Welcoming the light of spirit, man becomes eternally revitalized in the pool, or source, of creation. Likewise, modern Christian and Gnostic thought, sights the gospel of John 4:14 paraphrased, 'But whoever drinks the water I give will never be thirsty. the water I give will become a spring of water gushing up inside that person, giving eternal life.' and John 4:5, 'I tell you the truth, unless one is born from water and the Spirit, he cannot enter God's kingdom. Human life comes from human parents, but spiritual life comes from the Spirit.' As such, the initiate flows into the infinite waters, rather like Loa-Tsu's ancient teachings concerning the circulating Way of Zen, or the Collective pool of the Unconscious in another sense, all the eternal and idealized formulation of God. Conversely, to accept the darkness involves the gradual degeneration of the physical body, absorbed into a myriad of worldly forms, each with its own reincarnate spirit, yet utterly unlike the once intact human soul. The sanctity of whose essence is central to the conceptualization of eternal life. To this end, the Pharaohs of ancient Egypt sought to preserve their original human form in flesh, in proper spiritual mortification techniques and in artistic renditions of themselves in sculpture and visible etchings. All this was done to insure their soul's safe passage into the eternal realm, past Judgment Hall and into the paradise of the afterlife, otherwise thought of as a union with the gods and evenhanded mankind.

Undeniably, the Judgment (20) arcana's imagery of fully realized man, or soulful man, does signal an ultimate death and rebirth of reality, both internally and externally. In the numerological sense, we return to The High Priestess (2) (compare Judgment (20), who causes a chaotic duality which is in turn mended by the matriarchal Empress (3) (compare World (21). Judgment (20) alarms the final division of all spirit and matter, in the metaphorical decision of the minotaur and Sphinx. However, in the end of the Tarot labyrinth, spirit and matter are reunited as one principle, the reality of God consciousness, the symbolic Heaven upon Earth mythified in most cultures and definitive belief systems. In the western tradition, Jesus Christ is the living metaphor, or archetype, of this union of spirit and matter. His existence reflects a beginning and ending, an Alpha and Omega, as he himself phrases it. Furthermore, his references defy temporal exactness and enter a kind of Jungian Collective Unconscious, which persists omnipresent throughout the duration of existent time. For example, in John 11:25, Jesus declares, 'I am the resurrection and the life. Those who believe in me will have life even if they die. And everyone who lives and believes in me will never die.' As such, Jesus is psychologically linked with the past, present and future, simultaneously. This restates the concept of the spaceless and timeless realm of the Supreme Being. Hence, we witness in the metaphoric fusion of spirit and matter, the next golden age of existence which is aptly represented in the last and ultimate arcana, The World (21). Accordingly, Judgment (20) seems to indicate, in its similarity with Revelations and the Egyptian Book of the Dead, an individuals risk of losing a new awareness of this fully ordained Heaven upon the earth. Having refused to accept the divine light at the end of the initiate's progress, or journey, through the major arcana, the initiate has been beaten by the minotaur Judgment (20) and is justly denied entrance into the eternal World (21) arcanum of infinite fulfillment.

At this point, we examine the figurative social resurrection of the dead at the commencement of reality, when spirit and matter become one. If at the moment of death, a single human being steps into God consciousness, he or she has entered the often mentioned, spaceless and timeless realm of the Supreme Wisdom. Hence, should the physical world of man (spirit and matter) come to a crashing, cataclysmic end, ten thousand years after that individual's singular death, his or her resurrection into the post-world, Heavenly plain, would nevertheless come instantaneously in that individual's once mortal awareness. Logically, the transition would not be recognized by the individual who has been in the timeless, spaceless suspended animation of the Almighty Being. The initiate, unhampered by physical time, would move directly from his death into the Heaven created at the end of time. In this light and in a single moment, all of mankind simultaneously joins in the fellowship of its own miraculous existence. Moreover, The Creator in his equality, reunites all men and woman from all time and disparate stations of existence, into a single and equitable confederation of permanent consciousness, at one with the singular awareness of the all-encompassing foundation of being. This realm will be elaborated still further in our discussion of the World (21) arcana, which culminates the royal path and transcends The Fool (0) into the allegorical wholeness of self-realization

Appropriating this conceptualization of Judgment (20) and its intricate concern with eternal life, we need to anatomize its visual appearance in our dream. On the surface, the card may be warning us not to lose the spirituality of our waking worldly behavior. However, on a much deeper level, the arcana symbolizes the exact moment in time when an individual must face himself in a truthful assessment of his own personal merit and virtue. The darkness, often mentioned in this section, concerns the lies within oneself, the hiding of ones soulless actions in life. The dream inquires if we are we prepared to face the light of honest exposure? The Unconscious may be aware of an individual's real progress toward enlightenment and now forces the hand. In all cases, the key revolves around the knowledge of self and its honest internal verdict. Before we can be judged by God, symbolic of not only Himself, but also, society at large, we must first surmise ourselves. If we are worthy of the light of truth, we can return to the existence of earth and assist in the creation of a veritable Heaven upon its sacred surface.

THE WORLD (21) (Tarot Major Arcana) In the examination of The World (21) symbolism, we address both ecclesiastical visions of paradise, as well as philosophical interpretations of a worldly Utopia. At first, the two paths toward eternal fulfillment, may seem radically different. However, we will succinctly observe how and why, both these separate tenets operate as one fully functional mechanism, designed to guide an individual toward the context of a cohesive society.

In order to accomplish this, we must first turn to the conceptual meaning of morality and social ethics in general. In the orthodox spiritual tradition, we observe the position of 'Goodness' as a conscious effort to achieve a sociable fairness which effects the whole of the community. In this sense, we find a built-in balance of human involvement and care. Within this communal nurturing, the individual is subordinate to his entire people. In this light, no man strives to advance personal gain at the expense of his brother, neighbor or fellow man. In fact, great measures are taken in the form of laws, or commandments, to insure this selfless behavior. We find in this order of tantamount existence, where each man and woman cares about the entire populace more than him or herself, a link with a unifying principle, or God, which is simultaneously concerned with each and every individual. As such, human beings do not need to be overly concerned, about their own needs, rather, in this pious observance of social equality, man pleases his creator and is taken care of one at a time. Since, this conceptualization of a sympathetic and benevolent God is beyond man, He is attributed to these laws, or commandments, of human justice. However, man lives and dies and experiences extreme and profound difficulties, in his worldly existence. This causes many men to question this caring God, who seems to have abandoned their particular needs and human consolation, in general. To this end, man begins to ignore the needs of his fellow man, in favor of accumulating his own requirements. Gaining power in the world, man loses his sense of communal unity and increases his personal force and desire, until he has conquered away all his fears of hunger and destitution. This behavior becomes symbolic of man's fall from grace.

In answer to this fierce individualism, religious and political leaders, most of whom have already surrendered to this personal temptation of gain themselves, provide man with a two-fold vision which is meant to guide them back toward the equality of spirituality under their just creator. The first image details an angry God, who is intolerant of man and his greedy, obsessive behavior and prepares to destroy the whole sinful lot of them. The second image depicts a forgiving God, who is willing to return man to the splendor and sanctity of His own presence, if and only if, each and every man and woman willingly changes their selfish, anti-social ways upon the earth. Naturally, there is only one way to explain this metaphor, or vision, of divine reward or punishment, which lends it a logical placement in the world. Herein, we introduce the meditation upon eternal life. Only in the vision of life after death, may we find an instantaneous return to the face of God. Now, whether this Supreme Being will be angry or pleased with our chosen actions upon the earth is what we literally need to question. Accordingly, the concern of morality is returned to the earthly plain of existence. Man, in order to find eternal happiness and avoiding eternal pain in the process, needs to return to his selfless behavior, in faith of a divine reality (God) far greater than himself.

In the Judgment (20) arcana, we examined some of the connections between judgment day and eternity. We theorized the possibility of all life after death occurring simultaneously, a mass awakening in the context of this very same judgment day, occurring at the end of time. Appropriately, we are finally and definitively judged at this moment and there is no turning back whatsoever. Nevertheless, we deliberately omitted a key discussion concerning the temporal worldly occurrence of this end of time. Legitimately, we can never know the exact date of such a cataclysmic event, however, we can speculate on the ideal futuristic climate for such a phenomenon to occur. In this, we explore the connection between the secular and nonsecular Utopian visions of a projected and desired, paradisiacal society. The concept of an evolving community of man which gathers information and slowly incorporates this information into a clearer understanding of its own future goals, is one which is readily accepted in today's world, if not essentially adopted. Notwithstanding, modern philosophy continues to gear the human race toward an inevitable communal mind, which concerns itself with the whole of man, in context with each and every individual being. To this end, we seek to break down the barriers of historical prejudices and age-old fears. Slowly, but surely, wisdom of diverse cultures are comprehended and the world grows ever smaller, falling within the visible scope of reason. We are now able to deal with our fellow men and women and demonstrate our actual respect for each soul and his or her society. In time, we realize the common thread of our humanity and formulate a meeting of minds. However, we soon discover the ideal sanctity of this meeting, or confrontation, involves a serious discussion concerning the absolute means necessary to provide social justice and individual contentment for all human beings, who now seek to altruistically come together. In this time, the great and final swell of individuality will rationally be felt, as each side offers its own 'wisest' solution toward world peace and reconciliation. In this heated debate, the spectacle and history of man may become reignited and create a towering inferno of hatred and animosity which could very well block the entrance into a Utopian reality, perhaps forevermore. Consequently, this would be the reasonable climate for an active judgment day, both physically and spiritually. Man, having done everything in his power to bring about peace, would now be facing his figurative self. This is the whole of society, rather than the individual, facing its reflective minotaur and Sphinx. In this struggle, the contest between love and hate is fully waged. The aftermath of this struggle would explore the Utopian world of a Heaven upon Earth, or man's final and complete acceptance of the miracle of his own kind. If conversely, humanity deems itself unworthy of continued existence, absolute death and extinction is always an option. The creation of atomic weapons and the senseless disregard of the natural environment, signal two proponents of this willful destruction. Sigmund Freud spoke about the Death Instinct within man, which seeks to utterly destroy itself out of existence. Although this behavior has been deemed fashionable and hip in a modern world whose future seems dark anyway, the truth instead weighs heavily on the alternative human tenet, which is a decided will to live (as long as we possibly can). All told, both philosophers and theologians search for the eventual Heaven on earth, where mankind is well taken care of and mutually supportive of his world. In this we find an ideal world of spirit, or the fusion of spirit and matter. All realities have merged and we live in loving harmony.

The Hebrew letter for this World (21) arcana is Tau, which means cross, or balanced connection. As we have seen earlier, the archetypal image of Jesus upon the crucifix, presupposes this fusion of spirit and matter, and furthermore, marks the metaphoric resurrection, beyond all life and death. In as much, this heaven on earth, signals the highest plain of existence, bringing full circle the wisdom of the almighty and His once cast out creation. The numerological interpretation of the World (21) arcana agrees with this logic. Accordingly, the World (21) path is linked with the High Priestess (2), or separation, and The Magician (1), or world order, finally completing its indicative descending pathway into The Fool (0), or faithful enlightenment. In this sense, the Fool and the World become one and the same, the symbolic alpha and omega of purposeful human existence. Moreover, the connection of these Major Arcana, return us to the allegorical Empress (3) or (2+1+0) figure, which indicates an acceptance of all reality in her certain and immaculate matriarchal fashion. In a vivid representation of this exact connection, the World card depicts a welcoming female-like figure, who is beyond all opposites, including spirit and matter and male and female itself. She is the hermaphroditic allusion to celestial being, the center of all reality, which empowers, while transcending the four elements of creation. On the outside corners of the card itself, we find the bull, eagle, lion and man, which represent these four elements, as well as, the heart, mind, spirit and will of man. The wreath which surrounds the male/female figure and welcomes the world of man, signifies the peaceful union of everything that ever was and everything which will ever be. He/she is the completion of the Major Arcana and the beginning of everlasting wisdom.

The appearance of The World (21) card in our dream, implies all the love and faith we carry within us, in the context of our waking world. Moreover, it demonstrates the promise which this behavior offers to the overall existence of man. Our actions are reflected in society and have a profound impact upon our immediate as well as, our distant future lives. If we long for a Utopia, or eternal paradise of being, we need to actively strive toward this goal. We cannot lie back and complain about all the outside evils presented in the world of man. Alternatively, once confronting our own personal spirit, we must do what we can to improve the actual quality of life on earth. This includes full acceptance of humanity and its complex condition. We must view existence as a whole, fully understanding the undeniable chain-reaction of our behavior. In as much, we need to treat humanity and nature as our own children, because in every way, we are the guiding light into tomorrow and forever.

The End of the Tarot Arcana

The Keys

TAR PIT The conceptualization of the Tar pit revolves around the stagnation of self and all its possibilities. Due to its extreme nature, the pit may refer to repression which halts our entire living process rather than certain isolated elements within that life. As such, these limitations may be very abstract and all encompassing. For example, we may be referring to a difficult childhood or a problematic marriage. In either case, an allusion is made to permanence and this may need to be addressed by the dreamer, especially if the dream is recurring and/or occurs quite often.

TATTOO The image of a tattoo elicits deep passions concerning freedom, aggression and perhaps, anti-social behavior. As such, the dream tattoo may be reflective of our escape from social norms and/or constraints. Moreover, since a tattoo is permanent, our unconscious may be illustrating a fixed determination concerning our iconoclastic new lifestyle. Furthermore, a tattoo is symbolic of the symbol itself, embodying an image which portrays the spirit of the individual who wears it. In this sense, the tattoo can be viewed as a complex icon which elucidates the alliance of portrait to artist, artist to subject and subject to portrait.

TEA The symbolism of Tea may refer to calm repose and a temporary cessation from the difficulty of everyday life. Moreover, the drinking of tea may depict a delicate contemplation of being. As such, we need to explore where we drink the tea and why we drink the tea. Moreover, we need to examine the symbolism of hot liquid, which may involve a delicate warming of emotion, and the cup itself, which may illustrate rather complex feminine sensibilities including passion, love and childbirth. (see Water) (see Cup)

TECHNICAL: The Technical dream may imply complicated workings in our life which function in painful, yet dynamic symmetry. As such, our unconscious may be illustrating the combination of all our responsibilities and endeavors and demonstrating the effect of this conglomeration upon our psyche. In as much, we need to determine the complex process of our waking life and whether or not it needs to be simplified. Perhaps, we function well in this stressful prism of reality, in which case, our technical skill may come fluidly and with apparent naturalistic ease.

TEETH: In the dream sense, a loss of Teeth refers to our feelings about aging and death, especially in a dream involving the loss of teeth or the rotting of teeth. Moreover, the conceptualization of bad teeth may refer to our fears about poverty or inadequacy in a relationship or social situation involving status. We may be illustrating feelings of ineptitude in our occupation, social sphere interaction, or even in maintaining the responsibilities of our family life. In this sense, a sort of forward regression may be taking place where we view ourselves obsolete in our present environment. Accordingly, the image of perfectly intact teeth may imply hunger, aggression and sexuality which seeks to bite into present realities. (*see* Bite) (*see* Mouth) (*see* Jaws)

TELEPATHY: Examining the theoretical approach of Carl Gustav Jung's collective unconscious, (*see* Collective Unconscious) we find the internal and personal world of individuality, linked to the external world of an entire human species. Compounding this theoretical union, with the elaborate system of retaining unspoken details about one another in family and loving relationships, we begin to witness a seemingly mystical, yet entirely corollary understanding of the human nexus. Further clarifying, in a relationship, we begin to know the thought patterns and in fact, the very thoughts (and feelings) of our mutual partners, whom with we share life's experiences. When these individuals are no longer involved in our immediate experience, we nevertheless retain a part of their fundamental being. Accordingly, the collective unconscious and the unconscious dreaming mind, occasionally bridge together to 'see', 'hear' and 'feel' these individuals, especially in times of intensely high levels of stress or anxiety, and even though they are literally thousands of miles away from us. For example, Mrs. Rosalie Richardson, a respected editor in broadcasting, conveyed a dream she had experienced involving an old boyfriend from her teenage years. She had not seen or thought about this man in over fifteen years, yet one night he suddenly appeared in her dream full of life, charismatic and entirely animated. Both he, Rosalie and the entire group of 'kids' who hung out together in that particular period of her life materialized in the dream landscape. Mrs. Richardson went on to explain how her once boyfriend was not only curiously lively, but also bright and vivid in rich chromatic hues of color, while she herself and her other friends appeared drab and essentially black and white in demeanor. Several months later, she learned that her resplendent ex-boyfriend in the dream had passed away after a long period of suffering illness. After mourning the loss of a once dear friend, Mrs. Richardson's dream came flooding back in her memory. Reflecting on the strange vision, she recalled a book she had read based on channeling spirits. In this book, she recounted, a certain 'spirit' chastised the working medium for his lack of knowledge and understanding in the fundamental matters of reality. The spirit alluded to the drab darkness of the medium's ignorance and his limited use of a fantastic elemental soul. In this instance, Mrs. Richardson understood the vivid, knowing spirit nature of her friend, who at the moment of his dream arrival, no longer joined the ranks of the one-dimensional, earthbound living... (*see* Clairvoyance)

TELEPHONE: The Telephone has become such a normal part of our existence, we barely acknowledge its ever present reality. However, in a dream landscape, its appearance is almost always symbolic of communicating with someone who is virtually unreachable. This is why we often dream of receiving telephone calls from departed loved ones, famous persons, angels or even God. In this sense, the call generally refers to a warning or communication about ourselves or our loved ones which we cannot perceive for ourselves, for whatever reason. As such, the phone voice may refer to a part of our consciousness (belief system, desires etc.) which is repressed and barred access from our reality in waking life. Nevertheless, the phone metaphor reaches beyond that line of repression and rings in the news of the self, directly to our waiting finger tips and eager ears.

TELEVISION: The bright screen in virtually every home and known as T.V. illuminates our existence with fragmentary images of the entire world of perception. As such, in a dream, the television screen becomes the dream within a dream. Its images reflect the concerns of our unconscious who recreates them through memory. The purpose for this image within an image centers around the need for focusing in on its intended message. Our dream may be revealing a media medium for comprehension of data. Accordingly, we need to watch the 'show' and determine its symbolic language.

TEMPTATION: The conceptualization of Temptation in a dream sense, involves a symbolic desire. That is to say, what tempts us in our dream may represent deeper longings and/or wishes, than the single objects which are witnessed in the dream itself. For example, gazing hungrily at a candy bar in a chocolate shop window, may illustrate a perceived separation from the sweet, good things in life. We may feel guilt in procuring the more precious experiences offered in existence. In this sense, temptations become a sort of meeting ground between craving, physical needs and moral, judgmental, spiritual restraints per se. Akin to a scale of decision, temptation asks us which way we want to go; the way of indulgence or the way of abstinence. From a psychological point of view, the middle ground is perhaps the healthiest and obviously best balanced ethical existence, the space between the demon and the zealot. (*see* Demon) (*see* Devil)

TERMITE: Since a house is representative of the self, the image of Termites may well involve forces eating away at the fabric and very foundation of self. The conceptualization of infestation involves a slow process wherein tiny pests, symbolic of obstacles and dilemmas, gradually accumulate into swarms, which eventually cause us unimaginable turmoil. Appropriately, we need to address our difficulties in waking life, one problem and solution at a time, thereby beginning the business of reducing their overall impact upon us. In this way, a step-by-step healing procedure may begin to take effect on our psychological perception of the world around us.

TERRACE: The view from a Terrace symbolizes our gaze at the outside world, from a comfortable vantage point. In this sense, we may be illustrating high spirits and/or lofty results in our undertakings. In an archetypal sense, we are akin to kings and queens who address their courts with towering and commanding status; status which may in fact be unreachable to us, were it not for these convenient and relatively democratic terraces. In this sense, in a capitalistic society, the more successful one becomes, the more elevated of a terrace he or she may be privileged to enjoy.

TEST: In a dream, a Test may refer directly to being challenged by some force (institution, society) greater than oneself. As such, the dreamer is asked to prove knowledge and/or ability. In waking life, these tests of merit occur quite often. However, in the psychological sense, these recurring test dreams may imply a fear of performance in quite specific terms. In as much, cases where dreamers score high results in examinations are exceedingly rare. Predominantly, we find anxiety and difficulty in the test undertaking. Naturally, many of us abhor the thought of having to certify our relative worth. In the case of the test dream, we are absolutely rebelling against the entire concept. (*see* Quiz)

THREE: The number Three, or the triad, involves the unbreakable strength of spirit. Moreover, the first odd numeral illustrates uniqueness and the principal dialectic creation born of dualism. As such, the number three becomes a new beginning on which to build the ultimate dualism of four (*see* Four), or two twos. Herein, lies the strength of the number, embodying a completion and an introduction simultaneously. In the dream sense, three-sided figures represent permanence and the infinite potential of transfiguration. Note the resilience of the triangle and taken one step further, the great pyramids based on the same geometric design. (*see* Tarot Major Arcana: The Empress (3) arcana)

TIE: The idea of being Tied up in a real sense indicates the removal of freedom. To be bound in a dream landscape reveals a forced restraint upon oneself by outside forces and/or situations. As such, our unconscious reminds us we may not be exercising our full potential freedom. Furthermore, the dream may imply that a person is tied in knots, symbolic of complication and hard misunderstanding. We may need to simplify matters, thereby unwinding their knots and otherwise cut free from the physical, mental or spiritual noose they insistently become. In another interpretation, independence requires a certain amount of courage and responsibility, therefore being tied up illustrates a way out of this accountability without remorse or regret. In this sense, being tied may refer to sexual indulgence without condemnation, guilt or liability. We cannot be blamed for actions we are forced into and cannot hope to escape (even if we ourselves purchased the rope, straps and/or handcuffs!). (*see* Knot)

TIGER: As opposed to a lion, which exhibits nobility, the Tiger remains wild, untamed and inhumanely ferocious. However, because of these characteristic traits, the tiger is thought to represent sexuality in all its unlimited carnal release. Moreover, the strength of the tiger comes to symbolize a powerful sexual partner who assumes control of the entire experience. In the potent imagery of the leaping animal, we interpret a leap of instinctual faith in ones abilities, sexual or otherwise. In the Chinese zodiac, the tiger personality is seen as aggressive and courageous, yet also as a deep thinker who dwells within his or her own being. The connection with our deepest primal memory is rather complex in that it demonstrates our fiercest survival instincts, as well as our profoundest union with earth and her natural elements. The tiger dream may explore the tenets of our intuitive behavior and all its inherent consequences in a so-called 'civilized' world.

TIME: In the dream sense, Time refers to our concern about temporal elements. For example, a dreamer may be expressing anxiety involving his or her difficulty with punctual deportment, in a dreamscape where he or she arrives late for a high-profile business meeting, wearing only polka-dot shorts. Another example of temporal dreams, revolve around the repetitive image of a clock, or symbolic 'clock-watching' behavior. Moreover, a dreamer may be depicting the reality of becoming a slave to time, when the concern of the physical hour dominates all other dream considerations. (see Clock)

TOILET: The image of the Toilet may represent the lowest position of our relative humanity, that is to say, the reality of our bodies eliminatory functions. In this sense, when we become nauseous, incontinent and otherwise irregular, we almost instinctively and entirely automatically run to the proverbial toilet. Besides its obvious function (the miracle of plumbing!), the reason we escape to the john, may involve our first lesson of bodily control and proper human behavior, that is: Toilet Training. Ergo, in our time of need, we return to our roots and root understanding of a solution to our discomfort and the elimination (disappearance) of our bodily waste. The combined reality of our inescapable animal nature and a hope to effectively hide this nature, may be involved in the dream analysis of the toilet. Accordingly, the john may symbolize guilt and/or a rationalization concerning our animal needs and/or functional behavior. (see Feces)

TORCH: The age-old symbol of the Torch involves victory and outright power innate in humanity's control over flame. Moreover, the image of fire held in hand invokes dominance over the natural world, including and especially, the world of darkness (night). In yet another sense, the torch represents real wisdom which blazes through the darkness of ignorance. In all cases, the hand-held flame acts as a trigger and catalyst of fortitude, both internal and external. Therefore, in a dream landscape, the actions involved around the manipulation of the torch and that which is illuminated by its fire, may reveal the potential of our personal and/or social abilities, dynamic and mighty as any metaphorical flame. (*see* Lantern) (*see* Ablaze)

TORNADO: The symbolism of the Tornado may refer to the real possibility, yet not certainty, of chaotic danger in our life. As such, we need to determine which facets of our waking condition may place us in the potential path of this harrowing peril. Moreover, the image of solid structures dislodged and uprooted, may involve a threat which concerns our deeply rooted psychological fabric, including perhaps, the equilibrium of our home and family life.

TOWEL: The concept of the Towel may involve wiping away the wetness of ones drenched emotions and moving into another psychological plain. Furthermore, since a towel is associated with the completion of cleansing oneself, our unconscious may be illustrating the conclusion of a purging event. In other words, we may be implying to ourself, that we have paid our dues and are prepared to begin anew. As such, we may need to evaluate conditions, relationships or situations in our waking life, which may in fact be resolved and/or readied for transition into another and entirely new stage of experience. (*see* Water) (*see* Wash)

TOY: The image of the Toy carries with it the reality of our childhood. In this sense, we need to interpret our feelings about the toy. Are we almost unnaturally drawn toward it? If so, we may be exhibiting signs of regression which may in turn signal difficulty in coping with the complexity and responsibility of our present waking life. On the other hand, if the toy is discarded, we may be displaying feelings of wasted youth or intolerant youth, which may indicate mental barriers which need to be overcome. Naturally the color and type of toy is essential in the meaning of the entire dream sequence. (*see* Wall) (*see* Wagon) (*see* Child)

TRAFFIC: The idea of Traffic is synonymous with being held back from ones goals. The reasons for this personal cessation are many and varied, however, the predominant cause involves the accumulation of many individuals with the same purpose and intent as ourselves. Consequently, a dream involving traffic may illustrate a personal psychological struggle to succeed or be left behind. Moreover, our unconscious may be revealing a feeling of personal anonymity, thereby relinquishing our individuality into the grand mix of society at large. This loss of identity, may in turn, act as the very catalyst which holds us back from our goals and subsequently, impedes all forward progress we may have enjoyed on a self-created and entirely individuated path of life.

TRAIN: In the modern world, the Train harks back to an earlier age where transportation was slow, deliberate and entirely scenic. In as much, the train dream involves a survey of changing landscapes and metaphoric lives. In this, we may see a physical act of decision making, concerning our fundamental heading in life. Moreover, the image of one lover departing another by train represents a long, painful separation with much thought and lingering emotion on the part of both parties. This exaggerated parting implies a desperate hope for a last minute change of heart, perhaps directly proportional to the moving distance of the partner left behind. As such, we witness a moment by moment change of landscape, which changes our internal point of view of life in general and precisely. Accordingly, the train dream may illustrate our 'train' of thought and list of possible life options. However, if we find ourselves tied to the tracks and a locomotive train is steaming toward us, we may be implying disastrous life consequences based on erroneous decision making.

TRANSMUTATION: The concept of Transmutation involves man changing into animal. In this we see a visual transition of psychological states of mind. Metaphorically, the 'animal' represents our primal, ancestral and deepest consciousness. Conversely, the 'man' which undergoes change, becomes symbolic of our modern civilized world and the moral decision making, which takes place in that world. In the act of transmutation, our unconscious may be illustrating the relative levels of movement between these two internal worlds of our experience. Moreover, in cases of dream Zoomorphism, we find a direct balance and poignant interaction between our foundations of perceptual memory. (see Zoomorphism) (see Reincarnation)

TREE: The complex symbolism of a Tree involves wisdom, strength and silent contemplation. As such, the mighty tree reaches toward heaven with branches extended and digs deep into mother earth with stolid and laborious roots. In the dream sense, the image of a tree may refer to our spiritual and/or well-balanced heading in life. Accordingly, a bowed tree may indicate a harmful or destructive path taken in life. Conversely, a rounded and spiraling tree may illustrate a wealth of rich experience in ones animated journey. (*see* Oak) (*see* Evergreen) (*see* Joshua Tree)

TRENCH: The act of digging a shelter into the soil of earth may represent a return to the womb, in other words, regression back into the familiar territory of mother and childhood. In the illustrious dream scenario of a fox hole, where soldiers hide from bullets and violence, our unconscious may be illustrating a fear of being exposed and targeted by outside forces. Taken together, we witness the symbolism of the Trench as it involves insecurities and a refuge from painful realities. In yet another sense, a trench may represent a ditch which we unexpectedly fall into, most especially when we waver from our direct course of ideas, ideals and personal faith. (*see* Den)

TRIBE: The basic tenets of social interaction and group organization can be clearly focused on in the systematic study of Tribal behavior. As such, the tribe reflects the physical, mental and spiritual connection innate in highly interactive human beings. Consequently, the tribal dream illustrates our innermost union with one another and moreover, the universal implications of this elaborate network of association. Accordingly, we witness a transfiguration toward nature's spiritual source when we embrace the family of man and deeper yet, the interconnectedness of ALL life on earth. (*see* Taboo) (*see* Ritual)

TROPHY: In the dream sense, a Trophy may refer to a richly deserved reward given in life. Accordingly, our unconscious may be illustrating the merit of our time spent on a noble and perhaps difficult, project. However, a trophy lost or imparted to a competitor, may symbolize resentment involving a lack of desired recognition for our efforts. Furthermore, if the trophy is broken or damaged, we may be indicating a spurious social or interpersonal appreciation for our laborious task.

TRUNK: A Trunk may be symbolic of restless behavior which entails incessant travel. Furthermore, the clothing and necessary belongings found in a trunk suggest ones possessions and acquisitions appropriated in life. Therefore, a single chest of goods may reflect a simple or meager existence, while a truckload of trunks (i.e. commodities) illustrates wealth, power and perhaps old wisdom. In an alternative dream landscape, we may find ourselves burying a chest, or conversely, searching for 'buried treasure.' In both cases we may be illustrating a poignant concern about our economic well-being and subsequently, the security of ourselves and our entire family. (*see* Chest)

TUNNEL: The trip through dark, subterranean regions in search for light and a re-emergence into new psychological landscapes, may involve a narrow and difficult period in our life which searches culmination, redemption and a return to a freedom of movement. Furthermore, the concept of the Tunnel pertains to the peculiar restriction of claustrophobia, which roughly parallels a fear of death replete with isolated coffins and graves. In yet another variation, this tunnel image is equated with being trapped in the pre-existence of the womb, where hope for complete expression is yet to be fulfilled. Hence, we search for the light of birth and creation at the end of our long, dark tunnel of uncertainty and slow, yet consistent, development. (*see* Labyrinth)

TWINS: The symbolism of Twins may refer to different underlying characteristics in similar appearing entities. Consequently, the dream image of twins may refer to a split personality in oneself. In other words, this characteristic twinning effect may imply an internal argument which equally explores opposing sides of a particular conjecture. (*see* Double)

TWO: The archaic symbolism of the numeral Two involves the paradoxical nature and division of balance found in duality. Accordingly, the image of two items represents the partition of one item into two halves. Conversely, a reflection of one object may become a dual image of a single entity. In other words, two connotate the double-sided nature of existence. In the dream sense, two persons or objects may refer to two sides of a single story. (*see* Double) (*see* Twin)

TYRANT: In the dream sense, a Tyrant may refer to improper and self-serving leadership. Accordingly, we need to determine the motivations of our dream tyrant, and what this symbolic person tells us about ourselves. Moreover, we need to analyze any and all representational uses of force or aggression indicated in the dream landscape. In most cases, the Tyrant is not meant to be king, and implies a confusion in the natural order of things. (*see* King)

UFO: The image of a UFO, or space crafts in general, involves a dire hope for something entirely new in the realm of experience, which hold the key to deliver us from ourselves, in other words, the limitations of our reality. The UFO perceptively travels through space, and perhaps even time, and, in the very essence of their living breathing being, transcend all earthly realities. In this, they may in fact, seem able to solve ALL our self-imposed, yet nevertheless complex, ensnarements of civilization. This factor gives them unbelievable emotional, as well as, psychological appeal. It is assumed, that these beings immediately understand the troubles facing our world and once prepared, will begin the process of healing all the unnecessary wounds. Conversely, we may find a fear of aliens, which may involve a general insecurity about our own well being. In this sense, we may feel ever-vulnerable to an invisible enemy who observes us from the heavens. Alternatively, the alien who comes to conquer mankind and is instead defeated by (mankind), may involve a complex compensation concerning individual and social strengths, as if to say, even though we seem weak, chaotic and vulnerable, when we stand together, we can conquer the stars themselves. The dream itself therefore, is as complicated as the dreamer's psychological perception of the world. Accordingly, we need to determine the hopes and fears of the dreamer. Moreover, we may need to analyze religious or spiritual tenets to uncover the dreamer's relation and thoughts about an unseen outside force. Naturally, in many ways, aliens may be (and have been) compared to deities. (*see* Stars) (*see* Extraterrestrials)

UMBILICAL CORD: The symbolism of the Umbilical Cord refers to our attachment to maternal sustenance. In other words, in the dream sense, we may be expressing anxiety about supporting ourselves and otherwise creating a self-sufficient psychological and emotional foundation. Moreover, the image of cutting ones umbilical cord, refers to the forced removal of matriarchal nurturing, for better or worse. This dream image may imply the unconscious message that proper learning involves falling and lifting oneself back up. The self which fails to symbolically stand on its own represses its distinguished potential of individual freedom.

UMBRELLA: The symbolism of an Umbrella may refer to a hapless attempt to block out stormy and down-pouring emotions. However, the image of a parasol may represent well-defined social parameters in a romantic courtship. Traversing further down this line of thought, we explore the circle, or ring, of passion which circumscribe lovers embraced under an umbrella in the coursing rain. Accordingly, in the dream sense, we need to interpret the color, shape and practical use of the visually stimulating dream umbrella.

UNCLEAN: In a very real sense, Unclean objects or persons have become symbolic of evil or demonic activity. The primary reason for this archetype centers around the connection with wild (life) and therefore, inhuman behavior. Another name for the devil is Beelzebub, which can loosely be translated as 'lord of the flies', consequently, we once again witness this thought construct of foul and unclean realities linked with otherworldly evil and chaos. In dreams, we find levels of uncleanliness and subsequently, at times, we behold only certain body parts unwashed. These respective body parts may illustrate differentiated aspects of our guilt or moral fear. For example, dirty hands may represent deceitful manipulations recently transpired, including perhaps, deviant sexual transgressions. (see Cleaning)

UNCONSCIOUS, THE: To understand the Unconscious, it is necessary to first analyze the cognitive processes of the human brain. The mind, such as it is, provides us with instantaneous reception and transmission of an almost infinite array of information. Information, is the abstract term for the reality perceived by one or all of our five senses. Each of our sense organs is specialized to differentiate subtle distinctions in the specific reality which that organ is adapted to perceive. For example, our sense of hearing 'listens' to waves of sound within a wide spectrum of audible frequencies. Likewise, our sense of smell recognizes the most minute shades of separate fragrances found in the world. The most complex of these senses, is our sense of sight, which involves spatial relationships such as depth, height and distance, as well as, three-dimensional shapes and the entire prism of visible color. Over countless millennia, the brain evolved these sensory organs to 'reach out' and process the outside world. As such, in the action of this sensory perception, the brain receives information in all its focused complexity and is therefore able to accurately coordinate this elaborate information with all other forms of sensory input. In this sense, the mind builds information into memory and memory in turn strengthens with each correlation of experience. Therefore, if separate units of sensory input are continuously repeated in sequence our mind essentially will link them together. Over time these continuities become our worldly perception and supply the background for our individuated points of view.

When we lie down to sleep, we bring our fears, concerns and daily elations, all still fresh in our memory, into our dream consciousness. This dream consciousness is referred to as the Unconscious, because it contains all the sensory information gathered over a life-time by the human brain via the continuous operation of the sensory organs. In the process of dreaming, our unconscious reveals the furthest elaboration and deepest memory traced on the human being's mind. In this elaboration, or clarification, of memory, our brain illuminates a series of (visual, auditory, olfactory etc.) sensations to best understand the present application of reality. This series of sensations act as a language of symbols (and archetypes) and serve to create the dream landscape such as we know it.

Naturally, the complexity of memory experiences and the huge storehouse of recollected sensory perceptions associated with them, reveal an outstanding number of dream images, which taken together, appear nonsensical and perhaps even random. Appropriately, the dreamer needs to sort out the more powerful and/or poignant references found in these images and in this manner, akin to a cryptographer, decipher the message offered by the unconscious and its life-time of experience. Furthermore, examining the Collective Unconscious, we witness how the individual mind may tap into the racial memory of humankind, revealing innate tendencies and preferential aptitudes in a diversity of intelligence variants. In all these tenets, we find a phenomenal union of consciousness and an overall cohesiveness of being... (*see* Collective Unconscious)

UNIVERSITY: All the elements and various aspects of higher education may be prevalent in this dream scenario. Moreover, our academic history (or future) directly effects our occupation and livelihood. Therefore, University dreams may reflect anxieties or relative concerns about our financial stability, present or future. In another sense, our unconscious may be illustrating facets of our social interactions or simply reminding us about crucial lessons or beliefs (theories) once held. Naturally, any significant or traumatic experiences which occurred in college figure prominently in the overall dream interpretation. (*see* School) (*see* Academy)

UPHILL: In the dream sense, an Uphill journey refers to a difficult path taken to reach an emotional or psychological summit. As such, our unconscious may be illustrating the persistent courage and fortitude necessary to achieve worthwhile goals. However, an uphill battle, may also imply the very real possibility of failure. Accordingly, we may need to access our abilities and our relative fears. Are we able to scale the mountain of our own apprehensions, anxieties and perceived limitations? The dream may hold the answer we desperately need to discover and utilize in our waking experience. (*see* Wall) (*see* Path)

URBAN DREAM: The complex conceptualization of the urban environment, replete with droves of people, loud noise, confusion and hyperactive energy in general, may refer to a specific psychological drive. This drive or desire, may involve fully embracing the sheer exuberance of crowded and diversified city life, or conversely, running from its chaotic madness. Naturally, this distinction is based upon our relative perceptions about urban life. In either case, it may need to be said, that bright lights can be entirely illuminating AS WELL AS utterly blinding. In this sense, we see that reality, unlike a sometimes prejudiced perception, is always a two sided coin.

URINE: In the dream sense, the expulsion of Urine, may refer to a release of pressure. Moreover, since urine is primarily water, we may be expressing the removal of an internalized and impassioned relationship. However, since urine also removes potential toxins, our unconscious may be informing us that this purging may in fact be healthy and cleansing. Consequently, we are now able to drink in new and fresh waters of experience. (*see* Baptism) (*see* Water)

URN: The complex symbolism of an Urn refers to a personal shrine or sanctuary for memories of deep and eternal love. In this sense, the memorial vase which contains ashes of a loved one, or simply flowers, conveys a physical space embodying the immaterial emotions of love, devotion and respect. As such, an urn may be compared to an icon, in that it symbolizes far more than the sum of itself. Appropriately, in the dream sense, an urn may refer to the embrace and unabridged acceptance of our abstract feelings which we sometimes lose sight of in the physical world. (*see* Ashes)

VALLEY: The image of the Valley carries with it the promise of fertile lands, exaggerated activity and a safe haven for human life. Furthermore, this sanctified geographical womb implies an invitation into sexuality, love and ultimately, family. All in all, we seem to be witnessing a desirable and secure plain of existence. However, the reality of the valley is divided by the mountain dwellers who were perhaps removed from the fertile plain or simply denied unmolested entry, due to a lack of force or social standing. In this sense, we find the archetype of the valley of shadows and the biblical terminology of the valley of death (into which 600 men rode and alas, never returned). In the dream interpretation, we may need to determine whether or not the valley is in fact desirable and/or safe for our entry. In turn, we find the complexity of this dualistic dream image narrowing down to its minute individual components. As such, every tree, fruit and resource in general obtained in the dale, glen or vale, may be beneficial and fulfilling to our well being, or conversely, poisonous, rotten or barren of any prospect of vitality, whatsoever. Hence the term, 'How green is your valley?'

VAMPIRE: The complex symbolism of the Vampire involves seduction, sensuality and death. In this diversity of meaning we find unique elements of contrasting images. The first and most obvious paradox is that of hot-blooded lust and cold-bodied death embodying the same individual via the drive and hunger for rich and animating life-blood. The second contradiction is the vampire's civilized nobility paired off with his animal (vampire bat) ferocity and aggression. Lastly, in the inconsistencies of this creature, is its attractive lure and fairly converse, horrendous, long-fanged and generally monstrous behavior. Accordingly, in the dream sense, our unconscious may be utilizing this complex dream figure to demonstrate extreme and diverse feelings involving a situation or individual (if not oneself), whose charm may be ultimately harmful. In this sense, a vampire may represent an addiction to drugs or alcohol, or conversely, a romantic obsession involving a partner with little or no emotional concern for the relationship itself. (*see* Impale) (*see* Bleed) (*see* Shark)

VAULT: The complex image of a Vault involves a powerful arched structure which supports a heavy roof. In the symbolic sense, we may be referring to the psychological support of our abstract conceptualizations. In medieval times, artists such as Michelangelo, were encouraged to paint enormous cathedral ceilings supported by vaulted architecture (ex: Sistine Chapel). This representation of God's work was presented in a symbolic sky buttressed by a powerful and upright faith. Accordingly, in the dream sense, we may be illustrating a stolid conviction in some person, or idea. Moreover, since vaulted architecture is sometimes used in mausoleums, our faith and belief may concern unshakable wisdom imparted by deceased loved ones.

VENTRILOQUISM: In the dream sense, Ventriloquism may involve deception and otherwise, speaking out of the corner of ones mouth. Moreover, the image of a puppet which blurts out words which are not its own, may refer to politicians and political figure heads, who read speeches created not by themselves, but spin-doctors, trained in the art of propaganda. Taken together, we see the symbolism of hollow, and therefore, untrustworthy, individuals appearing in the context of our waking life. Furthermore, we may be referring to our own parroting behavior which emulates some other person's language, behavior and original ideas.

VICTIM: To be Victimized involves power and the desperate lack of it in ones own life. A natural and beneficial human trait involves a keen awareness of vulnerability in a particular situation. Normally, we strive to remove ourselves from these vulnerable situations and locations as quickly as possible. However, in waking life, we often find ourselves forced to remain in physically, mentally and spiritually hostile environments simply to make a living (occupation) and otherwise exist in a modern aggressive society. When we repress these feelings of victimization, they loom large in our unconscious and we may find ourselves submerged in nightmares where we are relentlessly pursued and/or tortured. Psychologists almost universally recommend facing and challenging ones tormentors in a dream landscape. In theory, when the dream abusers have vanished, we may gain courage to face those who seek domination over us in waking life, whether they be bosses, criminals or even (and sometimes especially) loved ones. (*see* Attack)

VIKING: The symbol of the Viking involves relentless aggressive behavior in the acquiring of goals. However, although these Vikings did in fact, plunder for gold and valuable goods, they nevertheless should not be confused with pirates and other outlaws. The reason for this justification is centered around the cultural acceptance of their practices and the subsequent social, rather than individual, motivation which prompted their ventures. Accordingly, the Viking is not anti-social, but rather ultra-social, in the minds of his people. Hence, the appearance of a Viking in a dream landscape, may refer to an aggressive exertion toward some valuable and gregarious goal. For example, an Olympic swimmer, may illustrate a dream image of a Viking ship which rows relentlessly toward shore and the gold (medal) it offers.

VILLAGE: The dream Village may be symbolic of simplicity and childhood reassurance. Naturally, these two factors of our psyche are indeed intricate and entirely complex in their own right. Accordingly, we need to closely analyze all the features of the village landscape. The internal social interactions combined with the accessibility into the communities inner sanctum (bar, general store, festival, church etc.), especially by a stranger (the dreamer and dream cohorts), may illustrate the psychological layout of social stability, status and ultimately, adaptability. Therefore, a harsh, alienating village, may represent an unconscious learning ground (or stage) for unstable or ill-advised waking behavior. On the other hand, an idealic wonderland may involve fantasy and wish-fulfillment revealing various and perhaps pernicious, forms of regression; which is of course, an example of a dream being far more problematic than a nightmare. Another facet of this dream landscape involves the Village Idiot, who may represent ourselves, and as such, may be yet another tool utilized by the unconscious to demonstrate elements of our personal folly. However, it must be remembered that the archetype of the fool (or Idiot), carries much wisdom in its ability to perceive the world with an empty (open) mind which sees and learns with earnest integrity and spiritual faith in the ability of self.

VINE: The image of the winding Vine which covers our home (or castle?) with its lush growth and long reaching artery-like network of stems, may symbolize our ancestry, family, or the roots we've planted in the community of our upbringing. In this sense, the conceptualization of ever-reaching tendrils, may be positive in their skeletal support of oneself and ones rich history. However, these same vines may represent a trap or prison imposed by the moral structure of ones family, town or entire nation. Furthermore, a restrictive image of vines may involve ethical fears concerning sex and other naturalistic impulses which may bind us in blind emotional passion. In yet another interpretation, our dream may be alluding to the intellectual institutions known as the 'ivy league' schools, famous for their old coveted buildings (and edifices) covered in rich vines of ivy. In this case, we may be expressing a concern about our education, learning or knowledge in general. Accordingly, our occupation or the occupational aspirations once held (or still hold) may be intimately involved with these ivy league dream visions.

VIRGIN: The complex symbolism of the Virgin, refers both to purity AND potential. As opposed to the eunuch who is rendered sexually incapable, a virgin is the embodiment of unblemished coitus and therefore, sanctified motherhood. In this sense, a pharaoh gave birth to noble children, from the bodies of his cluster of virgins. Taken one step further, we see the image of the virgin Mary, who remains intact, even after the birth of baby Jesus, who becomes a sort of symbolic super-nobility, or 'king of kings.' Along these lines, we see the dream image of the virgin pertaining to spiritual harmony and the potential for higher love and ideal motherhood. However, the virgin reflection may involve a repressed fear of sexuality or the difficulties of childbearing, or relationships in general. As such, we need to determine the behavior and demeanor of the dream virgin for apparent similarities with, or radical differences from, our own waking experience.

VOICE: In our dreams, a Voice primarily represents an internal and very personal part of our understanding, which we somehow distance from the self we wish to personify in waking life. As such, the dream voice becomes our own knowledge disembodied and therefore acceptable to our belief system and ongoing personal agendas and/or philosophies. Naturally then, the voice is primarily a balancing force in our overall psyche. For example, a timid person may find a powerful narrator in his or her dream landscape, who eggs them on to perilous and inspiring adventures, while a reckless daredevil, may hear a voice of calm reason and various warnings about the merits and outright intelligence of caution. Additionally, the unconscious may utilize voice dreams to work as reminders of role models who exercised influence over our life, and who's 'words' remain with us.

VOLCANO: The image of the Volcano is extremely symbolic of the disruption of stability and good firm ground in general. The red, hot lava, which flows from this mountainous eruption seems to indicate emotional disruption. Suitably, since earth is associated with womanhood, we may gather that this gusher involves extraordinary feminine characteristics. These features may include evaluations of relationships, child-rearing and occupational difficulties due to sexist bias. In any case, we find the rumbling volcano to be a fine descriptive metaphor for increasing stress levels which eventually reach the boiling point and explode figuratively over the entire landscape in a torrid and inescapable flood of emotion.

VOMIT: The purging of toxins from within is graphically symbolic of throwing away harmful persons or situations. Interestingly enough, that which is regurgitated is often initially perceived as grand, sweet and entirely desired. In this sense, we witness a physical metaphoric reversing of intake or acceptance. The violence of Vomiting seems to reveal the real danger involved in the reality of that which is only symbolically discharged. Consequently, our dream may be indicating that our actions are rapidly dragging us into peril and we must reverse our drastic behavior, thereby releasing the poison which has internalized itself into our waking reality. (see Stomach) (see Regurgitate)

VOODOO: In the dream sense, the practice of Voodoo may involve a complex fear of castigation and death caused by our own immorality. Comparable to many religions, Voudon stresses humility and worship offered to a God or Gods. However, as opposed to many creeds who threaten punishment to the immoral in the realm of the afterlife, voodoo promises immediate retribution in the form of priests, who are extremely capable of providing a 'hell on earth', here and now. Accordingly, the dreamer may be experiencing a very real anxiety about his or her sinful behavior and the immediacy of its harsh retribution.

VOYEUR: The symbolism of the Voyeur may involve a physical alienation from life's activities, which are instead experienced vicariously. Accordingly, in the dream sense, a voyeur may refer to a person who watches or imitates our own behavior, or conversely, our own jealous observation of a some other person's actions or life-style. We may need to determine the exact nature of this dream estrangement and compare the physical scenes observed by the voyeur, with our own imaginative explorations. Along these lines, the invasion of privacy committed by this Peeping Tom, may reflect a direct probe by our conscious awareness into the unconscious ocean of our repressed memory.

VULTURE: The dual symbolism of the Vulture involves both a struggle for survival and a wish for death. In the dream vision, flying vultures embody a forewarning of our own psychological or emotional death. In this particular case, our demise should be evaded by every method at our disposal. This is perhaps why the vultures reveal themselves in the representational sense. This revelation gives the dying victim something to think about before giving up the struggle. Conversely, a dream vision involving the birds eating carrion, may be reflective of our own parasitic behavior which may take advantage of the destruction, or loss, of another. Appropriately, we need to analyze all other elements of the vulture dream landscape, including flight, heat, the desert, absence of water, and the full connotation of death itself.

WAGON: The little red Wagon, which carried our toys and goods reflected the beginnings of our intimate association with tools and technology. In this sense, our dream may be alluding to simpler times and simpler tools necessary for successful endeavors. In an age of space satellites and mainframe computers, virtually incomprehensible in design and repair maintenance, even to the very persons who operate and rely on them day in and day out, wagon, shovel and pail dreams have become far more commonplace.

WAIF: Although sensationalized in our current media and modeling industry, perhaps because of its natural allusion to fragile and certainly reckless youth, a Waif has nevertheless primarily symbolized poverty and a lack of basic needs. As such, we need to examine the reasons, if any, for this inadequacy and metaphoric malnutrition. Moreover, we need to determine if repressive behavior forbids the intake of these needed requirements. Therefore in a dream, we may need to analyze the fears, repulsions and conversely needs and realistic desires of the waif figure.

WAKE UP: To Wake Up in ones dream implies the rousing of a crucial realization, which may have been overlooked by a sleeping (lazy, wandering, delusionary) mind. Moreover, since waking involves opening ones eyes, we may be alluding to clarity of vision in understanding an object or person who has always (or at least previously) been present in our field of experience. In another interpretation, our waking up, may signal a spiritual, mental or physical form of calling, or enlightenment, to 'wake up' others around us who are sleeping through the fulfillment of their own lives. This sort of zealot dream scenario, occurs quite often, and therefore may provide a desired psychological quiet. This may be accomplished by building relevant status in the perception of self. Moreover, ancient Persians believed in reverse dream interpretation. In which case, the dream of waking up implies a necessity to dream, or live out ones dreams, in waking life. It is interesting to note that all these dream interpretations carry a common thread of undeniable spiritual transcendence.

WALK: In the dream sense, Walking may refer to our perception of the world and the society around us. Accordingly, as we walk through a dream landscape, we may need to interpret every facet of the series of images which we come across. Moreover, any changes of direction, or relative obstacles, should be noted and analyzed. However, the natural and casual ease of walking, usually implies a slow, contemplative sense of well-being. (*see* Journey) (*see* Path)

WALL: The powerful symbol of the Wall represents personal barriers which seem impossible to cross, penetrate and overcome in general. Unlike a gate or fence, which implies security with controlled accessibility, the thick, ponderous wall neither receives entry nor allows escape. It is both a physical, as well as mental, stronghold. In the psychological sense, the wall is built up by the self, brick by brick and cinderblock by cinderblock. Each segment of this wall represents a disillusionment found in life's experience, for example, a bad relationship or childhood trauma. Most people overcome these stumbling blocks of social and personal reality and attempt to move on after each occurrence, remaining as intact as possible; depending of course, on their relative severity. However, when these blocks seem to appear continuously and with an exaggerated frequency, we begin to fundamentally link their causal relationship. As such, we focus on our own personal characteristics and their limitations which we realize trigger the cause and effect machination of these stumbling blocks. Naturally, if this complex socialization occurs at an early age (which it usually does), we have a tendency to accept full blame or at least full responsibility, for all these aberrations from normal behavioral interaction. When this self-depreciation occurs, we unconsciously stack the stumbling blocks, brick by brick and cinderblock by cinderblock. Over time, we find ourselves trapped within the insurmountable wall of our own creation. In waking life, this barrier figures prominently into all our decision making, weighing as heavily as it does on our perception of self-worth. The dreamer may need to slowly disassemble this wall, brick by brick. Conversely, if the dreamer finds him or herself building a wall, an active and acute unconscious may be signaling that their is still time to reverse our course in life, enabling free access to separate realities. As such, we may begin to learn to accept our limitations and moreover, the limitations of others who are unable to perceive inconsistencies in their overall picture of reality, causing them discomfort, fear and personal uncertainty in their own life.

WALTZ: The art of the Waltz involves coordination and sensuality, yet with a ritual adherence to accepted social themes. In this, the waltz is roughly comparable to tribal dances with rules of communal organization and status. The free-spirited dance of peasantry has little in common with the terse, gallant pageantry of the courtly waltz. In the well known fairy tale where Cinderella arrives at the king's royal ball with her glass slippers, we witness far more than a festive dance. We see instead a rite of passage into power and wealth, where shoes are not meant to be sturdy and flexible (usually ideal for dance), but rather fine, delicate, smooth and yes, sexual glass slippers, on which to magically transport a would-be princess in her courtly waltz. As such, our dream may represent an aspiration for social order and recognized status. Furthermore, it may involve a fantasy concerning our overlooked grandiloquence in the world of our waking life. Moreover, our unconscious may be reminding us about the level of dedication and knowledge (remember the glass slipper!) needed to achieve our lofty goals in life, including love and the creation of family. (*see* Dance)

WAND: The image of the magic Wand symbolizes the force of pointed will which bends and in some cases, creates unimaginable potential. The elements of sexuality related to this phallic object date back to ancient times where it was recorded that the phallus routinely transformed into a writhing serpent possessing a semi-divine pleasure principle. However, the wand as staff is most prevalent in written history; the sturdy axis toward heaven and God which equates balanced leadership the measure of its lowest focal point, under which, all men and women serve a common cause. Accordingly, we need to determine the full intention of the magic wand in our dream landscape and who (if not ourself) wields the stalwart staff.

WANT: The expression of ones desires or wishes may stem from a lack of fulfillment which cannot be satiated by these or any other material agents. A Want, or overbearing craving for people, things or sensations in general, may illustrate an open void into which these realities free-fall without leaving anything permanent, or at very least, substantial, in their wake. Conversely, a spiritual desire or journey may involve the surrender of ego and the subsequent gratification achieved by material greed. In a dream, we may need to analyze the real worth and significance of what is coveted, to discover its symbolic draw into the waking experience of our unique psyche.

WAR: In life, a human being is constantly confronting battles of one sort or another. When these battles seem to wage on incessantly without any hope of peace, we may find ourselves experiencing recurring dreams involving War. In such cases, we need to determine who is our enemy and why this person or persons seeks our destruction. Often, the enemy revealed is ourselves, more exactly, mental limitations imposed upon our acceptance of self. We may be revealing paranoia about our social relationships. Trust is often a necessary ingredient in positive alliances, therefore, when this trust is broken, we may feel an act of war has been instituted upon our psyche and prepare for the ultimate battle of our liberation and personal honor. Naturally, it should be remembered that peace involves sacrifice and equal points of submission on both sides. Psychological mercenaries

achieve very little in life other than the booty of other mercenaries. (*see* Explosion) (*see* Imbrue) (*see* Impale)

WAREHOUSE: A Warehouse is a place for storage and set aside
valuables. In this context, it is roughly comparable to the human unconscious, which stores information into memory and
is therefore readily prepared to transport this wealth of knowledge into our waking consciousness. Consequently, our dream
may represent an act of manipulating the fluctuating inventory
of our personal cognizance. In an interpretive sense, we are retaining the items of memory which we desire and may wish to
use and returning all other superfluous and somewhat metaphorical memorabilia.

WARMTH: In general, feelings of Warmth are comforting, reassur-
ing and nurturing. Maintaining a balance of hot and cold, a
warm environment is perfectly suited for warm-blooded human beings. As such, we may be referring to overall feelings of
well being, good health and secure calm. These conditions lead
to eloquent and well thought out survival skills, both personal
and professional. However, in a dream, we may need to determine exactly which elements in nature provide us with this
warmth. For example, if we are warmed by a pool of blood, we
may be expressing conflicts in our sacrificial or martyrdom behavior. Conversely, a warm fireplace, hot tea and a loved one
all in close proximity may illustrate a general contentment.
Naturally, as in all dream analysis, we must compare the dream
reality to our waking reality. If the two are polar opposites, we
may be experiencing wish-fulfillment, which may or may not be
recommended, dependent on the waking world view of the
dreamer. For example, a soldier stationed in an igloo in Gnome,
Alaska may do well to dream about flirting with and romancing
beautiful hula girls on a warm beach in Hawaii. On the other
hand, a 'happily married' father of three, living in Teaneck,
New Jersey, may be expressing personal anxiety or sexual repression if he revels in this same dream. As in other theoretical sci-
ences, everything is relative.

WARNING: Everyday life is inundated with Warning devices,
from alarm clocks and red lights, to sophisticated weather-
scanning orbital satellites. In each case, a signal is registered to
inform the human mind of sudden change and the subsequent
and necessary behavioral changes needed to successfully adapt
to each reality transition. A warning signal witnessed in a

dream may symbolically express similar behavioral responses to allegorical situations. For example, if a voice yells stop, we may need to freeze our actions and assess the wisdom of certain waking realities we are about to become immersed into. Conversely, a bell (as in a boxing ring), may signal a new beginning and the stealth, caution and strength necessary to perform productively in this arena. Warning signs employ age-old archetypal stimuli, such as loud noises, bright lights and annoying repetitious wailing. In most cases, we human beings are well aware of the down-side of our actions, due to our internal warning mechanism (in a dream, or otherwise), however, overpowering motivations including ego, desire and youthful exuberance, often may cause us to ignore the flashing light, blowing whistle and shouts from the crowd to stop, until its too late! This is usually when the legal system takes over...

WARRIOR: The symbolism of the Warrior involves a struggle within oneself to find the strength necessary to survive in a harsh and violent environment. The superior motivation in this process is the reality of being destroyed by a stronger and better prepared fighter. In this sense, the representative notion of 'kill or be killed' is still entirely relevant in today's competitive society. Accordingly, the unconscious of a dreamer may be illustrating a necessity to dig down deep inside oneself for the courage, fortitude and determination needed to stand up and fight for worthwhile goals.

WART: A Wart may symbolize a feeling of appearing grotesque to the society of people encompassing ones life. Moreover, because of its association with a witch's nose and witchcraft in general, a dreamer possessing this defacement may feel as though they have been cursed, or cast aside from social interaction, by a malicious person or a peculiar situation beyond their immediate control. The dream image may indicate a serious and ongoing concern, given that a wart is difficult to remove and may last a long time. In an interpretive sense, we must ascertain the exact location of the wart and analyze the symbolic implications of this particular body part and its relative disruption.

WASH: The active image of Washing involves the removal of unclean, harmful realities. In the action of cleaning oneself (or ones goods) with soap and water, we withdraw what is perceived as 'base' elements of our physical environment. These elements have become symbolic of a 'devil's playground' of flesh, dirt (soot, grime etc.) and dust (germs, viruses). Therefore in cleaning, we regain the emotional purity of self, roughly emulating the spotless spirit and image of 'God's work.' Naturally, if one continues this action of absolution, dry, wrinkled and raw skin may shriek in consummate denial, the supposed wonder of any godhead whatsoever. In another interpretive sense, we find the conceptualization of relinquishing responsibility for unethical or unsound judgments. Hence, the phrase, 'I wash my hands of the whole matter', initially uttered in text by Pontius Pilot, but almost certainly used earlier by a number of great men and women who needed to step away from sticky predicaments with uncertain popular results. Stickiness, naturally being another physical rudiment of evil design, in need of being washed away. (*see* Water) (*see* Unclean) (*see* Basin) (*see* Baptism)

WATCHING: In dreams, Watching represents personal suspicion as well as various levels of paranoia. This sort of investigative imagery may result as an unconscious compensation for elusive and perhaps distrustful behavior enacted by the dreamer. However, the distinction must be made whether or not this suspicion is well founded. For example, if in a dream, a mother continually watches her three year old playing in the yard, she may harbor concerns about the child's real safety in and around her dwelling. In this case, the watching is merely cautious. On the other hand, if in a dream, an ordinary working man suddenly feels as though ALL his work mates and friends are mysteriously scrutinizing his actions and eavesdropping on his personal conversations, this man may be exhibiting a strong form of paranoid psychosis. In another interpretive sense, we may need to consider relative objects observed in dreams and determine their symbolic significance to the dreamer. For example, watching a clock and observing the ballet-like dance of a Bottle-Nose Dolphin as it spins above the surface of a crystal clear pool, elicits two quite different meanings. Unless of course, you happen to be a marine biologist/dolphin trainer, who happens to be late for a lecture and demonstration at the Public Aquarium and Waterworld.

WATER: In the symbolic sense, Water refers to the diverse states of our entire emotional capacity. Accordingly, every time water appears in a dream landscape, we represent the fluid, ever-changing and insubstantial characteristics of our own sensitivity. Moreover, clear, untainted water intimates spiritual purity and cleansing. (*see* Baptism) (*see* Boat) (*see* Drown) (*see* Rain)

WAX, DRIPPING: The image of Dripping Wax may involve the potential for passionate emotions which leave a decided effect upon our psyche. (*see* Ablaze) (*see* Fire) (*see* Melt) (*see* Candle)

WAX DOLL: As a society, we have long experienced a fascination with Wax Dolls and wax museums. Soulless, yet vulnerable duplications of ourselves, intimately associated with flame in the heated detail of their creation, these wax figures have ceaselessly amazed us. Furthermore, in the historic and ritualistic sense, wax dolls have archetypally represented a sorcerers tool, a sort of magic mirror, which may well be manipulated to affect and inflict a depicted personage. Taken together, this golem-like formation of a human likeness, may illustrate a complex metaphorical insecurity about either our physical or spiritual body. As such, the pliable nature of a wax doll may be fully indicative of manipulative behavior enacted upon us by outside individuals or forces, or conversely, our own shaping and molding deeds enacted upon our families or close associates. Since heat and flame is involved in the melting of wax, we may need to address our anger and otherwise intense emotional responses in the entirety of these examples.

WEATHER: In most cases, Weather is compared to our emotional states of mind. Consequently, we may feel gloomy and gray, bright and sunny, cold and distant, or enigmatic and moody (rapid weather shifts). There is more to this particular archetype than simply psychological behavior responses. In a biological sense, it has been discovered that weather and location, which produces a variety of disparate levels of ionization (a form of electrical activity in the immediate atmosphere), effects us directly by changing the intricate relations of our neurological operation. As such, certain southwesterly winds and low incoming storm fronts, have been known to drive people mad, while high altitudes and conversely low altitudes (at 0 sea level) with crisp weather patterns, seem to elicit ideal and socially accommodating internal pleasure. The only major difference in these two atmospheric environments is high and low levels of ionization in the surrounding air. Taking all this into account, we need to fully examine the weather conditions in our dream and all responses relative to it. This way, we may be able to determine the level of 'symbolic' as opposed to 'actual' reality of the message obtained from the elaborate, weather-inspired dream imagery.

WEB: The intricate pattern which creates the dual reality of beautiful lure and deadly trap demonstrates a stunning archetype of human experience. As such, we find ourselves at times drawn toward realities which appeal to us, even though we are fully cognizant of their danger. In fact, as Sigmund Freud argued with his theory on a human death instinct, an internal predisposition which craves self-destruction, the danger itself, may invite us further into the very situation. The spider Web dream may offer some insight into this odd behavior in our own waking life. Heeded as a symbolic warning, we may need to analyze particular situations or relationships which seem beautiful in their intricacy, detail and all-encompassing invitation, but which may in fact wait to ensnare us in their complicated and preconceived net of involvement. (see Knot) (see Rope) (see Zig-Zag)

WEEDS: Although Weeds are generally perceived as unwanted realities which spring up into our lives, they can also be viewed as strong, simple and honest forces of nature which refuse to be denied. In this sense, a child who grows quickly and sturdily is often referred to as a weed. We may need to determine if the weed grows in our yard, a neighbors, or out in the wild. Moreover, we may need to analyze our dream reaction to the weed. In this line of thought, we may come to learn to accept the weed as an undeniable and inescapable example of nature's supreme rule. (see Garden)

WEIGHT: The implication of Weight in a dream scenario may involve a heavy burden or a significant and extremely serious decision encountered in ones life. Linked with the idea of weight, is support and naturally, the lack of it. When we talk of 'Holding the weight of the world upon our shoulders', we are saying that we are over-burdened and cannot easily support the gravity of our intentions. In this sense, we examine the quality of support, which is a crucial archetype in the psychological analysis of self. Accordingly, if a person is well grounded, well balanced and effectively creates a sound support base, he or she may be able to carry more 'weight' and responsibility than someone who is shaky all over. In fact, in the not too distant past, an overweight boss was considered well-proportioned for the importance of his position and looked every bit the role model of leader. Similarly, women who would be considered overweight by today's standards, were regarded as ideal maidens and objects of desire, able to bear children, satisfy a husband and raise an entire family. As the culture changes, so does its ideas of role models. Unfortunately, the pendulum of social mores often swings too far in an alternate direction. This being the case, obese people are chastised and made to feel inferior because of their weight. They may become despondent, depressed and shrink away from normal social interactions and activities found in day to day life. As such, the weight dream carries certain implications for overweight persons which are exclusive to their experience. In as much, the reality of support becomes superseded by the need to be supported and this support network becomes more and more difficult to find as depression increases the cycle of food and fulfillment.

WHITE: The dual symbolism of the color White involves both purity as well as frigid detachment. In the sense of its stark, light-reflective brilliance, white embodies components of clarity, simplicity and intelligibility. On the other side of the coin, we find cold isolation and alienation in this severe, glaring and pallid landscape. (*see* Antarctica) (*see* Winter)

WIDOW: In the dream sense, a Widow may refer to a sense of personal loss. Of course, this deprivation may involve the parting of a loved one, but may also concern a dissipation of a part of oneself. For example, when an individual in a relationship feels a loss of passion for their once desired partner, a dream landscape may characterize this feeling in the form of a widow or widower.

WILD: Although man seems to have conquered the so-called Wild world with the elaborate efforts of his iron and mortar civilization, the fact is, he has only hidden himself from the natural tenants of its universal existence. Accordingly, the wild nature which is ever-present within himself, still burns vividly and displays hunger, passion and freedom, the latter supremely ironic, since freedom is billed as the major strong point of this stainless-steel man-made environment. Nevertheless, the wild impulses of man remain, and the theoretically tame society of man has found difficulty in dealing with this unfortunate internal paradox. Dreams serve as the mediators in this internal battle of metaphysical belief systems. The dream is not afraid to hunt, run, scream, act with total abandonment, and one more thing, the exercise of freedom. This way, in waking life, we can return to our safe existence without hurting ourselves or others around us. As a message from our unconscious however, we may need to heed the reflection of the dream and act (with caution, and within the limits of the recognized law) on the impulses of our wild instincts. (*see* Jungle)

WIND: The rush of air which serves to push and pull us in ominous directions may entertain the visual equivalent of being led around by outside influences. Moreover, the Wind, which is naked to the human eye, may imply that these forces are not revealed to us, or deliberately deceptive, or simply misleading in their interaction with ourselves. From another interpretive view, we should analyze not only the force of the wind, but also its relative temperature. Is it cold, painful and numbing, or is it warm, intoxicating and inviting? Moreover, does the wind blow any object away from us? If so, what is that object (or person), and what is our exact relationship to it? Lastly, are we able to retrieve that item, or does it appear to be lost forever? (*see* Ice) (*see* Zephyr) (*see* Boat) (*see* Antarctica)

WINDOW: The symbolism of a Window involves the appearance and acknowledgment of an outside world of vast possibilities. In this sense, the window may represent a focal point of the dreaming mind itself. Accordingly, the transparent glass directs our immediate attention on the dream landscape found within its frame. Moreover, the sunlight allowed into a home, is representative of reason and wisdom. Accordingly, we need to pay special attention to all objects and persons seen through our cordial pane of glass. (*see* Glass) (*see* Drapes) (*see* Light)

WITCHCRAFT: The complex symbolism of Witchcraft refers to a unifying force which underlies nature and the archaic earth magic used to tap into this well of power. Consequently, any irresistible spells cast over a dreamer, may be represented in dreams as a form of sorcery, or Wicca. Moreover, the naturalistic aspects of this earth magic contain feminine precepts of spirituality, including heightened sensual awareness and a matriarchal similitude. Hence, female wisdom may be implied in the overall dream meaning. (*see* Aboriginal) (*see* Hex)

WOLF: In the dream sense, a Wolf represents beauty, solitude and pride. As such, its wild nature is elevated to a status of high passion. In this sense, a wolf is not a killer, but rather, a seducer. Consequently, when a wolf appears in a dream landscape, its symbolism is that of the noble loner who asks for nothing yet deserves the world of our respect. The interpretation of this dream may involve a dreamer's self-confidence and composure in a variety of social situations, which he or she can move in and out of with relative ease and grace.

WOMB: The conceptualization of the Womb involves complete security and sanctity. The chamber of birth exhibits life entirely provided for, without worry of harm, survival responsibility, or the isolation of solitude. The image of mother and child as one, represents a sacred union of love, creation and selfless sacrifice in the image of the pregnant woman. In a real sense, this dream is quite different dependent on whether or not the dreamer is male or female. The primary reason for this is found in the example of the male, who has no concept of a having a womb, only the regressive warmth and protection which it archetypally offers him. In the case of the female dreamer, we find a complex analysis of the womb concerning fears about the sacrifice and responsibility of childbirth, mingled perhaps with the quandary of sexual pleasure versus obvious social expectations involving procreation. (*see* Bottle) (*see* Child) (*see* Childbirth) (*see* Fetal Position) (*see* Umbilical Cord)

WOOD: The symbolism of Wood involves the complex connection of nature and man. In one sense, a wood structure or house built rather than a steel, brick or plastic one, may imply naturalistic ideals in the psychological framework of an individual. On the other hand, an ancient oak tree chopped down to obtain wood to make a house, may imply an unhealthy domination of nature. Accordingly, we need to understand our respectful association with wood in the dream landscape, and in a very real sense, our symbolic affiliation with forests and wilderness in general. (*see* House) (*see* Tree)

WORM: The symbolism of a Worm in a dream, may imply an introverted behavior which attains much intelligence, but very little wisdom, gained from experience. In this sense, the worm represents a frail innocence which is entirely vulnerable. Moreover, the exposed defenseless nature of the creature implies weakness and a general lack of courage. Accordingly, a worm appearing in a dream landscape, may illustrate wall-flower behavior and a general fear of social confrontation or interaction.

WREATH: In the dream sense, the symbolism of a circle of flowers, or Wreath, refers to eternal love, respect and admiration. Moreover, since a circle, or ring, implies infinity and order, an

KEYS TO YOUR DREAMS
295

encircling of flowers may indicate a natural and spiritual eternity of life. In this sense, a wreath may be representative of the concept of an immortal soul. (*see* Circle) (*see* Flower) (*see* Ring)

WRITING: The communication of complex ideas through an organized redistribution of letters or symbols, creating words, is singular to mankind as a species. With the introduction of Writing, language as we know it, blossomed into a pool of knowledge and information which could be passed not only to our neighbors, but also, carried on to successive generations. This well thought process outlined the foundation and upward cohesive structure of society and civilization itself. As such, it is no accident that writing figures prominently in the psyche of the human population. Our dreams resort to primal archetypal images to covey messages from the unconscious into the waking conscious. Therefore, to communicate the very art of communication itself, our dreaming mind will present the image, or gesture, of writing. Moreover, this communiqué may involve a direct continuity of thought which would be absurd and unreasonable to explain in metaphor. In other words, the dream is spelling it out for us in plain English, if we choose to read and understand. If written progressively, the countless examples of authors and poets who received entire passages of their famous verse in dreams, would far exceed the length of this humble manuscript. Accordingly, we need to analyze all the particulars of the writing dream, the penmanship style, the parchment used, the writer's inspiration, and especially, the words themselves. (*see* Letter) (*see* Book)

X-RAY: The symbolism of X-Rays naturally involves looking through things. In other words, in the dream sense, we may be expressing a desire to see inside a person (if not ourselves), both physically AND mentally. This internal inspection may involve finding good qualities inside a person, as well as exposing bad characteristics, or ill health, within that self.

XYLOPHONE: (*see* Accordion)

YACHT: The Yacht dream concerns a luxurious and relaxed social happening or overall atmosphere of good feeling. Whether fantasized or not, the fanciful ship carries with it a notion of emotional ease and a lack of worry. It is very rare that we should dream about a yacht caught in a stormy sea, unless the dreamer fears being way in over his (or her) head, in a financial deal, investment or style of life, which may sink... (*see* Boat)

YAK: The long-haired Asian ox known as a Yak, is a paradoxical dream figure because it simultaneously represents the sturdiness and reliability of a four-legged, domestic vegetarian (akin to a cow), and an exotic and arguably rare beast, admired by easterners and westerners alike, the world over. Therefore, our dream may be expressing a double-meaning and otherwise split feeling about a certain person or situation in our lives. By and large, the qualities of uniqueness and dependability, taken together, add up to a formidable and perhaps precious person, entity or happening.

YAMMER: Loud confusion, especially verbal confusion, may indicate frustration concerning an inability to communicate ones ideas or the converse and exasperating experience of confronting an avalanche of ideas and opinions from others, none of which are useful or applicable to our own neural experience. Alternatively, the hostile nature of an animal's yammering, may be indicative of a warning against danger, or an otherwise threatening event. It may be necessary to piece together decipherable bits of information in the confused chatter to reveal single examples of what may in fact be troubling us in waking life.

YANK: The action of pulling at someone or something with violent passion in ones dream, may demonstrate a desperate need to free that person or object away from its present position. Perhaps the subject is in a station or posture of symbolic paralysis. However, it should be remembered and noted, this freeing of an object, may carry with it a need to possess or 'recapture' said object, or individual, into ones own (the dreamer's), psychological ensnarement.

YARD: The symbolic conceptualization of a Yard which maintains larger than life tools of human civilization (pumps, trains, ships etc.), may be indicative of our day to day machinations which propels us through a complex world. Conversely, the Yard which outlines our house or apartment building may be reflective of our synthesis or communication with the land itself. As such, we may need to examine the naturalistic condition of our physical property. Is the grass green? Are the trees tall and thriving? Are the flowers in bloom? Additionally, childhood games played in yards, reflected in bright toys, playground rides and sand-boxes, may illustrate regressive behavior or an age-old drive which our unconscious clearly displays. In this sense, we need to examine the condition of the childhood items. Are the toys broken? Are the swings rusted? Or conversely, is everything shiny and new, as though time has not passed since our animated youth. It should be remembered, that our concept of waking time is irrelevant to the unconscious, which utilizes time as a symbolic communication of a psychological state of mind.

YARDMASTER: The Yardmaster is the feared and revered embodiment of our external machinations. In this sense, this dream figure is akin to a foreman who oversees our physical actions and moreover, our ability to usefully perform in all levels of society: private, public and professional. As such, the yardmaster may represent our insecurities and fears concerning our direct abilities and the harsh realities of their possible outcomes. However, if we ourselves are depicted in the body of the yardmaster, we may be illustrating a complex control over our environment. This blunt characteristic may elapse in our waking experience in the complicated network of our elaborate social interrelationships.

YARN: The concept of a Yarn, refers to a fanciful story which is not meant to be taken seriously, but which may contain certain elements of wisdom. In the alternate usage of the word, Yarn, used for weaving, is often thought of in the sense of a playful kitten's ball of yarn. Once again, and perhaps not as coincidentally as one might expect, yarn contains an element of play and tomfoolery. As single strands of material which are interwoven to create imaginative knits, the individual strand of yarn is comparable to the single element of truth, the cohesive reality, found in the tall tale called a 'yarn.' Taken together, the image of yarn in our dream landscape may refer to a playful person or situation, which nevertheless, reveals to our waking selves, a necessary truth or decisive wisdom.

YAWN: The immediate association of a yawn may be that of boredom, weariness, or outright exhaustion concerning some aspect of our waking behavior. However, there may be certain oral and/or sexual allusions involved in the gaping image of the long, relaxed yawn. Furthermore, its catchy, mimicking quality may illustrate an imitative interaction enacted ourselves, or by others, in our immediate sphere of experience. We need to analyze who in fact yawns in the dream, and what precedes (or causes) the automatic response, if anything at all.

YEAR: The conceptualization of the Year may involve a concern about aging and the passage of time. Alternatively, the importance of significant events which may have occurred, or will occur, and cause profound changes in our day to day life, may be alluded to in our complex dream vocabulary. In this sense, we may be illustrating our more elaborate concerns, fears and desires involving time, which is in some sense our analytical, scientific perception of life and human physical reality, such as it may actually exist. On the other hand and metaphysically speaking, metaphorical comparisons can be made with the notion of the horoscope, in essence, the predicted future, which may need to be psychologically wished for, in the shape of some semblance of hope.

YEARBOOK: The image of our Yearbook carries with it the people we once were and alternatively, the persons we were meant, or promised, to become. We may be expressing a concern about our relative station in life and how we managed to end up as the people we are today. The friendships and loves once maintained in our early youth certainly formed and manipulated attitudes which we carried later in life. Our unconscious may be referring to these early stages in life in the embodiment of the yearbook. Moreover, this preserved, fragile moment in our personal history may reflect a seemingly insurmountable mental block or delicate neurosis which may need to be addressed. Along these lines, elements of repressive behavior may be singularly indicated in this dream context.

YEAST: The idea of potential, symbolized in the raising of bread, may be illustrated in the dream motion of yeast. Any and all depictions of growth refer to maturation and significant transitions. us in coping with these difficult irreversible realities

Bread itself is symbolic of flesh and nourishment, as such, yeast may refer to inner and crucial growth in our personal life. the combined fulfillment of our mind, body and spirit completes the story of our adulthood, and furthermore, our humanity. Therefore, we need to analyze and interpret this dream image thoroughly, as it may concern significant transformations and transfigurations in our immediate experience.

YELL: The action of forcefully pushing out internal agony, which may be otherwise suppressed is purposefully actualized in the dream Yell. In our dream consciousness, we are able to express feelings which are difficult to accept or even cope with in our waking experience. The yell, in and of itself, is not at all a negative behavior trait. In fact, in the animal kingdom, the scream is used instinctively as a warning, challenge or general release of intense emotion. Moreover, loud yelling prepares the endocrine and adrenaline systems for physical confrontations and critical battles, including territorial and mating. The dream scream therefore, reflects a necessary physical response to stressful stimuli which may need to be emulated in waking life.

YELLOW: The complex symbolism of the color yellow may involve light and warmth, as well as, sickness and/or cowardice. Accordingly, we need to determine if the yellow entity in the dream landscape is displaying its normal ocher color, or if it has become this color due to some cowardly or pusillanimous behavior.

YESTERDAY: The conceptualization of Yesterday may refer to remorse concerning unchangeable events. As such, we understand that yesterday is gone and cannot be recaptured or replayed. The suddenness and completeness of the passing days of our life relate the reality of conclusions and resolutions to the direct machinations and decisions of our conduct, function and belief system. In other words, yesterday illustrates consequences which we must accept. A crucial part of the maturation process involves standing behind our choices and decisions, even if they have failed or been proven unacceptable. As such, we learn to admit our own errors in judgment and at times, entirely human ignorance. The replaying of yesterday in our dream, may serve to reveal our mistakes, or conversely, our triumphs, in order to learn from our unique and personal actions. Often in life, we are faced with permanent loss, allusions to firm conclusions and completions in our psychological development, may aid.

YIN/YANG: The balance of our masculine and feminine aspects, may be alluded to in the dream image of the yin/yang symbol proper. In ordinary life, we are often asked to behave quite differently, dependent on certain situations. For example, our sensitive, or feminine side, may be required in certain difficult scenarios, such as dealing with the personal needs of our loved ones, or handling a profound bereavement and mourning suffered by a close and personal friend. Conversely, our strong, or masculine side, may need to be called upon to address situations where we need to stand up for ourselves, our beliefs or simply our motivations. Habitually in life, we choose to favor only one of our internal gender traits. The yin/yang dream may indicate a need to find equilibrium in our complex emotional spectrum in order to become ever more complete in our humanity and human potential.

YOGA/YOGI In the dream sense, a Yogi refers to our inner meditations and the conviction of our spiritual path. The stillness and quiet of the yogi represents the archaic wisdom of fusing body and spirit. In theory, when the body and spirit become one, all physical and spiritual limitations are absolutely erased, allowing the master fakir to come and go as he pleases, guided by vision, sense and insight. (*see* Journey) (*see* Path)

YOKE: The symbolism of a Yoke refers to the burden we must carry in waking life. Accordingly, if the burden is too heavy, our unconscious may be revealing the excess tasks and responsibilities which hold us down, or basically enslave us. Conversely, if the yoke is light and well-balanced, we may be illustrating the worthwhile nature of our supportive efforts concerning work, family or social commitment.

YOUTH, FOUNTAIN OF: In the dream sense, a vision of The Fountain of Youth, may represent a wish-fulfillment to regain the strength, vitality or even beauty of our youth. This escapist dream confronts the profound tribulation of aging and exposes a society which is insensitive to the very real needs and desires of the elderly. On the other side of the coin, if an individual ignores the dream fountain entirely, he or she may be displaying a sublime acceptance of self and the divine order of nature's unfolding.

ZEAL: Enthusiasm and excitement in a dream, may well represent a foreshadowing of some joyous event or sudden good news; for example, the arrival of a child. Conversely, Zealous behavior may be a reactionary reflection of a lack of emotion to good fortune, or performance approval, which occurs in ones own waking life. In either case, the exact nature of the dream zeal should be analyzed and interpreted comprehensively for a deeper and perhaps, complete understanding, of the unconscious message revealed.

ZEBRA: The symbolism of the Zebra refers to the perfect symmetry and unity of opposites. Moreover, this visual balance found in nature demonstrates the unanimity of life itself. Furthermore, since the zebra, unlike a horse, is a wild animal who lives in a naturalistic landscape, we may surmise that freedom and latitude, play a major role in this dream imagery. Accordingly, we see the inherent liberation found in the instinctive and fluid co-existence of opposites in our remarkable world.

ZEITGEIST: When a certain historical fashion (or mood) is reinstated in a dream, we may be fantasizing about that particular way of life. Naturally, we may be indicating a dissatisfaction with our own period of time and the life it has offered us. However, it should be understood that the human mind and spirit transcends social norms of any period. As such, in the USA, we are very fortunate to be able to create our own appropriate sensibilities in todays date in time, in other words, the present. Therefore, an old-fashioned person can live alongside a modern person in this rare world of a theoretical freedom of choice.

ZEN: The Zen dream involves mysticism that transcends language and behavior in all its forms. Accordingly, we may be expressing in the Zen scene, a life-style free of rigid spiritual rules created by, for and toward God, or, an otherwise complete system of personal enlightenment. In this way, the dream may be illustrating a belief in self and an acute faith in the infallible direction, administration and course, of that self. Moreover, we may need to interpret the theatrical behavior performed in the self-same Zen dream imagery, as the movements may reveal hidden truths which may need to be explored extensively. In this sense, we need to analyze particular body parts and the reflex actions they display through the overall spatial environment.

ZENITH: In the dream sense, an absolute Zenith may illustrate potential and/or formidable goals. It may be essential to interpret the dreamer's reaction to the vision of the zenith atop the horizon line. Is the dream character striving to push the absolute limit of his or her being, or is he or she thrown into chaos at the prospect of tackling or associating with such a seemingly insurmountable apex of human or worldly existence?

ZEPHYR: The warm caressing breeze called a Zephyr, may be a fairly accurate representation of stoic contentment, that is to say, a gentle, natural calming of internal emotions. In most cases, this sort of ease and tranquillity occurs after turmoil and a difficult period in ones life. The zephyr may be the affirmation of a moral life and otherwise confident soul. However, a normal element of dream language finds sudden changes in environmental forces. Therefore, the dreamer should be aware if the warm breeze grows harsher and gradually more difficult to bear, until he or she finds him or herself in a deadly sandstorm, the unconscious may be signaling a warning. The warning reminds us to be cautious of the seeming ease which certain aspects of our lives may now display.

ZEPPELIN: Apart from the well-publicized Hindenburg disaster, the usual image of a giant blimp-like craft which flies with effortless majesty over the horizon, illustrates a grand promise and the singular and eloquent overcoming of a seemingly impossible feat. In an entirely separate interpretation of this ship, we find the shape and formidable presence of the Zeppelin may imply a phallic symbol of bold and dignified proportions. In any case, the huge craft is an example of human possibility and the emotional effectiveness of human grace. It combines quiet beauty, simple elegance and gargantuan size and strength. Taken together, this symbolism may refer to large accomplishments which should, can and will be made by the dreamer in waking life.

ZERO: The appearance of a Zero account figure, or the visual representation of the center of the mathematical line, both refer to a fresh beginning and an otherwise restructuring of self. The absence of finances may naturally illustrate a fear of economic devastation. however, more than likely, the bankrupt figure carries with it the conceptualization of 'creating ones fortune', both physically and metaphorically. Moreover, the absence of money may imply spiritual wholeness absent of perhaps burdening material possessions. All this conjecture is influenced by the dreamer's perception of the value of the 'almighty' dollar.

ZIG-ZAG: In a dream, Zig-Zagging behavior may be symbolic of indecision and wavering sensibilities. However, analogous to the insect world (ex: moth), a chaotic pattern of movement may conversely illustrate a defensive strategy taken or planned in the near future. The dream conceptualization of a moving target implies that a person or group of persons, may be aiming negative attacks in our direction, (either real or imaginary). In a rather complex analysis and interpretation of this dreamscape, the zig-zag motion may be recreated on paper, or on video, in our waking life, to determine the intricate weave or pattern formed by the repetition of our movement. The subsequent significance of the web-like creation in space and its revealing body language, may be indicative of our unique behavior patterns in day to day life.

ZIPPER: The combination of metal and the alternate covering and exposing of flesh may be illustrative of a harsh sexuality, or a sexual relation with dire consequences. The article of clothing which is zipped or unzipped may refer to a fascination with that particular body part which is revealed (boot, jacket, pants = foot, chest, groin). Furthermore, if the Zipper should become ensnared in flesh, we may be illustrating a material and perhaps unnatural approach to our own sexuality and/or overall physiology.

ZODIAC: The twelve aspects of the astrological wheel, symbolic of birth and behavior, also maintain one of the four elements of fire, water, air and earth. In this sense, we need to analyze which sign is alluded to in the dream, especially if the sign is different from the birthsign of the dreamer. If all the signs of the Zodiac are present, the dreamer may be referring to the art of astrology itself. Naturally, a concern about ones future, in essence, ones horoscope, may be implied in this straight-forward dream scenario. (*see* Astrology)

ZOMBIE: The undead in dreams generally refer to persons, or more appropriately, situations which refuse to go away. The unnatural and grotesque appearance of the Zombies may refer to the monstrous reality of a human problem which grows in significance with time and the inability to vanquish its perplexing nature. In the archaic sense, a zombie, akin to a golem, is a soulless creature, made entirely of earth and flesh and therefore, bears no relation to a deceased loved one. This ghoul is rather an archetype of our own long-standing fears and perceived shortcomings, returning night after night to haunt and torment us with the simple human frailty of our own selves.

ZOO: The complex symbolism of a Zoo revolves around the separate animals characterized in the dream itself and their relative condition and/or behavior. However, the sheer number of diverse animals in the dream landscape may also play a part in the overall interpretation. In this sense, we may be expressing a series of conflicting emotions and desires which reveal themselves in the specific animal which we observe. Moreover, the fact that the animals are locked in cages may refer to the long standing repression of our passions and drives, which would explain their possible sickly and otherwise strange appearance.

ZOOMORPHISM: The complex symbolism of Zoomorphism refers to the connection of human and animal characteristics. Consequently, the image of a being with half-human and half-animal parts alludes to the dual expression of both of their respective physical natures. That is to say, wild, untamed and instinctive versus civilized, restrained and moral behavior in general. Appropriately, we need to examine the paired representation of the zoomorphic form and place it into the significant psychological make-up of the dreamer who conceives this unique entity in the context of his or her physical world of experience. In this, we may need to determine if the dreamer's 'animal' sense increases or decreases relative to ones 'human' sensibility. The wild or civilized bearing in the physical manifestation of our dream, may be illustrating an extreme course of action in our waking life, which may have rather distressing and perhaps unexpected, consequences in our social relationships. However, if our opposing natures are equally balanced and the dreamer feels a fluid ease and control of experiential behavior, the unconscious may be revealing an ideal symmetry in our physical, psychological, and spiritual self. This healthy, well-balanced personality is known in psychological terms as a Self-Actualized individual.

Index

Final Word

The world we view within ourselves is the resonant memory of our deepest and most furtive experiences. Each night we journey further and further into this realm of self. What we learn in memory yesterday, has becomes a part of the fabric of ourselves today. Hence, each night we become further enmeshed in creation and we will continue to grow in that infinite spectrum of 'comprehensive' being. In an unmistakable fashion, our dreams mirror, echo and scrutinize our most subtle of positions in life's revolving kaleidoscope. When we finally open our eyes, our dreams still live there within us, gracefully woven into the infinite tapestry of our being.

Pleasant dreams

A&B Publishers Group
Send for our complete full color catalog today!

*(hc pricing)Also available in hard cover   **Prices subject to change without notice**

Mail To:A&B PUBLISHERS GROUP · 1000 ATLANTIC AVE · NEW YORK · 11238
TEL: (718) 783-7808 · FAX (718) 783-7267

NAME:_____

ADDRESS_____

CITY_____ST_____ZIP_____

Card Type_____Card Number_____

Exp_____/_____ Signature _____

We accept VISA MASTERCARD AMERICAN EXPRESS & DISCOVER

About the Author

R. M. SOCCOLICH studied Psychology, Theater and Literature at Glassboro University and at Hunter College of the City University of New York (CUNY). After graduating, he continued intense study for several years into the human mind and its collective historical development. He has followed humanity's progressions and digressions over a period of fifteen years and in the process has focussed upon the source of our universal beliefs and our deepest fears. He has traveled the labyrinth path of thousands of generations of mankind and witnessed first-hand the subtle variations of our highest and most deeply held perceptions of "The Truth"

His first book *The 100 Steps Necessary for Survival on the Earth* is a culmination of his studies and details an elaborate human history and its wholly apparent and critical initiative. He has co-sponsored a series of titles called *The Survival Series* which includes *The 100 Steps Necessary for Survival in the Global Village* which unraveled a dramatic view of society's most intimate series of upcoming adaptations . The series also includes several other thought provoking titles.

This encyclopedia of archetypal symbols and their universal interpretation showcased the author's deep commitment to research and the ultimate psychological imperative of the world's people. His latest project, co-authored with Sam Chewas *Mischievous Acts and Repercussions*, addressees Karma and its elaborate bizarre and far-reaching impact.